Nisei/Sansei

In the series

Asian American History and Culture

edited by Sucheng Chan,
David Palumbo-Liu,
and Michael Omi

A list of books in the series appears at the back of this volume

Nisei/Sansei

Shifting
Japanese American
Identities and Politics

Jere Takahashi

Temple University Press
Philadelphia

Temple University Press, Philadelphia 19122

Copyright ©1997 by Jere Takahashi

All rights reserved

Published 1997

Printed in the United States of America

Text design by Nancy Johnston

⊗ The paper used in this publication meets the requirements of American National Standard for Information Sciences—Permanence of Paper for Printed Library Materials, ANSI Z39.48-1984

Library of Congress Cataloging-in-Publication Data
Takahashi, Jere, 1943–
    Nisei/Sansei : shifting Japanese American identities and politics / Jere Takahashi.
        p.   cm. (Asian American history and culture)
    Includes bibliographical references and index.
    ISBN 1-56639-550-X (alk. paper)
    1. Japanese Americans—Politics and government. 2. Japanese Americans—Social conditions. 3. Japanese Americans—Ethnic identity. I. Title. II. Series.
E184.J3T316   1997   97-22408
305.895'6073—dc21

For my Mother and Father

Contents

Preface

MY PERSONAL EXPERIENCES HAVE BEEN AN IMPORTANT starting point for this study, which began nearly two decades ago as a doctoral dissertation. Growing up as a Japanese American in the post–World War II period, I developed an interest in the issues of race, identity, community, and culture as I struggled to sort them out in my own life. My parents' experience in Topaz, Utah, one of ten concentration camps where Japanese Americans were incarcerated during World War II and my birthplace, made me wonder why they were imprisoned and what significance mass incarceration had for my parents, family, and other Japanese Americans. These long-standing concerns converged with the dramatic social changes of the 1960s and 1970s, and the racial tensions and conflicts of those times. The emergence of the Asian American movement, especially the political activism of Japanese American youth who were coming of age, captured my attention and kindled my interest in the transformations that were taking place.

These issues prompted me to explore empirical and analytical questions: What political shifts transpired among Japanese American youth in the late 1960s and 1970s? Was it a dramatic departure from the prevailing political style within the community, or was it something that resonated with political themes and expressions from the past? Also, why did some Japanese American youth adopt a new political style? Was this shift a matter of generational change, or was it a manifestation of other dynamics and social processes as well? Specifically, did race and the changing racial formation of the times come into play for Japanese Americans? Finally, did this activism represent a passing fad or did it reflect a transition in political and racial consciousness that would affect the future political styles of this group? This book attempts to answer these questions.

After reviewing documents, newspapers, and numerous oral histories and interviews that had been collected in the 1920s, 1940s, and the 1960s, I began a field study of Japanese Americans in the San Francisco Bay Area. I conducted 40 in-depth interviews with a diverse group of informants in the San Francisco Bay Area who represented a variety of age cohorts and who were knowledgeable about Japanese American life as a result of their own experiences growing up in regions of California where Japanese Americans were concentrated. Through their personal narratives I wanted to understand the key issues they confronted as they came of age and the major historical events that impacted their lives. I also hoped to explore various dimensions of human agency and develop "sociohistorical portraits" that would illuminate the shifting identities and political styles of Japanese Americans from the 1920s to the 1970s.

Because of my field research location and my pool of interviewees, the post–World War II sections of the book have a Northern California emphasis. Although I considered interviewing additional people of various ages outside of Northern California, I decided to stay with the original interviews. I felt that new interviews that were gathered in a different time period and social context would change the quality of my data and make comparisons difficult. I hope that this book will prompt new studies that flesh out regional differences and similarities more fully, as well as invite new accounts and analyses of political activism.

Having gathered my interviews nearly two decades ago, I wondered about the contemporary significance of this book. It struck me that the current attention to race and ethnicity at all levels of society, the debates around multiculturalism and diversity, and the questions of racial inclusion and the meaning of being an American are issues quite similar to those that this book touches upon in a different historical period. I find it somewhat ironic that issues, such as affirmative action, that were salient in the 1970s are prominent today. This book also addresses issues that may be relevant to new Asian American communities, particularly the racial and generational dynamics that appear to be an important feature of their social and political life.

Regarding terminology and pseudonyms, because of the specific historical time frame of this study, some of the terms that I use derive from their contemporary usage in the 1960s and 1970s. For example, I use the term *blacks* in reference to African Americans, and the term *Third World* in reference to people of color in this country, although its implications then had more to do with being a colonized or oppressed racial group. I also employ the term *Japanese* interchangeably with *Japanese American*, particularly in reference to the "Japanese community." When I make specific reference to Japanese from Japan, I refer to them as *Japanese nationals*. I created pseudonyms for individuals who are cited or quoted in the text, unless they gave permission to use their actual names. I did not change the names of public figures or individuals whose names appear in public documents.

This book would not have been possible without the cooperation and collaboration of those individuals who were willing to share their life experiences with me. Some have become friends with whom I have been able to keep in touch over the nearly 20 years since I first interviewed them. I am impressed that so many of them, especially those who came of age during the 1960s and 1970s, have maintained their political perspectives as they managed the many changes that have occurred in their lives. Also, special thanks to Joe Oyama, Yas Sasaski, the late Toshio Mori, Chizu and Ernie Hyama, Paul Takagi, Florence Hongo, and others of my parents' generation who were valuable sources of inspiration.

For intellectual guidance and support, I am deeply indebted to Troy Duster, Ronald Takaki, and Bob Blauner. Their teachings and writings have been an important influence in my thinking about the issues of race, identity, politics, and human group life that are central to this project. Their encouragement and advice have been a vital part of my intellectual as well as personal development. I am grateful for their mentorship and friendship.

Throughout this project, I received encouragement and guidance from Yuji Ichioka, who shared with me his materials and vast knowledge of the Japanese American experience. His critical comments and writing on Japanese American history have been integral to the development of this book. I am grateful for his friendship and support. Over the years, Lane Hirabayashi has helped me in many ways by sharing his work, providing valuable insights about the changing character of the Japanese American experience, and offering timely observations and critical comments. I extend my thanks and I wish I was as conscientious in reciprocating. For their thoughtful suggestions and critical observations, I want to thank David Wellman, David Minkus, Deborah Woo, Isami Arifuku, Art Hansen, and David Yoo.

Many thanks to Dana Takagi, Keith Osajima, Don Mar, Don Nakanishi, Elaine Kim, and Ling-chi Wang for helpful comments on the early phases of my research and their encouragement. For their personal support, I want to thank Greg Mark, Gerald Shimada, Pat Hayashi, Janice Koyama, Janice Tanigawa, Francisco Hernandez, Barbara Davis, Grace Massey, Weichi Poon, and Janice Otani.

A special note of thanks to Lisa Hirai for her research assistance and help with the tedious task of proofreading, and the numerous other ways she helped me. For her patience and assistance in the final stages of the book, thanks go to Janet Francendese at Temple University Press. For her copyediting and assistance in the final stages of preparation, thanks to

Betsy Winship. Thanks to Ford Hatamiya for allowing me to use his art for the book cover.

I have had the benefit of working with two series editors. To Sucheng Chan, the founding editor of the Asian American History and Culture series, I owe a special debt. Without her encouragement, I would not have taken on this project. During the ebb and flow of revising the manuscript, she exercised patience and provided constructive criticism. She reviewed every aspect of the manuscript and gave detailed comments and suggestions for improvement. This book would not have happened without her help. Special thanks to Michael Omi, the series' social science editor. He read every chapter and provided useful comments and helpful suggestions. His theoretical insights and criticism certainly benefited my work, and his unwavering support and willingness to help me flesh out issues and sound out problems aided me immensely. Equally important have been his friendship and counsel over the many years we have been associated.

Finally, my wife, Terri, and my daughter, Annie, and family never wavered in their support and encouragement. They were a special inspiration and helped me through the difficult times. I cannot fully express the depths of my appreciation.

Nisei/Sansei

Introduction

DURING THE EARLY 1960S, THIRD-GENERATION JAPANESE Americans, the Sansei, were poised to participate more fully in the mainstream of U.S. society than had any previous generation.[1] According to one observer, most of this generation had "grown up ... in relatively comfortable circumstances, with the American element of their composite subculture becoming more and more dominant."[2] Moreover, their dress, social conduct, and avoidance of such "extremist" forms of behavior as delinquency and political radicalism suggested that they were becoming very much like their white American counterparts.[3] Such behavior led *Newsweek* magazine to report that Japanese Americans were "outwhiting the whites."[4] In many respects, Japanese Americans appeared to be following the classical generational progression established by European ethnic groups who had arrived in the United States before the turn of the century.[5]

By the late 1960s, however, many Sansei began to chart a very different course in their approach to the larger society. Questions regarding their identity, culture, and political behavior became the focus of discussion and debate as key assumptions about their capacity to integrate into American society became problematical. College-age Sansei, for example, began to view race and ethnicity quite differently than their counterparts had done in the early 1960s. Those who embraced the ideals of integration and "assimilation" started searching for new perspectives that would help them understand their position in the United States. Others, for the first time, affirmed their ethnic identity and cultural heritage after having suppressed them during the early part of their lives. Still others, who experienced tremendous ambivalence about their identity and social status, launched a process to clarify or redefine for themselves the significance of race and ethnicity in their lives.

1

Perhaps most startling to outside observers were Sansei who developed a political and ideological orientation remarkably different from the one that their Nisei predecessors had held in the 1950s and early 1960s. These Sansei rejected accommodationist and assimilationist politics and instead pursued the political tactics of protest, confrontation, and mass action—methods patterned after black activists.[6] Institutions of higher education and the ethnic community became important sites for political action and racial change. Establishing Ethnic Studies and Asian American Studies programs on West Coast campuses was one of their primary concerns.[7] The involvement of Sansei students in the Third World strikes at San Francisco State University and the University of California, Berkeley, clearly illustrated this approach towards institutional change.[8] In their communities, Sansei leaders also focused attention on building alternative community organizations to provide legal services, health care, drug programs for youth, nutrition programs for the elderly, and low-cost housing. Ideologies informing this new political orientation ranged from local, liberal tenets to Marxist–Leninist world views.[9]

In contrast to earlier generations, Sansei activists also exhibited a very different kind of consciousness about interethnic and interracial politics. Their desire to unify various groups of Asian Americans and to form coalitions with blacks, Chicanos, and Native Americans was an important part of their emerging ideology. Bridging the racial and ethnic divide by linking their community organizing efforts with those of blacks, Native Americans, Chicanos, and other Asian Americans was an important part of their political strategy. Overall, this transformation in racial identity, culture, and politics signaled an important shift among Japanese American youth in their approach to race relations, one that contrasted sharply with the Nisei's political emphasis on gradualism, reliance on the legal system, and faith in educational achievement and hard work as a source of social mobility.[10]

This cultural and political divergence between the Sansei and Nisei in the late 1960s poses an interesting contrast in what I refer to as political style—the conventional notion that politics is the "art of the possible," where "the political artist must seek to create new things within the limitations imposed by tradition and the materials with which he or she works."[11] Some accounts have characterized Japanese Americans as a nonpolitical community.[12] Although Japanese Americans have been seen as cautious or conservative in their dealings with the larger society, or as disconnected from the electoral political arena, the notion of political style suggests that Japanese Americans have devised strategies and methods to advance their concerns and interests despite having been segregated from the political mainstream or having lacked the necessary political resources to make an impact on the political process.

The notion of political style, however, involves more than looking at Japanese Americans as political artists. It refers to their total efforts to define themselves, to challenge their racially subordinate position, and to carve out a meaningful space for themselves in American society. These total efforts include a reliance on their cultural resources, the formation of competing perspectives and ideologies, as well as the development of political organizations and networks, and their efforts to participate in mainstream politics. The notion of political style also involves both personal and social action: it includes the daily struggle of Japanese Americans to advance their individual interests, as well as their collective efforts to promote racial change in ways that fit their circumstances.[13] Such a conception portrays Japanese Americans as active parts of the sociohistorical process.[14]

The emergence of a new political style spearheaded by Sansei activists in the late 1960s poses an interesting contrast to those accounts that characterize Japanese Americans as a monolithic community whose members are nonpolitical and unfortunate victims of oppression. The emergence of Sansei activism points to an internal diversity and complexity in Japanese American identity, culture, and politics that represent a "buried past."[15] A recent account of the Issei, the first generation of Japanese immigrants to set foot on these shores, shows that they in fact had developed competing ideological orientations and a range of defensive political strategies to safeguard their interests in response to racially restrictive and exclusionary laws and policies.[16] Thus the existence of competing political styles has been an integral part of Japanese American "political history."[17]

These shifts in political style, as well as the tensions within and continuities between generations over the issues of identity, culture, and politics, point to complex issues in the relationship between Japanese Americans and the larger society that require analysis and interpretation. This book about the changing political styles of Japanese Americans between the 1920s and the 1970s adopts an approach quite different from earlier sociological studies that emphasized their cultural or economic adaptation to the larger society.[18]

Ethnicity-Based and Economy-Based Approaches

Most studies of Japanese Americans that examine their relationship to the larger society are informed by what Michael Omi and Howard Winant refer to as "ethnicity-based theory," a paradigm that emphasizes an immigrant group's "adjustment" and "incorporation" or "assimilation" into the dominant society.[19] The predominant view is that Japanese Americans have been part of the grand scheme of assimilation in American society where a minority group goes through a number of stages that had been originally coined by Robert E. Park as the "race relations cycle": contact, conflict, accommodation, and assimilation. This model was refined by Milton M. Gordon to include seven stages that identify where a particular group stands in its path towards complete assimilation. According to Gordon, structural assimilation, preceded by acculturation, is the key stage that marks full institutional participation in the larger society. For ethnicity theories, then, the main concern has been to identify the stage or the position on the assimilation continuum that Japanese Americans occupied.

As a result, earlier ethnicity-based studies have tended to study Japanese American political involvement and activism primarily as a feature of their level of acculturation or assimilation into the larger society.[20] For example, Ivan H. Light, in his comparative study of ethnic entrepreneurship among blacks, Chinese, and Japanese in America, offers an intriguing analysis of the moral dimensions of ethnic politics.[21] He suggests that traditional restraints and codes of "ethnic honor" which sensitize Chinese and Japanese Americans to the paradoxical norms of white society— that Asians should "achieve" yet maintain their subordinate "place"—pose a sharp contrast to the more universal and rational values they acquire through political assimilation. Thus old-world values which undergird the moral communities and organizations vital to ethnic entrepreneurship become less binding as the acculturation process enables Chinese and Japanese Americans to develop a better understanding of democratic values and the benefits of "modern" political action. Consequently, it is possible for the "political brotherhood" of the first generation to shift to the protest politics of the third generation as voluntary organizational life and universalistic, rational, and status-oriented values gain ascendancy.

In a recent and new variation of the assimilationist theme, Stephen S. Fugita and David J. O'Brien have provided an innovative analysis of the Japanese American experience.[22] In keeping with ethnicity theorists they posit that Japanese Americans are structurally assimilating into the mainstream of American life, but with an interesting twist: they suggest that Japanese Americans have been able to maintain their ethnic affiliations and sense of community by adapting their traditional culture and social organization to structural constraints within the larger society.

Such a duality has interesting implications for the political involvement and ideological perspectives of Japanese Americans. Fugita and O'Brien maintain that the persistence of ethnicity among Japanese Americans can and does serve as a basis for political participation. In contrast to most ethnicity-based studies, they posit that political activism is not simply a product of increased acculturation and greater involvement in the larger society, but is a phenomenon enhanced by the persistence of Japanese American ethnic group life. For example, in their analysis of three different types of Japanese American communities, they found that voluntary affiliation with ethnic organizations provided the very foundation for increased political involvement. Although they discovered generational and regional area differences depending on the political issue, Fugita and O'Brien also show that various forms of voluntary organizations rooted in the traditional Japanese ethnic culture provide an important political resource—a resource that ethnic groups that have structurally assimilated into the larger society have lost. In this respect, the persistence of ethnicity among Japanese Americans offers the potential for political mobilization on a community-wide basis, as it did for Japanese Americans who came together to support the movement for redress and reparations in the 1980s.

In recent decades, economy-based models have also been used to examine the changing patterns of ethnicity among Japanese Americans. Perhaps the best example is the middleman minority paradigm.[23] According to this scheme, middleman groups are numerically small, relatively powerless, and limited to specific occupations that are fairly lucrative but that place them in a buffer role between the masses and the elite. The group's political involvement is then seen in terms of its economic position and corresponding interests. Occupying a status above other racial groups but below elite groups, members of the middleman minority find it in their interest to avoid politics or to be politically conservative in order to preserve the delicate balance between privilege and oppression.

According to Edna Bonacich and John Modell, groups like Japanese Americans historically find themselves in such a position because of their economic motivations.[24] As sojourners who came to the United States for quick material gain, the Issei could fill only certain economic "niches" in agriculture that enabled them to amass highly liquid assets. As they encountered economic and political racism, the Japanese withdrew into their own enclaves, remained culturally autonomous, and avoided participation in local politics. Even though these sojourners eventually became settlers who made America their home, it is implicit in the middleman perspective that Japanese immigrants passed on this ethic of economic accumulation but political avoidance to succeeding generations. In this respect, economy-based studies identify the importance of economic structures in understanding an ethnic group's social position and reveal some of the limits in social mobility that confronted Japanese Americans.[25]

While both approaches are highly useful in dealing with the cultural and economic aspects of the Japanese American experience, they may also point us in a very different direction conceptually. First, by casting Japanese Americans as being set between the dominant and subordinate groups, thereby leaving them little room to maneuver, the middleman approach can be limiting. Such a paradigm would not lead us to predict that Japanese Americans would develop political styles counter to their pre- and post–World War II political orientations, voicing concerns on such issues as redress and reparations. Second, by conceiving of Japanese Americans as a middleman-minority group that is situated between whites on the one hand, and blacks, Chicanos/Latinos, and Native Americans on the other, this approach tends not to emphasize the racial nature of the experiences that Japanese Americans share in common with these other racial groups.

Third, earlier ethnicity-based studies tend to flatten the political complexities of this group by conceiving the nature of their political life primarily in terms of the electoral system rather than looking at their diverse and often competing efforts to gain full citizenship. Moreover, because ethnicity-based studies focus primarily on acculturation, interracial marriage, and civic identity, they do not emphasize intragroup diversity, racial and ethnic conflict, and change in race relations.[26] As Robert Blauner has indicated, assimilationist studies generally view minority groups as moving along a unidirectional path without recognizing that they may have been forced to assimilate under conditions very much contrary to the wishes of the group members themselves, who may actually desire an alternative direction.[27] As a result, we only get a partial picture of the overall efforts by Japanese Americans to shape their identity, retain their cultural heritage, and develop political strategies, techniques, and perspectives in dealing with race relations.

Fourth, a number of ethnicity-based theorists tend to study Japanese Americans mainly in relation to white society and emphasize their social and economic achievements compared to other minority groups. Pointing to low rates of crime, delinquency, and mental illness, and high median income and educational levels, those scholars usually place Japanese Americans in opposition to other racial minority groups and tout them as an "exceptional" group that has surmounted racial barriers within a period of only two generations.[28] Some scholars attribute the Japanese Americans' success to the compatibility between their ethnic cultural values and those of the American middle class.[29] Others attribute it to their ability to organize socially—a key feature of their cultural legacy.[30] This kind of "exceptionalist" explanation places Japanese Americans squarely within the traditional framework of the "immigrant analogy."[31] As a result, Japanese Americans are equated with European ethnic groups, in contrast to other racial groups. This is not to deny that Japanese Americans have indeed shown great upward mobility. Unless we examine the extent to which their social and economic advancement can be explained solely in terms of ethnic culture, however, ethnicity-based studies will provide only a partial understanding of the complexities of the Japanese American experience.

Imaging Japanese Americans in terms of their success is very much related to the tendency of ethnicity-based theorists to merge the ethnic and racial features of their experience and to ignore race as a basic stratifying principle within American society. Such theorists assume that prejudice and discrimination become less salient as a minority group becomes acculturated and more fully integrated into American life.[32] Consequently, we do not get a sense of how the racial dynamics and political complexities of the larger society affect the political style of Japanese Americans, such as how other racial groups may influence their political thinking and strategies. Theories that view Japanese Americans as a "model minority" group overlook the mixed character of their social and racial position and affirm the notion that Japanese Americans are an anomaly exempt from racial subordination.[33]

Finally, while there is agreement that generations are a key sociological dimension in the Japanese American community, most ethnicity-based studies tend to treat each generation as a relatively homogeneous group.[34] Issei, Nisei, and Sansei are usually depicted as having their own characterological traits, as well as being relatively uniform in their beliefs and behavior. Whatever political variations exist are said to be differences between generations. For example, the first and second generations are considered accommodationist by tradition, while the third generation's militancy, greater level of acculturation, and ability to be vocal are said to result from their Americanization.

More recent ethnicity studies, however, have identified variations within the Japanese American community, as well as continuities across generations regarding "political attitudes, ideologies, and affiliations."[35] Ethnicity is analyzed as a resource for political organizing. Continuities in ethnic organizational life and opportunities for maintaining flexible ethnic affiliations through voluntary organizations are what have enabled Nisei and Sansei to come together around key issues such as redress, but have allowed each group to take a different stand on such matters as identifying themselves as Asian Americans. It is recognized that there are significant differences among Japanese Americans in terms of political party affiliation and orientation, as well as differences among Sansei by geographical region. For example, Fugita and O'Brien found that Sansei with rural roots tended to be much more sympathetic to the Nisei Farmers League and the latter's conservative political outlook than were urban Sansei.[36] Much of this variation is explained by experiential differences and the divergent degree of structural assimilation. Thus the manner in which ethnicity operates and the form that it takes often vary across generations. Accordingly, a particular group's political affiliation, behavior, and ideological outlook are not necessarily similar to those of other segments of the Japanese American population.[37]

More attention should be given to the social and historical process through which intragenerational differences and tensions arise and intergenerational continuities take shape. For example, field researchers working in close contact with interned Japanese Americans during World War II observed a tremendous amount of political continuity between the Issei and Nisei, the overt differences between them notwithstanding.[38] Both generations rioted and organized protests against camp authorities. At the same time, Nisei draft resisters in the camps showed a marked diversity of political thought and action.[39] The continuity between and differences within generations were both rooted in the generational complexities that characterized political life within the pre–World War II community, especially as the war between the United States and Japan became imminent.[40]

An Alternative Approach to Political Style

While cultural and economic adjustment, accommodation, and assimilation are an integral part of the culture and history of Japanese Americans, the political styles of Japanese Americans are discussed in this book as expressions of their complex and dynamic relationship to the larger society—a relationship shaped by both structural forces and the actions of Japanese Americans themselves. Such an approach emphasizes their efforts to determine their identity, retain their cultural heritage, and develop political strategies, techniques, and perspectives that address their racial position, and how these facets of their experience resonate with the racial dynamics and political complexities of the larger society. Viewed this way, we will see an ethnic group that is not simply moving along the path of assimilation or striving to preserve its ethnic identity and community, but one whose members have been working to secure a place in the larger society and whose efforts are marked by internal diversity and struggle, ambivalence and questioning, as well as community solidarity and cohesive group action. Only an approach that casts Japanese Americans as part of the historical interplay between human subjects and structural forces can help to capture those aspects of their experience that have not yet been studied in detail. The concepts of racial formation and generational change are an integral part of this analysis.

Racial Formation

According to Omi and Winant, race is central to the way in which American society is organized. Racial formation constitutes a complex and dynamic process where the "meaning of race is defined and contested throughout society, in both collective action and personal practice."[41] Because the racial categories that emerge from this process are continually formed and transformed, racial formation refers to "the process by which social, economic and political forces determine the content and importance of racial categories, and by which they are in turn shaped by racial meanings."[41]

The contention that race operates at both the personal and structural levels of society and that "the racial order is organized and enforced by the continuity and reciprocity between these two 'levels' of social relations" is especially significant because such a formulation acknowledges that macro- and micro-level phenomena like racial discrimination and racial identity are often reciprocal and interpenetrating realities that inform both personal and institutional life. Simply put, one's racial identity can be the basis for collective political action and vice versa.

In contrast to ethnicity- and economy-based theories, therefore, racial formation theory offers an important way to analyze the changing political styles of Japanese Americans in terms of the racial dynamics operating at both the personal and group levels. Three aspects of Omi and Winant's framework are especially relevant to this study. First, the notion of racial formation points to the importance of analyzing the efforts by Japanese Americans to shape their identity, retain their cultural heritage, and develop political strategies to improve their racial position in relation to major cultural, political, and economic changes in American society.[42]

Second, Omi and Winant's conception of race suggests that racial ideology may play a hegemonic role in the spheres of identity and political socialization, areas that have been an important part of the Nisei and Sansei experience.[43] Thus, rather than reviewing the development of identity and politics among the Nisei and Sansei in terms of assimilation, it may be more advantageous to see how culture and politics have been shaped by racial ideology during specific historical periods and within specific racial contexts, and how the hegemony of racial ideology has racialized the Nisei and Sansei. Such an approach is useful in answering the question of why Japanese Americans in general, and Nisei leaders in particular, responded to their internment with widespread cooperation.

Third, the concept of racial formation stipulates the importance of treating race as a dynamic "social and historical process" consisting of "*an unstable and 'decentered' complex of social meanings constantly being transformed by political struggle.*"[44] In short, such things as racial identity and racial institutions are continually reinterpreted and redefined as individuals and groups forge new racial meanings through "political contestation" in various institutional realms or "sites" within society including the family, the labor market, and the political system. Although Omi and Winant are primarily concerned about the dynamics of race in relation to major social movements and the latter's impact on the state, their conception of racial politics alerts us to the importance of analyzing individual political action because it is through the process of struggle that racial structures form and are transformed by the individuals involved.

An important feature of the transformative nature of racial politics is "the process of *rearticulation*."[45] For Omi and Winant, this is a key feature of social movements:

Social movements create collective identity by offering their adherents a different view of themselves and their world; different, that is, from the worldview and self-concepts offered by the established social order. They do this by the process of *rearticulation*, which produces new subjectivity by making use of information and knowledge already present in the subject's mind. They take elements and themes of her/his culture and traditions and infuse them with new meaning.[45]

The black movement, in their estimation, was pivotal because it demonstrated how black identity assumed new meaning and significance through rearticulation as the "civil rights movement linked traditional black cultural and religious themes with the ideas and strategies of social movements around the world."[46] This transformed identity, and subjectivity, in turn, gave rise to a new political agenda and strategies for action.

The notions of political contestation and rearticulation enable us to examine the development and persistence of Japanese American political styles in relation to historical and structural patterns in the larger society. Thus, within any given situation, we can examine how Japanese Americans draw from their cultural and political resources and operate as social actors who seek to redefine themselves, thereby carving out their own history within the structural limits of the times. In Marxian terms, they are people who shape their history but not always as they choose.

Generational Change

The changing political styles of Japanese Americans must also be analyzed in relation to the concept of generation. Scholars have called attention to the unique nomenclature used by Japanese Americans to identify each generational group and how generation is defined in terms of birth order and used as an analytical tool to explain variations in the group's behavior.[47] But, the existing studies have not looked closely at the historical and structural dynamics affecting the formation of generational groupings.

Karl Mannheim's work on youth and social change provides a useful way to examine how generations intersect with history and social structure. In his provocative essay, "The Problem of Generations," Mannheim distinguished between generational location, actuality, and units.[48] Generational location refers to members of a society who are in a common age group and who experience how the same social and historical forces limit their "modes of thought, experience, feeling, and action" and restrict the "range of self expression open to the individual to certain circumscribed possibilities."[49] The analytical value of generational location, however, is limited, according to Mannheim, since members of the same generation do not necessarily participate in the "common destiny" of this grouping. Those members of a particular generation who establish a concrete bond because they experience directly or indirectly the same social and intellectual dynamics in a period of significant change constitute a generation as an actuality. Furthermore, within an actual generation, separate generational units can form different groups when youth respond differently to their common experiences and forge an "esprit" based upon a shared political perspective. In this respect, generational units possess greater solidarity than do actual generations.[50]

Mannheim further states that generational units can establish new generational styles that are shaped by periods of "socio-cultural destabilization." He adds, however, that each generation does not necessarily develop its own style when the pace of change is either too rapid or too slow. These groups will graft themselves either to an earlier and established generational style or to a new generational unit which is "evolving a new form." But he cautions that new styles must still be perceived within the larger *zeitgeist* of the age. Each new generational trend, in the final analysis, tends to be a unique reformulation of the conservative, liberal, or socialist world view that remains stable from generation to generation.

Mannheim's conception of generation offers new ways of looking at generational change among Japanese Americans. Not only does it point to the fact that competing groups within a generation often emerge during periods of significant historical and structural change, it also identifies social processes involved when members of a generational group assume a dominant leadership role not only for themselves but for the entire community.

Applying Mannheim's conception to Japanese Americans, we can then examine whether they developed a rich political diversity during periods of intense social change and cultural destabilization. We can also consider whether a particular generational unit advocating an accommodationist style emerged within such a context and eventually assumed dominance within the Japanese American community. Such a discussion will provide the basis for comparing the different Nisei political styles that emerged during the political and economic crises of the 1930s with the ideologies and strategies generated by Japanese American youth in the late 1960s. By looking at generations in this way, we will begin to recognize that they often competed among themselves as they challenged the individuals and the institutions that denied them their rights as American citizens and permanent residents of the United States.

By viewing racial formation and generation as primary concepts, we can perceive the dynamic and complex nature of ethnic identity, culture, and politics in new ways. This approach will help us understand those complexities of the Japanese American experience that entail intragenerational tensions and diversity, intergenerational continuities, and the paradoxical nature of Japanese American social and economic mobility on the one hand, and the persistence of racial subordination on the other, as well as the ironic shifts in their political styles.

The "Sociological Imagination"

Methodologically, to ground the various themes involving political style, race, and generation, I have relied on the approach used by Richard Sennet and Jonathan Cobb and by David Wellman.[51] Their studies of racial and class responses to structures of oppression provide a valuable blueprint for combining historical and field research methods. They emphasize the importance of analyzing a person's life experience within the context of the major institutions of the society in which he or she lives, and demonstrate how such an approach could help us understand the impact of social structures on one's racial consciousness and political ideology.

In adopting such a methodology, I draw from in-depth interviews, historical sources, and participant observations to construct sociological portraits of Nisei and Sansei who came of age during periods of major social change. These individual portraits allow us to apply what C. Wright Mills calls the "sociological imagination": "to grasp history and biography and the relations between the two within society."[52] Through the interplay between personal life and social structure, major racial and economic trends and patterns that have shaped the political styles of Japanese Americans are identified.

This book is organized around four historical periods. Each one has a chapter that outlines the social position of Japanese Americans during a particular period followed by a chapter devoted to portraits that illustrate how individuals defined and responded to the racial tenor of their times. The concentration camp experience during World War II is not, however, paired with portraits, but treated separately, given its central importance to the Japanese American experience.

Chapter 1 offers an overview of the Japanese American community in the 1920s with special attention to the Issei legacy and their demographic characteristics. Chapter 2 examines the social and economic position of the Nisei prior to World War II and provides a context for assessing the Nisei political styles that are covered in the next two chapters. Chapter 3 contains four Nisei portraits that emphasize their political thinking and organizing efforts during this time of racial hostility and political and economic upheaval. Chapter 4 examines the responses of Nisei leaders to Executive Order 9066, signed by President Franklin D. Roosevelt on February 19, 1942, that authorized the evacuation and incarceration of Japanese Americans, and explores the impact of the internment experience on the ethnic identity of the Nisei.

Chapter 5 reviews the postwar integration of Japanese Americans by sketching the changes in their socioeconomic position in the 1950s and early 1960s, and considering the political and economic conditions that initiated important changes in their racial position. This discussion provides the backdrop for Chapter 6, which offers portraits of two Nisei whose lives and political styles resonated with those times.

The period from the 1960s to the 1970s is discussed in Chapters 7 and 8, which examine, once again, the changing social position of Japanese Americans and the rise of militancy in the late 1960s among Sansei youth who forged a new political style during the cultural crisis and racial unrest of the period. As in Chapter 3, Chapter 7 examines the link between generational location and political style within this context of sociocultural flux. Chapter 8 provides portraits of two Sansei who were deeply affected by the cultural destabilization and social movements of that time.

This study is not a political history per se. Rather, by analyzing political styles in specific racial and economic settings between the 1920s and the 1970s, I provide new insights about the nature of social action in the Japanese American experience and identify dimensions in their approach to the racial order that have not been emphasized before. The book closes with a discussion about the larger significance of studying Japanese American political styles and an assessment of the possibilities for the emergence of new approaches that may be crafted in the future.

The Issei Legacy

From Entry to Exclusion

TO UNDERSTAND HOW JAPANESE IMMIGRANTS, THE ISSEI, developed political strategies and expressed concerns for the "life chances" of their children, the second-generation Nisei, we must examine the social, political, and economic conditions under which the Issei struggled with their racial position in the United States. Three aspects of the social and economic position of the Issei generation are discussed: 1) their entry into the United States as cheap labor, 2) their changing economic position, and 3) their encounter with racism. Out of these experiences emerged a defensive Issei political style and a particular perspective on the socioeconomic problems facing the Nisei.

Entry to America

Japanese immigration to the United States commenced in the 1860s. In 1868, the first group of contract laborers (141 men, 6 women, and 1 child) went to Hawaii, but the major migration took place between 1885 and 1894 when approximately 30,000 contract workers "were brought to the Hawaiian Islands."[1] Immigration into the U.S. mainland directly from Japan and via Hawaii took place between the turn of the century and the passage of the Immigration Act of 1924. About 245,000 of the 275,000 Japanese who immigrated between 1861 and 1924 entered the United States in that 24-year period, with the majority coming to California.[2]

Before 1907 Japanese immigrants were predominantly young, single men from farming backgrounds with an equivalent of an eighth-grade education.[3] Most of these immigrants thought of themselves as *dekaseginin*, which literally meant "go-out-to-earn people."[4] The view that the Issei thought of themselves as sojourners who came to America with the basic purpose of making their fortune and returning home once they had accumulated enough capital was voiced by one Issei:

> Generally speaking, when a European emigrant is bidding farewell to his home, his intention is, perhaps, to go to a new land where he can start a new life.... The contrary is true of the Japanese whose only desire is to build a new home, not upon American soil, but in his native land. He desires to save a certain amount of money by a four or five-year struggle, and then, coming back to his own land, to start in business or become an independent farmer.[5]

But the crucial issue is not whether sojourning was the primary reason for immigration; what matters is that some Issei possessed a pragmatic vision—they knew they could earn the equivalent of two Japanese yen for every dollar earned in America. More importantly, they could secure an education in the United States by working their way through school.[6]

For Issei in general, however, their vision of America and their motives for immigrating were shaped within the political and economic context of Japanese society, where their opportunities for social and economic mobility were severely restricted. Land taxes—crucial sources of revenue needed to support Japan's efforts to industrialize at the turn of the century—placed an especially heavy burden on farmers in southern Japan who were key producers in a rice economy. At the same time a population growth spurt coincided with food shortages. These conditions, in what had been a stable social and economic environment, created significant financial hardships for the prefectures in southern Japan and prompted many residents to look to the urban areas and countries like the United States for economic opportunity.[7]

Meanwhile, U.S. capitalist expansion created a demand for cheap labor, first in Hawaii and then on the Pacific Coast, as well as major shifts in California agriculture. Three economic developments in particular affected Japanese immigration. First, during the 1880s, the shift from wheat to fruit production, which resulted from the introduction of new irrigation techniques, signified a major transition in California's economy. As these techniques gained widespread use after 1885, the amount of irrigated acreage increased significantly, as did the need for an additional source of labor.[8]

Second, the completion of the transcontinental railroad and various railroad lines—the Southern Pacific (1881) and the Atchison, Topeka and Santa Fe (1885)—incorporated California into the national economy and provided access to eastern markets.[8] The critical link between California's fruit crops and external markets was the refrigerator car, first introduced in 1888, which allowed fresh fruit and produce to be transported over long distances.[9]

Third, urbanization, which derived from the expansion of manufacturing and the rise of corporate capitalism, helped to increase the demand
for fresh produce.[10] The railroads played a significant role in this process by
facilitating the movement of settlers to the West Coast. Meanwhile, California became the supplier of fresh fruit and produce for cities throughout
the nation. Japanese began to enter in large numbers just as specialized
farming became a central feature of California's economy.[11]

Thus, at the turn of the century, Japanese immigrants filled the
increasing demand for cheap labor. Substituting to some degree for Chinese laborers who were excluded as a result of the 1882 Chinese Exclusion
Act, the Japanese worked the fields of the Pacific Coast and soon became
the major source of farm labor, numbering as many as 39,000 in the summer of 1909.[12] Issei farm workers were concentrated in the intensive crops
which included sugar beets, grapes, fruits, berries, vegetables, and hops.[13]
These crops were seasonal and required Issei labor to be highly mobile. By
1909 Issei labor was vital not only in California but in Idaho, Colorado,
Montana, Utah, Washington, and Oregon.[14]

Although Japanese laborers were located mainly in the agricultural
sectors of the economy, they also worked in the mines of the Rocky Moun-
tains and on the Northern railroads.[15] On the West Coast, they toiled in
the canneries, logging camps, meat packing plants, and salt works.[16] For
the most part, Japanese immigrants were isolated from the more lucrative
trades and the manufacturing jobs. In contrast to the Chinese who had
entered manufacturing industries prior to being driven out by white workers in the 1880s, Japanese immigrants were unable to enter cigar, shoe, and
garment factories because of anti-Asian sentiments and the monopolization
of these jobs by white workers.[17]

Issei found work under a contract system in which Japanese bosses
acted as intermediaries between their workers and employers. Each boss
generally collected a commission from his employer for each worker per
day of labor. By handling up to 1,000 workers at peak season, a railroad
labor contractor, for example, could easily reap $100 a day on a commis-
sion of merely 10 cents per man.[18]

Unwilling to accept their strenuous and exploitive working conditions
passively, some Issei workers became involved in labor organizing in order
to win better wages and work conditions.[19] As early as 1900, the Japanese
Labor League, an organization that had sprung from the Japanese Socialist
Revolutionary Party of San Francisco, struggled to free workers from the
contract system. Adhering to the ideal of working-class unity, the Labor
League recruited some 200 workers. Despite their initial enthusiasm, however, the Labor League did not succeed in its goals because it received a
great deal of hostile press coverage as well as acrid criticism from establishment leaders in the Japanese Association. The problem of maintaining

financial solvency compounded the Labor League's problems. But most important, the migratory character of the agricultural workers, coupled with the failure of the white working class to adhere to the principles of international class solidarity, made it virtually impossible for Issei workers to consolidate on a more cohesive basis.[20]

While the Labor League and its followers pursued class-based politics, numerous Issei workers showed strong antipathy towards labor organizing and union activity. Instead they yearned to become independent growers, which suggests that Issei laborers viewed their role as a transitional phase on the road to becoming petty entrepreneurs. Many struck out on their own, first as tenant farmers and then as small landholders.[21] This particular economic thrust, according to Modell, was in response to circumstances surrounding and within the Japanese community. The Issei confronted a unique racial situation in Los Angeles, an ambiguous color line that excluded them from some activities but allowed their participation in those which were "important to the economy and to the smooth functioning of business in the area."[22] As the economy prospered, Issei leaders embraced an accommodationist strategy that stressed "harmony and cooperation" and the need to earn the respect of white Americans through proper conduct, including Americanization activities, a reduction of behavior deemed deviant by white society, and the self-management of social problems. This response, combined with hard work and perseverance, was economically effective: by the late 1920s and the early 1930s, the Japanese had carved out lucrative niches which were "quite compatible ... with racial separation."[23] In a similar interpretation, Tetsuya Fujimoto points out that petty enterprise became the key to Issei survival for two important reasons.[24] First, the "ideology of white supremacy forced this immigrant group to cope with the techno-economic environment in particular ways, i.e., family-centered small entrepreneurial activity including family operated farms."[24] And second, the Issei shift to petty enterprise, particularly small farming, had been made possible by the changing American political economy. In California, the development of irrigation, innovations in transportation, and the rise of cities made intensive agriculture an attractive and necessary alternative for Issei laborers. It was this economic transformation that enabled the Issei to pursue intensive farming.

Changing Economic Position

Between 1900 and 1910, the number of Japanese farmers in California increased from 37 to 1,816, while the total acreage leased jumped from 35,258 to 80,232, and the amount sharecropped expanded from 19,572 to 59,001.[25] According to Robert Higgs, wage discrimination and barriers to economic mobility were major reasons that the Japanese moved towards independent farming, chiefly as tenants and sharecroppers.[26] Land leasing enabled large landowners to avoid risks and to secure substantial profits as the Japanese tenant farmers bore the burden of finding the necessary labor to work the land. Also, Issei farmers were willing to pay higher rents for the land than were white farmers.[27] Because the Japanese were able to produce higher yields, and thus higher profits, they could afford higher rents. But Higgs suggests other reasons for why white landowners charged the Japanese higher rates. If a large number of landlords were concerned only about their profits, competition for Japanese tenants should have reduced the prevailing "racial rental premium," so Higgs conjectures that the differential rate structure resulted from the persistence of anti-Japanese sentiments during the period 1900–1920. He further suggests that a racial rental premium should have vanished between 1920 and 1940, once the 1924 Immigration Act had been passed. Higgs' hypothesis is provocative and raises the possibility that both economic and racial considerations served the interest of white landowners to treat the Japanese differentially. Higher rents not only meant greater profits and a thriving economy, but also acknowledged the more privileged status of white farmers.

Issei tenant farmers were able to begin operations with little capital because some commission merchants offered financing in exchange for liens upon the crops, and shippers were willing to extend cash credit in order to secure control over certain crops.[28] The Issei had little alternative, if they wished to improve their economic standing. They were compelled to cope with poor working conditions to improve their land, and to expend the hand labor needed to grow fruits and vegetables. The demands of specialized farming also required entire families to participate in the production process.[29]

Between 1910 and 1920, the Issei reached their highest level of agricultural production in California as a result of the wartime prosperity and the demand for food. By 1920, they owned 74,769 acres, cash-leased 192,150 acres, sharecropped 121,000 acres, and contracted 70,137 acres.[30] What they produced was valued at $67 million and represented 30 to 35 percent of California's entire truck crops. They established "a virtual monopoly" on fresh snap beans, celery, and strawberries by 1941.[31]

In the first two decades of the twentieth century Issei urban enterprises also proliferated.[32] According to Yamato Ichihashi, the increased number of Japanese immigrants, limited occupational mobility, and discrimination against the Japanese in boarding houses, restaurants, barber shops, and so forth, required that the Japanese develop their own facilities.[33] In San Francisco, for example, "city trades" jumped from 90 to 545 between 1900 and 1909.[34] In the city of Stockton, small business establishments rose from 54 to 250 in the period 1909–1920.[35] In Seattle, 47 percent of the hotels and 25 percent of the grocery stores were Issei owned and operated by 1919.[36] The most dramatic changes took place in Los Angeles, where the number of businesses increased from 473 in 1909 to 1,806 in 1928.[37] This growth also corresponded with the overall expansion in California's economy, especially in Los Angeles after the turn of the century.[38]

Racial Exclusion

The very presence of Japanese workers as well as their subsequent attempts to secure a foothold in West Coast agriculture raised white fears of economic competition, the loss of white privilege, and the erosion of the myth of white superiority. Issei efforts to fully participate in American life were continually blocked by much of the same exclusionary and social control measures encountered by other racial groups. The efforts to keep these early Japanese in a racially subordinate position took the form of population control, segregation from American political life, and the denial of land ownership. As the targets of these measures, the Japanese experienced a much different reality than white ethnics who immigrated at about the same time.

Population Control

The small size of today's Japanese American population can be traced to earlier immigration policies and statutes shaped by a strong anti-Japanese movement. Unlike the large urban communities which European ethnic groups established in the East Coast and the Midwest, the growth of Japanese immigrant communities had been regulated by the Gentlemen's Agreement of 1907, which restricted Japanese labor immigration. In response to the decision of the San Francisco Board of Education to segregate Japanese Americans students, along with Chinese and Korean American students, from white students in 1906, compromise was reached between Japan and the United States, whereby Japanese American students would not be removed from San Francisco public schools if Japan would stop issuing passports to all laborers except those "who have already been in America and to the parents, wives and children of laborers already resident there."[39] As a result of the agreement, immigration to the mainland declined sharply for Japanese males. An executive order terminating the entry of Japanese by way of Hawaii, Canada, and Mexico further reduced immigration. The restriction, however, did not apply to *yobiyose* (relatives of settled immigrants), nor did it anticipate the entry of "picture brides." A moderate-sized influx of these two kinds of immigrants and the subsequent rise in the Japanese birthrate caused anti-Japanese labor leaders and politicians on the Pacific Coast to rekindle their exclusionary efforts, culminating in the passage of the 1924 Immigration Act. Arrivals decreased from 4,759 during the 1920–1924 period to 571 in the 1924–1930 period.[40]

The 1924 Immigration Act contributed to an abnormal age gap between the Nisei and the Issei compared to European ethnic groups. Japanese communities were divided into young and old. "In 1942 the median age of Nisei was 17 years," whereas it was 55 for Issei men and 47 for Issei women.[41] Aware of this disparity, an astute Issei sketched out the impending dilemma:

> What invites our attention is the great discrepancy in the age between the father and the babe. In many cases the father is a half-old man of fifty, while his children are only four or five years old. When the latter reach the age of twenty the former will be approaching the grave, if not actually in it. Time will come when our community will be made up of weak, half-dead old men and immature and reckless youths. Who will guide the young men and women of our community twenty years hence? There is no answer.[41]

A brief contrast with the white ethnic situation provides a glimpse of the political consequences of population control for the Japanese. Heavy Irish immigration to New York and Boston in the 1840s gave the Irish a significant plurality, a condition that made possible their subsequent rise and control over city politics.[42] A few decades later, the entry of Russian Jews into the New York area provided them a political base. Though these groups, too, were perceived by old-stock Americans as cheap foreign labor which undermined the native white standard of living, the consequences of the 1924 Immigration Act had been far less severe for the Irish, Italians, Greeks, and Jews.[43] They received immigration quotas based on the number of their countrymen in the United States in 1890.[44] Since many European ethnic groups had already established large communities by that date, compared to the Chinese and Japanese, their natural growth was not completely truncated by the 1924 Act. European immigrant settlements in America, therefore, possessed an advantage over the Japanese in terms of leadership development. Though generational differences between the immigrants and the American-born were acute, white ethnic groups have been more balanced in their age structure, making generational differences along political lines less severe though they were by no means absent.[45] In turn, this allowed for greater continuity in the development of community leadership over the long run.

Exclusion from American Political Life

The right to vote had been granted to European immigrants as a result of the Naturalization Act of 1790 that conferred the privilege of citizenship to free white males. Japanese immigrants struggled to win this same privilege through the courts, pushing their case all the way to the

Supreme Court, which denied naturalization to Japanese in 1922.[46] The Court's decision excluded the Issei from America's political mainstream and undermined their potential to amass political influence through the tactic of bloc voting. Without the franchise, they were virtually powerless compared to European ethnic groups to promote their own interests in the American political arena. Although many of the Poles, Italians, and Greeks hesitated to transfer their loyalties to America, the patronage system of city politics soon made them realize that the vote, when properly used, paid handsome material dividends.[47] Through ethnic associations, the Greeks and Italians became familiar with the potential benefits of being voters.[48] While the critics viewed political bosses and the spoils system as a form of exploitation, patronage, nonetheless, set the foundation for a local power base upon which white ethnics could construct a sturdy apparatus. Tammany Hall in New York City acted as an Irish stronghold for many years.[49] A few decades later, the Italians gained political influence with the mobilization of a bloc vote.[50]

Some scholars have argued that since the Japanese and the Chinese before them came to America as sojourners whose primary concern was to make money before returning home, they had no intention of establishing roots in America and hence had no political interests. The overemphasis on the sojourner notion, however, can become extremely misleading. Many Greek immigrants also came to America at the turn of the century as sojourners who displayed tremendous loyalty to their homeland, not unlike the cultural nationalism manifested by the Issei.[51] In fact, the Greek nationalist cause gained the greatest support from its overseas colonies. During World War I, many Greeks questioned their status in America. After serving in the armed forces and acquiring American citizenship as a direct result, many did transfer their loyalty to America and naturalization skyrocketed, largely in response to the campaign to promote Americanization.[52] With their newly acquired citizenship, Greek Americans intensified their political activism in the 1920s.

Japanese immigrants, like Greek immigrants, had also begun to manifest ties to America. In his study of the Japanese community in Seattle, Washington, S. Frank Miyamoto suggested that the period between the Gentlemen's Agreement (1907) and the Immigration Act (1924) was a "settlement period" during which women and nonlaborers came in greater numbers.[53] This was indicative of what was taking place throughout the Pacific Coast.[54] According to Yuji Ichioka, the influx of women between 1910 and 1920 "enabled many immigrant men to enjoy a settled family life which socially reinforced the economic foundation of permanent settlement."[55] Despite lingering intentions of eventually returning to their homeland, the Issei quickly shifted from "sojourners to permanent settlers" with the emergence of a second generation.[56]

Thus, in contrast to white ethnic groups who had access to two important resources—group size and naturalization—the Issei were fundamentally excluded from American institutions. Those with political aspirations were compelled to limit their activities to their own communities. Essentially, the Issei had to rely on their own limited resources to protect their economic interests.[57] White ethnic groups, on the other hand, had greater latitude in developing political organizations within the context of urban economic development and could secure direct access to local governments.[58]

Denial of Land Ownership

Besides prohibiting citizenship, the 1906 Naturalization Act set the precedent for California's enactment of a pair of alien land laws which were aimed at Japanese in agriculture. While the 1913 Alien Land Law contained provisions allowing the Issei to lease land for no more than three years in accordance with a prevailing treaty with Japan, the law's intent was clearly revealed by U. S. Webb, Attorney General of California:

> The fundamental basis of all legislation upon this subject [Japanese], State and Federal, has been, and is, race undesirability. It is unimportant and foreign to the question under discussion whether a particular race is inferior. The simple and single question is, is the race desirable.... It [the law] seeks to limit their presence by curtailing their privileges which they enjoy here; for they will not come in large numbers and long abide with us if they may not acquire land. And it seeks to limit the numbers who will come by limiting the opportunites for their activity here when they arrive.[59]

Thus Webb believed that a law preventing the Japanese from owning land for agricultural purposes would force them to abandon their stake in California and discourage others from coming in the future.

To soften the impact of the 1913 Alien Land Law, Issei agriculturists resorted to guardianship, a strategy that put the title to the land in the name of their citizen offspring.[60] It was not uncommon for Nisei who were of legal age to function as paper landowners for several Issei farmers. When officials realized that the Japanese were able to circumvent the restriction, the California legislature passed an amendment in 1920 which rescinded the provisions allowing the Japanese to lease agricultural land and negated the practice of guardianship. The State of Washington similarly amended its land law the next year.[61]

Scholars disagree about the long-term impact of these laws. Some argue that the Issei had successfully circumvented them, while others regard the land laws as crippling.[62] Masakazu Iwata, for example, demonstrated that the expansion of Issei agriculture, which reached a high point in 1921, when Issei accounted for 12.3 percent of California's farm production, tapered off in 1925 to 9.3 percent.[63] Many Issei vacated their farms seeking refuge in the cities, while others became migrant workers once again.[64] Still others concentrated their efforts on quick-growth crops.[65] By reinforcing their segregation from the economic mainstream, these laws probably heightened the Issei's sense of alienation from American life and intensified their feelings of subordination.[66]

Although it is difficult to determine precisely the impact of the land laws, they did regulate the acquisition of an important economic resource in a society where land ownership has been an important means of advancement. Armenians and Italians on the Pacific Coast have used their land as a foundation for power in local and state politics in much the same way the Jews of New York have used their small businesses as a source of political influence. Had the Issei been able to consolidate a larger agricultural base, their power potential could have been far more substantial.

In combination, these institutional limits restricted the Issei possibilities for developing a wider range of political strategies. Organized Japanese labor was isolated from the larger labor movement and their position as migrant workers hindered their capacity to sustain the organizations needed to develop a strong political base. Without citizenship, the Issei could not actively participate in electoral politics. And without the ability to expand their agricultural economic base, their potential for economic power was undermined. Under these circumstances, the Issei had little choice but to adopt a cautious and conservative style in dealing with race relations.

Defensive Politics

In response to their racial situation, the Issei developed a political style characterized by an extensive organizational network of prefectoral societies (*kenjinkai*), Buddhist and Christian churches, business associations (*kumiai*), and labor organizations to improve their social status and protect their economic interests.[67] Between 1900 and 1942, the "so-called Japanese associations" provided the most important source of political leadership.[68]

As the anti-Japanese movement developed in California in the early 1900s, the Japanese Association of America was formed to counteract the efforts of the exclusionists and to promote the social and educational welfare of the immigrant community.[69] By 1908, prominent Issei leaders had transformed the original association into an organizational structure that featured a "three-tiered hierarchy."[70] "Local Japanese consulates occupied the upper tier, while local associations represented the third tier. Situated on the middle level were so-called central bodies, which provided the link between the local consulates and local associations."[70] The original association became the "central body" that coordinated the activities of its affiliated "locals" not only in California, but in Arizona, Nevada, and Utah. In 1911, the Japanese Association of Oregon, which was organized in Portland, became the parent body for its locals in Oregon, Idaho, and Wyoming. The central body for the Pacific Northwest, which formed in Seattle two years later, coordinated its locals in Washington and Montana. As new locals arose in the Southwest region of the Pacific Coast, the Central Japanese Association of Southern California formed in Los Angeles to direct the affairs of its affiliates in Arizona, New Mexico, and Southern California. By 1915, the association's geographical span encompassed the Pacific Coast and several inland states (Idaho, Wyoming, Montana, Arizona, New Mexico, Nevada, Utah, Colorado, New York, Illinois, and Texas). In 1923, it had 86 "affiliated locals."[71]

Lacking citizenship and franchise, but needing to protect their farms and businesses, Issei leaders could not adopt an activist or a protest-oriented response to their subordinate status. The racial situation and the racial ideology of that period offered them few political options. To defend themselves and their interests, they had to develop a political style that featured several different strategies to counter the ideas and actions of exclusionists like Mayor James D. Phelan of San Francisco, who in 1900 had criticized the Japanese as undesirable and unassimilable.[72] To promote mutual understanding between the Japanese and white Americans like Phelan, the Japanese Association of America developed a public relations campaign to educate anti-Japanese agitators and their sympathizers.[73] Prior to 1924, the Association waged a prolonged battle against the exclusionists by disseminating pamphlets which were written to counter the inflammatory sentiment fostered by such groups as the Anti-Asiatic Association, the Alien Regulation League, and the American League.[74]

To counteract the exclusionists' criticism about the Nisei's dual citizenship, Issei leaders took concrete action. Because Japanese citizenship was automatically extended to children of Japanese nationals, regardless of their country of birth, anti-Japanese propagandists viewed the dual citizenship of the Nisei as a threat to the American body politic. Thus in 1915 the Northwest American Japanese Association petitioned the Japanese government to resolve this question so that the Nisei would not be the target of criticism. Japan responded in 1916 by allowing Issei parents to renounce their children's Japanese citizenship if they were 14 years old or younger. Children between the ages of 15 and 16 could themselves renounce their Japanese citizenship but those who were 17 years or older were required to satisfy their "Japanese military obligation" before they could do so.[75] The Japanese government further amended its nationality law when anti-

Japanese agitation intensified in 1924. Henceforth, "automatic nationality based upon paternal descent" was removed, while provisions were made to allow the Issei to retain their children's Japanese citizenship if they so desired.[76]

Issei leaders also took conciliatory action on the Japanese language school issue. Nativists were very critical of Japanese language schools because they supposedly retarded Americanization and promoted Japanese nationalism. Through a series of conferences, Issei leaders and educators debated the purpose, curriculum, and instructional materials of Japanese language schools.[77] Despite differences in perspective on the best way to proceed, Issei leaders revised their educational plan for the Nisei in 1912. Instead of preparing them to "enter the schools in Japan" by providing an education that covered intellectual, moral, and physical matters, they decided that the American public schools would provide the intellectual and physical aspects of their education while the language schools would handle the moral dimension of Nisei education.[78] As the exclusion movement intensified in California with the passage of the 1913 Alien Land Law, some prominent Issei stressed the importance of an American education for the Nisei.[79] Although the Issei, no doubt, accommodated begrudgingly to the exclusionists, their defensive gestures quite probably were the only options available to them under the circumstances.

To avoid conflict with white citizens, Issei leaders further proposed ways for Japanese immigrants to interact with white Americans.[80] In response to the agitation in 1923 to expel Japanese residents from the Rose Hill, Boyle Heights, Hollywood, and Sherman districts of Los Angeles, Sei Fujii, President of the Japanese Association of Los Angeles and newspaper publisher, issued a warning to the Issei community asking its members to change any behavior that offended white Americans: "It must be remembered . . . that if there is anything in our daily conducts [sic] which is repugnant to the good customs and manners of America and otherwise objectionable, we must be good enough to change it right away."[81] He believed that women should discard the practice of wearing "improper" clothing on the streets and the use of "unwelcome old customs." Men were to keep their premises clean, maintain friendships with American neighbors, and avoid foolish actions when misunderstandings arose with Americans, even when the latter acted "unreasonably" toward the Japanese.

By being unobstrusive and compliant, leaders like Fujii believed that the Japanese community could avoid troublesome encounters which might become catalysts for even more undesirable attention. The earlier anti-Chinese movement had made the Issei highly conscious of racial discrimination and cautious about their behavior.[82] Not all Issei, however, agreed with the Japanese association or leaders like Fujii. An Issei resident of Tacoma, Washington, for example, was quite distressed about such caution and called for a much more aggressive approach to the race problem: "Let us approach the Americans without fear and build our own strength and position in their midst till they withdraw their weapons and oppression and hostility."[83] While this critic called for an aggressive approach to the race problem, he did share with Fujii and others a desire to prove the worth and fitness of the Japanese. Both assumed that some change in the behavior of the Japanese, either compliance or a show of fearlessness, was the starting point for altering their treatment by white Americans. This line of argument differed basically from that of labor organizers who approached the race situation in class terms and stressed the need for worker solidarity. But overall, those who advocated protest or a mustering of "strength," like those who emphasized class politics, tended to be in the minority.

Employing defensive tactics did not mean that the Issei were not argumentative or indignant about the racism they encountered. For example, an Issei leader responded to anti-Japanese propagandists in the following way:

That the Japanese are not really an undesirable people, that they are in truth worthy to be assimilated finds indisputable proof in the very statements of the anti-Japanese agitators who preface their adverse arguments by admitting freely that the Japanese are sober, orderly, peaceful, industrious and enterprising, and in no way inferior to the Caucasian race. . . . And, admittedly possessing these characteristics, are not the Japanese wholly worthy of being assimilated? Then why not take a positive step in this direction? Why not make them a desirable integral part of American life and transform them into a valuable asset instead of permitting mistreatment and discrimination to make of them a liability to themselves and to the whole American people? Let rationalism rather than foolish sentimentalism rule.[84]

This leader appealed to Americans for fair treatment and the recognition of the Issei's potential contribution to American society in general. But more than logical argumentation and moral suasion were needed to defend their interests and achieve equal treatment.

To protect their rights and to promote their prosperity, Issei leadership used the legal system. In 1914, Issei leaders began efforts to secure the right to become citizens.[85] In order to counteract the 1913 Alien Land Law, they considered the use of diplomatic channels or the possibility of organizing a campaign to get a law passed granting them citizenship through Congressional legislation. But not wanting to rely on Japanese diplomats or public sentiment, they instead chose litigation hoping to obtain a judicial ruling that would make them eligible for naturalization by law and then push a test case all the way to the Supreme Court.

To ensure the best chance of succeeding, the Japanese association leaders supported Takao Ozawa, whom they considered an ideal choice for a legal test case because he more than satisfied all of the nonracial requirements specified by law. In terms of moral character and personal background, he was also an ideal candidate. As Yuji Ichioka described him, "Ozawa was a paragon of an assimilated Japanese immigrant, a living refutation of the allegation of Japanese unassimilability."[86] Despite some controversy and debate within the Issei immigrant community about the litigation strategy, a naturalization committee appointed by association leaders to oversee this legal campaign submitted the Ozawa case. In 1922, the Supreme Court ruled that Ozawa was ineligible for citizenship: as a Mongolian, the court reasoned, he failed to satisfy the racial requirements of naturalization which were reserved for free whites and persons of African descent.

Apart from the Ozawa case, Issei fought many legal battles to improve their subordinate status and to protect their economic interests. When they unsuccessfully challenged the alien land laws of California and Washington in 1923, the shocked Issei were compelled to seek out alternative strategies to maintain their livelihood.[87] After the passage of the 1924 Immigration Act, many Issei experienced a deep sense of "hopelessness and dejection."[88] Rather than amassing the political resources that enabled many white ethnic immigrant groups to secure social and political inclusion, especially at the local level, the Issei were excluded from full participation in American society. Within such a repressive racial and political environment, the future status of the second generation became an important issue in the eyes of the Issei.

Issei Concerns About the Second Generation

Aside from the questions of language training for, and dual citizenship of, the Nisei, Issei also worried about the Nisei's future. Although most Issei had achieved a level of economic stability either as petty entrepreneurs or as laborers, it was not all that clear that the Nisei would have a place in the economy, given the racial restrictions in the labor market.[89] The interviews conducted as part of the Survey of Race Relations (SRR) at Stanford University in 1925 and 1926 under the direction of Robert E. Park suggest that the Issei and those Nisei who came of age in the 1920s were vitally concerned about the limited life chances facing the second generation.

In anticipation of the problems awaiting the Nisei in the job market, some Issei believed that the second generation should secure as much education as possible. One man interviewed by the Survey of Race Relations, Dr. Peter S., indicated that he intended to provide every opportunity for his children to get a good education. His perspective was very pragmatic:

If the American born Japanese are to win a place for themselves they will have to excel in some special line, and that idea is quite largely responsible for the encouragement which Japanese parents give their children in school. In this connection we may learn a lesson from Japan. In Japan handicapped persons are not treated as they are in America, but they turn to some field in which they come to excel as when blind persons specialize in music. Likewise in America those who are handicapped on account of racial discriminations must make a place for themselves through excellence in some special field.[90]

Dr. S.'s notion of excelling in "some special line" because of racial discrimination is intriguing because his conception of education for the Nisei stemmed not simply from his cultural heritage, but also as a result of the limits imposed by the racial order.[91] In this respect, the Issei emphasis on education for the Nisei became a logical choice, given the labor market restrictions and the potential access to higher learning. The "special line" of education was thus an important strategy for winning a place within a restrictive environment.

This strategy, however, may have been much more characteristic among the professional and business segments of the community, whose members may have emphasized the role of higher education as a source of mobility and status. Like Dr. S., Professor Yamato Ichihashi of Stanford University, another respondent in the Survey of Race Relations, reflected on what the future might hold for his own son:

The young Japanese in America are going to have difficulties in fitting into industrial life. The racial mark of the Mongolian face is going to stand against them and I am not very hopeful of a solution in the immediate future. I have been thinking about this because I have a boy of six who will have to face the problem. I am planning to give him the best of advantages educationally in America, but I am also going to encourage him to learn the Japanese language so that he can go to Japan if he meets too many obstacles here. That part of it, however, I am going to leave to his decision, but I am going to prepare him to meet this situation.[92]

Despite the fact that Ichihashi occupied a position of prestige and status, he understood the objective racial conditions facing the future of the second generation. According to him, higher education, coupled with the ability to speak Japanese, were essential ingredients for survival. Had there existed a more egalitarian racial situation, we may infer that Ichihashi probably would not have emphasized either consideration as a precautionary measure.

While the Issei emphasized the value of education, not all of them defined it in the same manner. In contrast to the perspective of Ichihashi and Dr. S., Adjutant M. Kobayashi of the Salvation Army spelled out the need for more vocational education. He stated, "We must begin to think about the second generation of American-born Japanese. We must give them vocational training in art, carpentry, agriculture, etc."[93] Mindful of an incipient Nisei trend towards professional education and the impending saturation of professional positions within the Issei economy, and acutely aware of a racist job market in the larger society, he pushed vigorously for entry into agricultural occupations:

> It's my idea that we should develop in the Japanese children in America a greater interest in farming. In fact it is my ambition to start an institution to give boys training in poultry-raising, carpentry, agriculture, etc. Provision should be made for training the women in butter and cheese making, in general domestic science and secretarial work. This idea I have promoted for some time. I have read several of Booker L. Washington's [sic] books, but I have developed this idea before I had read about his activities.[93]

As for those Nisei who wished to pursue business, Kobayashi proposed a plan by which they would work with Japanese business firms that had branches in large cities throughout the world.

Although it is difficult to determine the impact of Kobayashi's ideas, they indicate that the Issei were cognizant of American educational currents and were familiar with the work of black educators like Booker T. Washington. Thus the ideas of men like Kobayashi were not merely Japanese in origin, but quite eclectic. While further research is necessary, Kobayashi's thinking tends to affirm the notion that the racial limits facing immigrants within the American context affected the way in which they devised strategies for coping with their circumstances.

In addition, Kobayashi's perspective tended to reflect the views of other Issei who urged the Nisei to return to the land.[94] By the mid-1930s, an exceedingly difficult period for Nisei old enough to enter the labor market, the reliance on Issei agriculture appeared to have been another special line, despite the earlier problems posed by the alien land laws.

The Issei fully recognized that regardless of the ability and superb academic performance of the Nisei, and despite the acquisition of the coveted college diploma, merit would not be sufficient to secure work in the larger labor market. Although the "older Nisei" were able to use their professional training by establishing themselves within the Japanese community, it seemed that the ethnic economy could not sustain the growing trend among the Nisei to seek white collar and professional occupations.[95]

At the same time, Issei leaders saw problems that Nisei might face in the agricultural economy. T. Takimoto of the San Francisco Japanese Association offered an interesting analysis of the prospective role of Nisei labor.[96] Reporting that the number of productive Issei workers had been declining since 1935, he estimated that the Japanese community in California would lose about 12,000 of its productive members by 1940—7,000 on the farms and 5,000 in the cities. The Nisei who were 20 years and older and who were born and still lived in California would number 13,000 by 1940, according to Takimoto. Taking into account potential migrants from Hawaii, he reasoned that the total number of Nisei would be about 15,000 by that year, with approximately 8,000 men becoming productive in five years. He also realized, however, that the Nisei flight from the farm to the city would create a loss in the rural work force. He anticipated that the lure of the city would result in fewer Nisei on the farm. He projected that by 1940 there would be 4,000 Nisei living in cities, leaving only 3,000 productive Nisei to replace the 7,000 farm workers who would be nonproductive by then. As a result, Takimoto feared that the Japanese would suffer the fate of the Chinese in agriculture, who also lacked successors due to the social consequences of the 1882 Chinese Exclusion Act. Without the infusion of new blood, Takimoto forecasted the decline of Issei agriculture, the life line of their own economy. Under these circumstances, efforts to find Nisei workers to fill the anticipated labor shortage gained even greater importance. Thus the question of Nisei job opportunity and the role of education hinged not only on a discriminatory "American" labor market, but also on the requirements of their rural economy.

Generational Relations

While the Issei pondered the future of the second generation in terms of their education and occupations in the larger society, they were also concerned about generational relations within the family and community. In comparison with the Issei, who were largely products of Japanese society, their offspring were deeply influenced by their American experience. Differences in values, experiences, language, and schooling were but a few of the sources of tension between the generations. Minoru Iino, an interviewee of the Survey of Race Relations, characterized this problem in the following way:

> Young people of our race in this country faces [sic] the difficulty . . . in the line of getting along with members of our "first generation." I have seen in many cases the evidences of constant conflicts between the members of our second generation and the members of the first generation due to the difference of their ideals and customs.[97]

Making these observations in 1926, he suggested that the generational problem was complicated by the fact that many members of the second generation did not learn the Japanese language because they considered it to be of little use as they did not wish to live in Japan. Although the Issei tried to teach the Nisei about Japanese customs and culture so that they might appreciate and better understand their parents, Iino was pained that so many Nisei despised their Japanese ancestry:

> They seemed to "look down" [on the] Japanese race which they belong to.
> I even heard that unpleasant word "Japs" from their own lips very many times.
> A Hawaiian born Japanese girl after divorcing a Japan born husband said to her friend, "Those Japs don't know how to treat their wives."[97]

Iino's explanation for Nisei behavior was that it was due to "half-baked Americanization." He qualified his criticism, however, by pinpointing the root of the Nisei problem:

> We must remember that although they are American citizens in a legal sense, they were not given full privileges of citizenship and opportunities in "whites'" society. So, their activities and happiness centers about [the] "Japanese village only."[97]

Sakoe Tsuboi, who arrived in the United States in 1923 after spending four years in Honolulu as a Japanese language school teacher, shared Iino's concerns about the generational issue. But taking a somewhat different view of the situation, Tsuboi made the following assessment:

> The freedom of and the independence of America brings the younger generation into conflict with their parents to a certain extent.
> They [Nisei] are progressive and the parents are conservative. Consequently, the parents do not interpret the things in the way that their sons and daughters do.[98]

Thus, rather than negating Iino's conception of the "half-baked Americanization" of the Nisei, Tsuboi's focus on the Nisei sense of freedom and independence seemed to complement it. In fact, the thinking of these men appears to have reflected the perspective of Issei leaders.[99]

A key source for closing the cultural and communication gap had been the language schools. These schools, in keeping with the Issei notion of remaining in America, had been designed to supplement Americanization ideals that were propagated in the Japanese culture. While "cultural nationalism" probably remained part of the spirit of these programs despite policy changes, imparting language instruction was not easy.[100] According to some observers, these programs had been ineffective.[101] For the most part, however, the Issei hoped that the Nisei would learn to appreciate their heritage, rather than disparage it, by becoming conversant in Japanese, thereby promoting greater amity between generations.[102]

Some Issei rejected the language school concept completely, fearing that Japanese instruction would interfere with learning English.[102] These sentiments were well captured by Nao Tashiro, a resident of Seattle and the wife of a small businessman, who was 44 years of age at the time she was interviewed by the Survey of Race Relations.

> I do not approve of language schools. I think it is too hard on them to expect the children to attend two schools at the same time. It is a strain upon their health. Besides they are Americans and it is much more important that they use good English than that they learn Japanese. I think too that a knowledge of German or French will be of more use to them in business and for cultural purposes than knowledge of Japanese. Japanese is a hard language to learn thoroughly and I never thought of insisting on my family learning it.[103]

Her emphasis on the use of French and German suggests a pragmatic outlook. The fact that she was a Christian and the wife of a small businessman may also have given her an assimilationist, middle-class bias. Moreover, her perspective was probably influenced by the anti-Japanese fervor still prevalent at the time of her interview. While other Issei may have had other motivations for opposing language schools, their concern for the most expedient adjustment to America was fundamental.

Despite some variation on the question of language schools, higher education, and occupational choice, the Issei seem to have had a strong desire to achieve what they termed *seiko*.[104] Traditionally having nonmaterial implications, *seiko* can be loosely translated as "success." However, the definitions of *seiko* expressed by the Issei who were surveyed by the Japanese American Research Project were diverse. Many envisioned it primarily in economic terms. Interestingly, the Issei respondents who considered themselves to be "mostly American" seemed to adhere to its classical meaning:

> *Seiko* is not necessarily monetary. I did not succeed in making much money, but I raised seven sons physically and morally. I call this *Seiko*.

> *Seiko* is not money but happiness. For the wife it is the happy relationship of the four generations of the line in the U.S.[104]

When Issei were queried about their career expectations for their sons, they were inclined to allow them to select their own occupations under the assumption that self-determination or choice would become a catalyst for success. Some seemed to believe that success was based upon hard work, diligence, frugality, and honesty, rather than luck.[105] Modell has hypothesized that the Issei transposed their aspirations for success onto their children because they had been denied the chance to realize their own ambitions within the restricted economic opportunities available in the pre–World War II period.[106] If he is correct, this would indicate a strong tendency towards material achievement and social mobility.

In any case, the Issei had been acutely aware of the racial restrictions barring Nisei access to the labor market. These perceptions suggest that we must ascertain how members of the second generation themselves eventually dealt with the racial situation they faced within the context of the Great Depression during which they came of age, and ask to what extent that context influenced not only their economic choices, but also their political perspectives and styles.

Chapter 2

Grant Avenue Blues

Pre–World War II Nisei Socioeconomic Position

WITH THE EMERGENCE OF THE SECOND GENERATION, the composition of the early Japanese community in the United States changed dramatically. In 1900, there were only 269 Nisei, but by 1910, their numbers had increased to 4,502. By 1920, the Nisei numbered 29,672 and comprised approximately 27 percent of the Japanese American population, largely due to the arrival of picture brides.[1] By 1930, the Nisei constituted nearly 50 percent of the Japanese population in the continental United States.[2] In California, the Nisei actually outnumbered the Issei in 1930, and comprised over 70 percent of the total Nisei in the United States.[3] Between 1930 and 1940, the Nisei population jumped from 68,357 to 79,642 while the Issei population declined from 70,477 to 47,305.[4] Thus, in 1940, nearly 63 percent of the Japanese population was American born.

Within this growing second-generation community, there was considerable diversity.[5] The largest segment of this population consisted of those who were born and educated in the United States. But in the same age cohort there were also individuals born in Japan who came with their parents to the United States in their early youth and were educated in American schools, as well as those who were born in Japan but were called over to the United States by their parents after receiving some part of their early education in Japan. Although these immigrant youth could not become naturalized citizens until after World War II, their experience was similar to their American-born counterparts and, in many ways, they identified themselves as Nisei. Those Nisei who were sent to Japan during their adolescent years for schooling were referred to as Kibei. Depending on whether they were educated in Japan during the 1920s and early 1930s or the mid and late 1930s, Kibei also had very different experiences and perspectives, an issue that we will examine in the next chapter.

Unlike other second-generation members of immigrant groups that served as an entering wedge into the larger society, the Nisei discovered that their chances for establishing a meaningful place in American life were as limited as they were for the Issei. Despite the fact that they were U.S. citizens who made every effort to acculturate and to gain acceptance, they were defined as "Japanese" and treated as second-class citizens. This contradiction between their political status and their racial position made it very difficult for the Nisei to adjust to the larger society as they came of age in the 1920s and 1930s.[6]

Education, Employment, and Racial Restrictions

Toshio Mori, an older Nisei and a writer who wrote many short stories about the pre–World War II Japanese immigrant community, was an astute observer and quite sensitive to the Nisei situation: "Most Nisei students followed the ideas and destiny of white students," he observed. "They had similar hopes and aspirations, and they saw their futures in the same way that their white peers did."[7] Nisei views about styles, tastes, beauty, and social activities were likewise similar to those of their white peers.[8] Like other students, the Nisei imbibed the democratic ideals that were dispensed in the schools.[9] They learned about men like George Washington and Abraham Lincoln; and they were taught to believe in the theory that "a person's progress was governed by his own ability and effort and nothing else."[10] According to Mori and Joe Oyama, the Nisei aspired to white-collar occupations and "clean work," rather than the agricultural and produce work which they considered to be demeaning.[11] Unfortunately for the Nisei, they discovered as they grew up that reality did not match the ideals they had been taught.

To prepare themselves for the future, many Nisei heeded their parents' exhortations to pursue higher education as a special line.[12] After completing college, however, the Nisei's life chances were circumscribed by the racial order. Nisei could not find meaningful employment or positions for which they were trained. Even before they became a critical mass within the Japanese community, the older Nisei, the first to seek employment opportunities and careers in the larger society, fully realized this problem. Chiye Shigemura, who was born in Seattle in 1904, had completed two years at the University of Washington at the time she was interviewed by staff members of the Survey of Race Relations project. Despite the fact that she was completing a college education, Shigemura was not optimistic about her future: "There is a great deal of race discrimination in the business world," said Shigemura. "No matter how well we may be trained in school the American business men will not give a Japanese a job if he can get a white person to work for him and it makes it very hard for us for although we were born here we cannot get work."[13] Chiyoe Sumi, another Survey of Race Relations interviewee, disclosed that she, too, was not at all sure about her future direction. Her father wanted her to be a pharmacist, a nurse, or a doctor. Sumi, on the other hand, was interested in becoming an elementary school teacher, but was hesitant about the prospects because of the racial limitations she perceived: "It interests me, but I don't know about teaching. If I could find a position in a school where there were mostly Japanese children it might be all right, but I don't believe I could get a position in any other school."[14]

The views expressed by Shigemura and Sumi, in large part, reflected the concerns that Nisei themselves expressed about their life chances. Another member of the older Nisei community who was familiar with this problem, Kazuo Kawai, was one of the few who had an opportunity to articulate publicly the position of the second generation. While a graduate student at Stanford in the 1920s, Kawai wrote an article, "Three Roads, And None Easy," that appeared in the May 1926 edition of *Survey*, a magazine that published the views of such intellectuals as Robert E. Park and Chester Rowell who were concerned about the Pacific Rim and "East-West" relations. Kawai seemed to have a solid grasp of the economic limitations facing the Nisei:

> Our community is not self-sufficient. We can't stand off and live our lives. We've got to find a place in American society in order to survive. And yet, no matter what our qualifications may be, evidently the only place where we are wanted is in positions that no American would care to fill—menial positions as house servants, gardeners, vegetable peddlers, and continually "yes, ma'am-ing."[15]

Although many Nisei tried to dodge the issue by avoiding situations or encounters where they knew they would face discrimination, something that would be quite embarrassing to them, they could not deny the existence of a racial problem.[16] Whether they lived in the Pacific Northwest, San Francisco, or Los Angeles, Nisei shared the same difficulties finding work outside the ethnic economy.[17]

Nisei Economic Kinship Dependency

By 1930, the occupational profile of the Nisei showed that they had become reliant on the Issei ethnic economy. Information from Japanese language sources provides a useful overview of the Nisei economic situation in southern California in 1930 (see Table 1).

Table 1   Comparison of Issei and Nisei Occupations, Southern California, 1930

Occupation	Issei		Nisei	
	Number	%	Number	%
Farming	7,376	57	261	32
Business	1,557	13	89	11
Hotel, restaurant	1,092	9	20	2
Fishing industry	911	7	6	0.7
Domestic work	809	6	40	5
Professional work	351	3	46	6
Office work, sales	190	1	300	37
Miscellaneous	181	1		
Manufacturing	169	1	29	4
Transporting	99	1	11	1
Handymen	76	1	11	1
Total	12,811	100	816	100

Source: Data collected by Los Angeles Japanese Consulate, 1930, reported in Zaibei Nihonjinkai, Zai-Bei Nihonjinshi [History of the Japanese in America] (San Francisco: Zaibei Nihonjinkai, 1940), 590–591.
Note: Table translated by Mabel Saito Hall, from files of Sucheng Chan.

Because of the Depression and racial segregation in the labor market, the Nisei, like the Issei, resorted to farming and small business.[18] Nisei also paralleled Issei participation in domestic and professional work.[19] In contrast to the Issei, the Nisei were heavily concentrated in the sales and office work category, but these occupations were largely within the ethnic economy. Few Nisei had the opportunity to work in white American businesses or firms, and those who did generally had blue-collar jobs.[20]

As World War II drew near, the Nisei dependence on the Issei economy had become much more pronounced.[21] In California, for example, roughly 14.5 percent of the Nisei were farm laborers who were unpaid family workers, 16.2 percent were paid farm laborers, and 18.3 percent were clerical and sales workers in 1940.[22] Assuming that most of these positions were connected to ethnic enterprise, we can estimate that almost 50 percent of the working Nisei who were 14 years or older were economically dependent on the Issei. The economic position of the Nisei in southern California clearly affirms this situation. In Los Angeles county, "40 percent of the women who worked, and nearly 30 percent of the men, worked without pay for their parents."[23] Outside of agricultural work, Nisei were concentrated in unskilled work, contract gardening, domestic service, and clerical/sales work. Although Nisei in these job categories were hired by white employers, they were given positions generally assumed to be reserved for Japanese.[24]

Beyond the system of economic kinship, the Nisei had very few options. Due to anti-Japanese sentiment, the Nisei were not likely to establish a successful practice in dentistry, optometry, or law in white society. The opportunity to develop professional practices within Japanese communities was also limited because the communities were large enough only to sustain the Issei and the older Nisei who had already established their professions.[25] Although civil service positions began to open up to the Nisei in some areas of California in the late 1930s, access was still limited.[26] Again, small farming and proprietorship were more viable options compared to professional work. For example, in 1940, only 2.1 percent of the California Nisei were professionals, while nearly 10 percent were famers and farm managers, and 6.1 percent were proprietors or managers.[27] Still, securing capital posed a formidable deterrent for Nisei who sought economic independence through small-scale enterprise.

Because their economic prospects were bleak, some Nisei sought employment in Japanese corporations that were located on the Pacific Coast and in New York. Some others went to Japan to make their fortunes.[28] Toshio Mori recalled that a number of Nisei who had been trained in college to be engineers went to Manchuria to take jobs on the Manchurian Railroad. Concurring with Mori's observation, Jim Kawamura said that they "didn't fare too well back there. Being a Nisei, you were a foreigner, so it was hard to get established."[29] Because the adjustment to life in Japan and Manchuria was difficult, these Nisei generally returned and found menial jobs that Mori described in the following way:

> Cal grads in business and engineering had to work as Grant [Avenue] import salesmen or work at a produce. Their average was one dollar a day which didn't go very far. Their wages hardly covered their expenses. They needed a suit; they had to get lunch; and if they lived in the East Bay they had to commute; so what was left over was not too much.[30]

A Nisei college graduate who grew up on a farm in the central California area was one of those Nisei to whom Mori referred. He offered a glimpse of what it was like to come of age at that time:

> When I graduated from college in the spring of 1939, I still had a secret ambition to be some kind of writer. I was clinging to this ambition but I felt that there were not many opportunities to develop in it. I knew that the Nisei were not accepted in very many economic fields outside the Japanese community. A lot of the Nisei students who graduated from college with me ended up on the farm and very few of them got places. Many of the city Nisei went to work as salesmen [in Oriental art goods stores] on Grant Avenue, or else they became gardeners or laborers. The Nisei used to joke that their only destination after getting their diploma was to work for cheap wages in a small

Japanese store. They did not have the optimism of the usual Caucasian graduates because they knew there was no demand for their
services.[31]

Having worked on Grant Avenue for five years after completing his college
course work in commerce, Kawamura echoed the fact that working on the
Avenue was a form of cheap labor: "Wages were very bad. It was [a] typical
Japanese firm type of thing. They didn't want you to organize a union. If
you join a union, they will fire you. [The] union wasn't strong there, just
like the sweat shop in Chinatown."[32]

It some respects the question of job opportunities, wages, and working conditions in the ethnic economy was a relative matter. Many Nisei
workers in the Pacific Northwest "drifted" from their hometowns to large
communities like Los Angeles. According to one Nisei observer, college
graduates from Seattle sought produce work in Los Angeles because they
considered work conditions there to be better:

> Work opportunities [in Seattle] were much more limited. Seattle only
> had cannery work for the Nisei and it was limited to a short season so
> that a lot of Seattle guys drifted down [to Los Angeles] after gradua-
> tion from college. Market work in Seattle was considered low class
> and they didn't want to do it up there. The guys in the Seattle stands
> worked 15 to 17 hours a day and the wages were much smaller than
> in Los Angeles. Seattle markets were not unionized at all so the
> employers took advantage of the Nisei workers. These Seattle fellows
> that I worked with were clean and trustworthy and a little older
> group than the L.A. bunch. Almost all of them had gone to college.
> Some of these fellows were pretty bitter about being pushed down in
> work like that but they couldn't do anything about it so that they
> gradually began to accept their position. They worked hard and they
> were still hopeful that someday they would be able to make some
> advancements although this dream was fading pretty fast.[33]

This movement up and down the Pacific Coast produced among the transient Nisei an unsettled feeling about the future. But as one Nisei observer
put it, they had to "make do" economically in light of their limited opportunities. Some Nisei turned to very specialized lines of work such as "chick
sexing," an occupation that was seasonal, and demanding, and considered a
field of ethnic specialization.

To circumvent the limited opportunities facing them, many of the
younger Nisei chose to continue their education instead. As a Nisei from
Los Angeles stated,

I was amazed to work with Nisei college graduates who had no ambition left. They were only interested in their weekly salary. I definitely became aware of how hard it was for Nisei after getting out of school, but it didn't sink in too much because I decided to go to school some more and get ahead.[34]

Using education to "get ahead" was also a way for Nisei to postpone their coming to terms with their problematical circumstances. One Nisei living in the San Francisco area could have been speaking for many of his peers when he commented,

I had no definite plans and I didn't know whether to go to J.C. or not. A lot of my friends were going to junior college. I guess most of the nisei kids just went on to J.C. after high school because there was nothing else to do. The nisei had a helluva time getting a good job because there was too much discrimination. They didn't get a chance ... like the hakujin kids. The hakujin kids were able to get good jobs if they had a high school education, but the nisei didn't have a chance even with a college education.[35]

By 1940, the median educational level for the Nisei, 25 years old and over, was 12.2 years as compared to the median of 8.4 years for the same age group in the general population.[36] Also, "by 1940, 22 percent of the Los Angeles Nisei males 25 or over had attended college; the figure for native whites was 21 percent."[37]

Although the Nisei adjusted begrudgingly to their social and economic circumstances, they still experienced great dissatisfaction since they could not find meaningful work or careers for which they were trained. Moreover, the disparity between their expectations and educational achievements, and their social and economic position was especially difficult for them. As one Nisei put it, "The majority were frustrated in economic activities and they didn't know what was going to happen to them next. They were seeking outlets but there did not seem to be many possibilities. Many ambitions were crushed in this harsh existence."[38]

Produce workers, in particular, were discontented with the long work hours, meager wages, and the lack of opportunity for advancement. One Los Angeles Nisei who was interviewed during the internment years expressed his feelings in the following way:

Three-fourths of the Nisei fellows and girls in the labor market during those years of depression were in the produce market work. I don't know how they looked upon it, but I did this kind of work for about a year and I found it most distasteful. It was hard work and the hours were long. The wage standards were horrible. Girls had to work 10 and 11 hours a day for about $15 a week and we didn't get paid for overtime. After the unions came in, it was a little better for the Nisei produce workers because they didn't have to put in such long hours. I think the Japanese market owners took advantage of the Nisei workers during the depression and they bled us for everything they could. One company for which my brother worked made the men put in at least 14 hours a day but the pay checks gave them only credit for 8 hours. The fellows couldn't say very much about that because there were plenty of Nisei around who would have been ready to jump at the chance to take their jobs.... I don't think I am exaggerating at all because it is a known fact that the Japanese produce and fruit stand market owners became very prosperous during the depression years.[39]

While most Nisei would have been thrilled to bypass the hard work and long hours associated with their low paying jobs, the reservoir of Nisei workers who were willing to take whatever jobs that were available to them made that an unlikely possibility. Perhaps, Leonard Broom and John I. Kitsuse best summarized the economic position of the Nisei when they stated that "the apparent choice for Nisei of staying in the ethnic community or breaking away was in fact no choice at all."[40]

Social Segregation

Racial restrictions in the labor market mirrored the limited opportunities of the Nisei to reap the social and cultural benefits of their citizenship. Although many Nisei associated with their white American peers in grade school, high school, and college, these relationships did not necessary lead to what sociologists call "structural integration." Despite extensive contact with their white peers, Nisei often drifted towards their Nisei peers for fellowship and social activity. During the early 1920s, one Nisei who spent his early youth in Napa, California, described his experience living in an area where there were very few Japanese Americans: "I mingled freely with Americans and [had] several close friends among them." But after he moved to Los Angeles, the situation changed. "At first I mingled almost entirely with the American children because I had been so accustomed to this in Napa that I considered myself an American and not a Japanese. In high school, however, I began to gravitate toward the Japanese pupils and began to feel slightly uneasy among the Americans."[41] A Nisei woman who grew up in southern California before World War II revealed a similar experience:

When I was a child I didn't have too many Nisei playmates and I played with all of the kids of the neighborhood. As we got older we didn't play with the other children anymore as we went around in our own groups. The reason for that was the city was quite prejudiced against the Japanese and the Caucasian kids soon learned it from their parents and the other older people. We felt more comfortable going around in our own group. My social life became centered around the Japanese church and the Japanese school. I was very conscious of a difference in race as I soon saw that the Japanese were looked down upon.[42]

Nisei who attended such institutions of higher education as the University of California at Berkeley also experienced segregration.[43] Although they attended classes with their white classmates and the two groups were friendly toward each other, according to Chizu Iiyama, a member of the Class of 1942 at UC Berkeley, the Nisei students still led separate lives. Nisei tended to "pal around" within their own circles and relied on church groups and organizations like the YMCA for more formal social activities. Nisei also encountered the discriminatory housing practices that were prevalent then. This situation led Issei and Nisei leaders to raise money to build Euclid Hall, a dormitory that accommodated Nisei students.[44]

While some Nisei were somewhat slow to become fully conscious about the race issue, they all eventually felt its impact. As one Nisei viewed their situation, "The Nisei were just beginning to wake up to the fact that something was wrong when the war came." He added,

The consciousness of the racial factor only entered into the sense of frustration and I didn't think in terms of overcoming it. It seems to me that it was too big a thing for one individual to solve. I just felt that the future might solve it in the natural course of time but I wasn't too hopeful about that. . . . I tried to build up a false picture of life by engaging in various superficial activity as I felt that these things would give me the mental stimulation I desired."[45]

For the most part, Nisei felt like outcasts in a hostile white world that failed to distinguish between Americans of Japanese ancestry and Japanese nationals.[46]

Some Nisei attributed the race problem to cultural differences. A Nisei interviewed by the Survey of Race Relations project argued, "I think that the great misunderstanding between Japanese and Americans are created not because of the mere difference in the color of our skin, and the structure of our countenance, but because of the great difference in our temperaments, language, custom and religion."[47] But most Nisei seemed to believe that racial discrimination was deeply embedded in society. One Nisei who moved to the Boyle Heights section of Los Angeles, after being rejected from the Belvedere district by white protesters, had this to say:

> . . . no solution of what ever kind can be introduced to solve this race problem, the problem of immigrants, the assimilation of these Orientals as long as there is physical difference. It is not economic, social or other problems that seem to be the cause of these prejudices, it is the color difference and nothing more. And so long as there are many races—there will be conflict no matter how America or the other countries tries to solve the race problem.[48]

Besides the social barriers that were part of the "racial etiquette" of their day, economic realities at home also restricted Nisei life, particularly for those who grew up on farms. Michi Nakada, who was the oldest of four children, remembered that having to help out in the family farm took all of her spare time. "Every day after school we would work and before school, [too], so we did not have what you call recreation and such, except when Dad took us on picnics; there was the constant thing of working."[49] Helping out on the farm or with the family business was expected and served to regiment Nisei life.

Generation Gap

Besides facing racial restrictions in the larger society, Nisei also experienced difficulties at home. Although they had been taught by their parents to understand and to appreciate their Japanese heritage, the Nisei were also socialized in American schools and influenced by American culture. They embraced the values, behaviors, and cultural style of the social mainstream.[50] Mrs. Iseri and Mrs. Takeyama, Nisei subjects for the Survey of Race Relations, described how different the Nisei were from the Issei in expressing themselves.[51] Both commented on the fact that Nisei revealed their emotions much more readily than did the Issei and that the Nisei often shocked their parents in front of guests when they expressed their emotions. Similarly, Seiichi Nobe, a Nisei living in Los Angeles, said,

> I have keenly felt that I would like my parents to understand me. I would like to be more of a pal with my father, but I can't. My father had a rather hard time in his early years and so he is very anxious to give us children the opportunities of an education. My mother holds to the old ideas much more than father does.[52]

As the Nisei acculturated to the American way of life, questions about personal appearance, personal habits (smoking, drinking), social activities (dancing), and dating and marriage became sources of tension and rebellion. Attitudes regarding these issues reflected clear generational and cultural differences between the Issei and the Nisei. Chiyo Otera, a Survey of Race Relations interviewee who was born in Japan but grew up in Seattle from an early age, said that when questions about social behavior came up, she found her parents to be too restrictive: "I often felt rebellious against the repression to which I was subjected, but I have modified to some extent now and have concluded that they did not impose these restrictions upon me to make me miserable but because they considered it was all for my good."[53] Iseri and Takeyama also noticed that as "times goes on," the Issei allow "young people to have much more freedom" as compared to 10 years earlier. Said Frank Ishi, a Stanford graduate: "I feel there is a considerable gap between my parents and myself.... I differ in my ideas and my outlook but I go about my business and do not disturb them."[54] Such differences were often due to the influence exerted by different mass media. Unlike the Issei who read primarily Japanese language newspapers which received much of their information from the Domei News Agency in Japan, the Nisei were informed by American newspapers and radio.[55]

Generational differences were certainly exacerbated by language problems. Although most Nisei attended Japanese language schools, few could be considered fluent Japanese speakers. Another Nisei interviewee of the Survey of Race Relations probably put it best when he stated, "I feel that I cannot go to my parents for advice when I have a problem to face because there is a language barrier between us and I couldn't make them understand me nor could they make me understand them.... Because of this difficulty in communication I have to work out my problems by myself."[56] When it came to finding comfort and understanding, Nisei had to rely on their brothers and sisters. Nobe stated, "My older brother and I, however, have had the same problems and we understand each other and get along together very well."[57] Otera echoed Nobe's sentiments about parental problems and found comfort in the fact that she could talk to her brother. However, not all sibling relations were close. What is especially interesting is the gap between younger and older Nisei. The more acculturated the Nisei, the more they exhibited American behavioral patterns. Ishi specifically mentioned that he felt a distance from his younger brother who spoke less Japanese than he did and was more concerned with personal pleasure:

In America the young people tend to break away from their parents. This is particularly noticeable in my brother, who is next to me in age.

He is in high school but I have to watch him to see that he goes; he would rather go fishing. He also goes to a lot of moving picture shows. I go to an occasional moving picture show, and I prefer to go to high grade concerts, grand opera and to plays in the standard opera houses, or on the legitimate stage.[58]

Younger Nisei growing up in the late 1930s were preoccupied with the same problems. Facing limited opportunities in the larger society and experiencing a generational gap at home, the younger Nisei were easily distracted by their immediate situation because their future was so bleak. Activities like poker, pool, fashion, and gang life became outlets for Nisei who were disgruntled about their future prospects.[59] Within this social context, organized activities also became an important part of Nisei life. Athletic leagues, church-affiliated organizations, YMCA and YWCA groups, social clubs, and civic groups became the focus of activity for many of the younger Nisei and, in some ways, a deterrent to delinquency.[60]

International Crisis

While the racial and generational problems greatly affected the Nisei, so too did the international situation in the 1930s. U.S.–Japan relations bore directly on the American public's perceptions of Japanese Americans and consequently the status of Nisei. After the passage of the Immigration Act of 1924, the intensity of anti-Japanese propaganda and hostility abated to some degree, although the issue of Nisei citizenship continued to be a source of agitation for some exclusionists and a cause for concern for Issei leaders.[61] When Japan escalated its military activity by invading China proper in 1937, anti-Japanese sentiment rose once again and set the stage for anti-Japanese legislation. In California, for example, a host of anti-alien bills directed at the Issei and Nisei were quickly introduced in the state legislature—an anti-alien corporation bill, an anti-alien fishing bill, and an anti-alien language school bill.[62] As tensions between the United States and Japan escalated in 1939, anti-alien fishing bills were introduced in the Senate and the Assembly by men like Sam Yorty of Los Angeles.[63] As political tensions reached crisis proportions in 1940 and the threat of war between the United States and Japan appeared imminent, the loyalty of Nisei to the United States became an issue and compelled them to examine their sentiments towards Japan.

Before World War II, Nisei often felt ambivalent about Japan and at times found themselves in situations where they were sympathetic towards Japan. As one Nisei put it, "I was prone to be sympathetic to Japan. . . . before the war. I even wrote a few articles defending Japan's aggression. It was a sort of racial defense. We all felt that we were alienated from America in some way and we felt a necessity to defend Japan because our own position was so precarious."[64] On the other hand, many were not at all torn or ambivalent about their pro-American sentiments. Against the backdrop of the 1924 Immigration Act, a Nisei commented that he generally took the side of the United States when any discussions came up about this subject.[65] Regardless of how they responded to the international crisis, what is important is the extent to which deteriorating U.S.–Japanese relations affected their racial position and set a political context within which they struggled to make a place for themselves in American society.

Chapter 3

"Lower The Anchor"

Formation of Nisei Perspectives

SECOND-GENERATION JAPANESE AMERICANS RESPONDED to their racial subordination and limited socioeconomic opportunities in the pre–World War II period in rather complex ways by formulating diverse ideologies, strategies, and styles. Four political styles that best highlight their responses to racial subjugation before World War II were: 1) the establishment of a cultural bridge between America and Japan; 2) the identification with American life; 3) the concern for "progressive" social change; and 4) alienation from American society. Although these styles are not mutually exclusive, I am treating them as ideal types in order to assess their unique and common features.[1] Each style also corresponds to a specific historical period. The concept of the bridge, for example, was in vogue in the late 1920s and the early 1930s, while progressive politics emerged in the late 1930s. The ideal of Americanism had been significant since World War I, but it became pivotal only in the mid and late 1930s. Although I will attempt to specify the historical relevance of each response, my objectives are to construct a portrait of an individual who adopted each style and to explore the key sociological forces contributing to its formation.

One of the central issues addressed in this chapter is the extent to which generational position influenced the political style of Japanese Americans, applying Mannheim's concept of the generational unit to examine whether the Nisei developed a unique political style. The existing literature on Japanese Americans discusses generation in terms of birth order and suggests that first, second, and third generations are distinguished by their particular characteristics and experiences. This chapter explores the possible continuity between generations and the diversity within generations, as suggested by the notion of the generational unit. I hope to provide a better understanding of the process by which a particular segment of one generation, under certain political and economic circumstances, sets the dominant style not only for its own generation, but also for the larger community.

A Bridge Between East and West

The Nisei originally responded to racial exclusion from the labor market and social isolation by attempting to synthesize the cultural imperatives of American life and their Japanese heritage into a coherent ideology and strategy for action. They promoted the idea that the second generation should become a "bridge" linking the East and the West in mutual amity. One way to understand this perspective is to look at the experience of one member of the second generation who advocated and shaped his early life around this ideology.

The Life of Kazuo Kawai

Kazuo Kawai, born in 1904 in Tokyo, Japan, came to America with his family in 1909.[2] Because his family was of aristocratic origin, it was expected that his father would become a soldier or statesman. Instead of maintaining the family tradition, however, the elder Kawai, who had developed an intense interest in Christianity as a university student, pursued a career in the ministry. He received his theological training in America and then returned to Japan. After a short time, the Reverend Kawai was sent to work among the Japanese community in Los Angeles, where he eventually became the "dean" of Japanese Christian ministers.

Shortly after his family settled in Los Angeles, Kazuo Kawai attended a primary school where he was one of a few Japanese students. He was a novelty; unable to speak English and mocked by others, he was forced to cope with feelings of loneliness. His mother was emphatic that he learn English; he did so at the expense of developing his Japanese language skills.

In 1912, Kawai's family moved to the east side of Los Angeles. Kawai recalled that the students at his new school were "poor and dirty little Mexican, Negro, Italian, Greek and Jewish children." Once he became part of the "gang," however, his negative first impression of his schoolmates faded. "I was now part of that cosmopolitan east-side population that was being molded by the zealous school teachers into good Americans," stated Kawai.

Although he was ineligible for citizenship because of his Japanese birth, he was heavily influenced by the Americanization movement that had been an integral feature of his schooling.[3] As a consequence, his view of Japanese immigrants was identical to the negative perceptions harbored by white Americans. At the time the 1913 Alien Land Law was passed, he recalled, "I didn't understand it, of course, and I thought that it was a needless trouble caused by some bad Japanese, whoever they were."

The development of Kawai's racial consciousness was a gradual process that crystallized between his junior high and high school years. His junior high school experience was particularly memorable. It occurred during World War I when Japan and the United States were allies. In a major school pageant, Kawai received acclaim from his classmates for his role in representing Japan. A bright and popular student, Kawai was proud of his ancestry and had little preparation for the racial problems that were in store for him. In high school he became cognizant of the "rotten" treatment accorded the Japanese. In contrast to the acceptance he received in junior high school, Kawai received little attention in high school, despite his ability. It was important for him to understand this change. He reasoned that the Japanese had created a "bad image" for themselves and that he was a victim of their poor reputation. Rather than blame the "Americans" who discriminated against him, he placed the blame on the Japanese.

As the racial inequities facing Japanese students became clear to him, Kawai sought the companionship of other Japanese students who had similar experiences. Thus began his "Japanese phase." Before high school, his friends were white students, as was also true for the other Japanese students at his school. In his autobiography, Kawai implied that the Japanese students intentionally associated with whites, although they were not overtly conscious of the reasons for their selective interaction. By the time they got to high school, however, their common isolation and lack of attention served to unify them. "But misery loves company and so, not by mutual attraction, but by common isolation, we became close friends," revealed Kawai. The color line instilled among these strangers a consciousness of kind and a sense of camaraderie.

The race problem remained a matter of great concern to Kawai as a college student attending the University of California, Southern Branch (UCLA).[4] Disillusioned with America at this point in his life, he pondered,

> I thought I was American, but America wouldn't have me. Once I was American, but America made a foreigner out of me—Not a Japanese, but a foreigner—a foreigner to any country, for I am just as much a foreigner to Japan as to America.[5]

The resolution to what Kawai defined as "foreigner" status came through his involvement in the Japanese Students Christian Association. His participation in a church conference at Asilomar, California was particularly significant. At this point he realized that he wanted "to live a life of greatest value" and that it would be most worthwhile to dedicate his life to an "ideal." The racial contact and conflict along the Pacific Basin were of special importance in this regard:

. . . I began to ponder over again some of the things I heard at Asilomar—of the fact of race conflict, of the white and colored races clash-
ing all over the world, but particularly over the Pacific Basin, of the
Occidental culture which had spread and expanded continually west-
ward, and the Oriental culture which had spread eastward until both
had half encircled the globe and now meeting across the Pacific Basin,
of the challenge which that situation offered for interpreters who could
bridge across the gap of the two races and the two civilizations, and
bring the two together in a harmonious meeting, to synthesize the two
cultures into a higher world culture. Then I thought of myself, racially
a child of the Orient, culturally a child of the Occident, neither Oriental nor Occidental, yet both Oriental and Occidental, embodying
within me the clash and the adjustment and the synthesis of the East
and the West, a microcosm reflecting the macrocosm of the world
problem of race and culture; I am both East and West, made into one
whole. I had at last found my field. The peculiar work for which I had
been ordained was to be just myself; my very self is [sic] an interpretation of the East and West; my life work would be that of an interpreter
of the East to the West and of the West to the East.[5]

The resolution of the racial contradictions in his life came from his discovery, to his pleasure and relief, that he was not compelled to be a poor imita-
tion of either an American or a Japanese. He had found an alternative
where he could be "authentic." He no longer had to face the disappointment of being "excluded from either side." As a cultural interpreter, he
could overcome his marginal position. As someone who could bridge the
cultural gap between East and West, he no longer anguished over his lack
of identity among "the mass of Americans."

By redefining his position in American society, Kawai established a
framework within which he could interact with white Americans and with
Japanese. By not having to reject one identity for the sake of the other,
ironically he became both: "Now I am more of an American, and also more
of a Japanese than in those junior high days when I was an American, or in
those high school days when I was only a Japanese."

Having found a perspective to guide his life, Kawai applied the interpreter ideology to his university work. Before entering the University of
California, his major interest had been literature. Given the grim realities
of the job market, however, he declared,

If I were to specialize in English it would be difficult for me to secure
a University position to teach the subject, but in the case of Oriental
history the very fact that I belong to an Oriental group will give me

standing. I am becoming enthusiastic about the prospects.... If I specialize in history there will be an opportunity for valuable service
either here or in Japan where I could teach American history.[6]

Thus racial restrictions in the job market steered him away from his
preliminary interests. But the notion of becoming an interpreter made him
optimistic about pursuing his university education at the graduate level. At
Stanford, where he completed his undergraduate training in 1926, Kawai
specialized in Far Eastern History. He received his M.A. (1928) and Ph.D.
(1938) degrees from the same institution. Taking a position at UCLA as an
instructor in geography and history, he found the opportunity to interpret
the "East to the West."[7]

As an approach to racial problems facing the second generation in the
prewar period, Kawai's articulation of the bridge ideal reflected the thinking of a number of prominent American and Japanese intellectuals, as well
as Issei community leaders. Dr. Gordon Sproul of the University of California, Berkeley, encouraged Japanese American students to become "cultural
ambassadors" who could promote cultural exchanges between America and
Japan. Similarly, Dr. Inazo Nitobe, one of the leading Japanese intellectuals
in residence in the United States, had this to say to young Japanese Americans living in Seattle:

> You are placed in a special position to interpret the East to the West
> and the West to the East that they may meet on common grounds to
> effect the principles of peace and mutual welfare.[8]

Nitobe, echoing Kawai's thought, suggested that the second generation
could be "good Americans" by using their knowledge of the English language and Americans, as well as their Japanese heritage, to promote
mutual understanding between the people of Japan and America.

Japanese diplomats stationed along the Pacific Coast reaffirmed the
interpreter ideology when they addressed Japanese American youth,
explaining that the Nisei could establish a "potential link in the chain of
Japanese-American friendship and understanding."[9] The emphasis on
improving foreign relations through communication and cultural exchange
fit squarely with the concerns of Japanese diplomats who urged favorable
economic relations in the aftermath of discord between America and Japan
over the 1924 Immigration Act.

The view that Nisei could potentially play a key role in future
U.S.–Japan relations was certainly not lost among such prominent Issei leaders as Kyutaro Abiko, publisher of the *Nichibei Shinbun*, a Japanese-language
daily newspaper based in San Francisco. In the wake of the 1924 Immigration Act, Abiko took the position that the future of Japanese communities

rested with the Nisei. "Being Japanese by descent but American by birth and education, the Nisei were ideally suited to become a future bridge of understanding between the two nations to dispel the ignorance which had been, in Abiko's opinion, the fundamental cause of the exclusion movement."[10]

In practice, Kawai's approach to the problems of employment opportunity and social mobility relied heavily on cultural alternatives and the adjustment of one's life to fit the exigencies of the times. The second generation's best opportunity, in this view, came from their ability to use their racial position and their cultural uniqueness to circumvent racism. The interpreter ideal accepted the prevailing racial order and did not criticize the institutions which excluded Japanese Americans from the larger society. Given the economic and racial conditions of the early 1930s and the political position of Japanese Americans in general, few other alternatives were conceivable and even fewer were possible.

But at the same time, Kawai's ideology reflected the perspective of the older and more privileged segment of the second generation. Men like Kawai were intellectuals. The notion of the bridge represented lofty idealism with regard to the role that the Nisei could play in domestic and international affairs. This idealism was shaped within the broader context of commercial contact between Japan and America. But we also must remember the unique social position of men like Kawai who were not eligible for citizenship even though they were socialized as Americans.

The majority of the Nisei who came of age in the late 1920s faintly recalled talk about the Nisei becoming cultural ambassadors.[11] For the most part only Issei and Nisei leaders discussed this notion, particularly between the mid 1920s and the mid 1930s, before tensions between Japan and the United States became acute. For the vast majority of the Nisei, the bridge ideal was an abstract intellectual notion that had little bearing on more pressing issues of livelihood and the desire to be recognized as Americans.

Identification with American Life

Whereas the perspective that the Nisei generation should identify fully with American life had been spearheaded by young Nisei professionals and businessmen, the emphasis on Americanism was put forward most clearly by the leaders of the Japanese American Citizens League (JACL). Although these two approaches were not mutually exclusive in the early and mid 1930s, the American ideal became the linchpin of JACL thought, especially as the international crisis between the United States and Japan escalated in the late 1930s.[12]

The ideal of Americanism was best articulated by James Y. Sakamoto when he commented about the future of the second generation in Seattle at the onset of the Great Depression:

The future is bright for residents of this community, but the bright-
ness depends upon their intent to settle here and to make homes here
that they may take their rightful part in the growth of the city. The
time is here to give a little sober thought to the future. The second
generation are American citizens and through them will be reaped the
harvests of tomorrow. Home, institutions and inalienable right to live
the life of an American, is the cry of the second generation and will be
the cry of posterity. It is high time to lower the anchor.[13]

The call to lower the anchor signified the nascent concern that the Nisei
identify themselves fully as loyal Americans and interweave their lives into
the fabric of American life. In order to assess the development of this particular response, we need to examine the formation of the JACL, the character of its leadership, its continuity with Issei leaders, its ideological
perspective, and its approach to electoral politics.

Creation of the JACL

The formation of the Japanese American Citizens League in 1930 had
been prefigured by earlier organizing efforts.[14] Between 1918 and 1920,
Nisei college students and professionals formed civic clubs in response both
to anti-Japanese propagandists who were critical of their dual citizenship
status and to their own limited career opportunities. In the San Francisco
Bay Area, these "post-collegiate study groups" led to the formation of the
American Loyalty League under the leadership of Dr. Thomas T. Yatabe.
This group quickly declined, however, when Yatabe moved to Fresno to
develop his dental practice. In 1922, Nisei in the Pacific Northwest organized the Seattle Progressive Citizens League, which bore no direct relationship to the San Francisco group. In response to the passage of alien land
laws, Issei leaders encouraged the older and more established Nisei to organize to protect the interests of Japanese Americans. Following a brief period
of interest, the Seattle group waned until James Sakamoto infused new life
into the organization.[15] Under his guidance, the Progressive Citizens
League reorganized under the theme of promoting American patriotism.

In the meantime, a statewide American Loyalty League was formed in
California in 1923.[16] Issei leaders in San Francisco played a central role in
stimulating Nisei leaders like Yatabe to organize the second generation.
The Japanese Association of America selected Nisei delegates from Fresno,
San Jose, Turlock, Oakland, Berkeley, Lodi, Florin, Monterey, Sacramento,
and San Francisco to participate in a founding convention. The greatest
support for this organization came from rural areas where anti-Japanese
agitation was strongest. By 1926, the Loyalty League had expanded to 16
chapters but suffered a sharp cutback in 1928 when it atrophied to six
chapters. Togo Tanaka has suggested three reasons for the dissipation of the

Loyalty League: 1) the Japanese Association withdrew its backing, thereby creating financial difficulties for the organization; 2) due to a lack of specific action programs, the Loyalty League failed to generate popular appeal among an extremely young second-generation population; and 3) Nisei leaders lacked the maturity and experience necessary to sustain the organization. For the most part, the professionally oriented leadership tended to be concerned about public relations with businessmen and political dignitaries in the larger community.[17]

Despite the collapse of these early organizations, they were significant because of their emphasis on American loyalty rather than ethnicity. This later led to the ultra-Americanism of the 1940s.[18] In addition, this activism reflected a close working relationship between Issei leaders and the older, professionally based Nisei leaders.

In line with previous efforts to organize the Nisei around the principle of loyalty, Clarence T. Arai, president of the Seattle Progressive Citizens League, met formally in California with such "prominent" second-generation leaders as Yatabe and Saburo Kido to discuss the creation of a national organization. In April 1929, Arai proposed that a founding convention for a new group, to be called the Japanese American Citizens League (JACL), be held in Seattle in the summer of 1930.[19] Although his proposal met with approval, an extensive debate ensued over the name of the organization.[20] Kido wanted a hyphen between the words "Japanese" and "American" in order to emphasize the ethnic ties of the organization, while Yatabe rejected completely the reference to Japanese. Ultimately, they agreed that the hyphen would be eliminated so that "Japanese" would simply modify "American" and that local chapters would retain the right to select their own name. The Fresno chapter, for example, retained its original name, American Loyalty League.

The following summer, a four-day convention gave birth to one of the most important second-generation organizations.[21] Between 1920 and 1940, the JACL expanded from eight charter affiliates to a total of 50 chapters with approximately 5,600 paying members.[22] Miyamoto's observations about the significance of the JACL in the Seattle Japanese community could easily characterize the JACL's role in communities throughout the Pacific Coast:

> Although the JACL became the leading Nisei organization during the 1930s, it was not an effective political group at that time because its leaders lacked experience and there were too few Nisei of voting age. It functioned as the Nisei's counterpart of the Japanese Association, kept the Nisei informed of political developments affecting the Japanese minority, combated prejudice and discrimination, and dealt with such community problems as education and social welfare.

Above all, the JACL served as a social medium for bringing Nisei together in conferences, banquets, and dances, and thus further reinforced the relations among the Nisei.[23]

As Miyamoto points out, in contrast to its social and communication roles, the JACL's political function within the community was limited because of the small number of Nisei of voting age and the inexperience of its leaders. Despite these limitations, however, it is important to consider the social and economic position of Nisei leadership and its corresponding ideological perspective in order to understand its political style and subsequent importance during the internment crisis.

JACL Leadership

Older Nisei in their late twenties or early thirties comprised the JACL leadership at both the national and local levels when the organization was founded. Saburo Kido, for example, was born in 1902 in Hilo, Hawaii and came to the mainland during the early 1920s. Dr. Thomas T. Yatabe, who was born in San Francisco in 1897, had been affected by the 1906 ordinance which barred Japanese American students from public schools and compelled them to attend a segregated school in Chinatown.[24]

Because of their generational location, JACL leaders were more familiar with the "ways of the Issei" and more attuned to the experience of the Issei than that of younger Nisei. Men like Kido were bilingual and could communicate easily with Issei leaders. At the same time, they were deeply aware of the prevailing anti-Japanese sentiments and the emphasis on Americanism. They witnessed this movement in the larger society and the prosperity of the Hoover years as they came of age in the 1920s.

Moreover, the "Old Guard," as they were referred to by the younger Nisei, were college graduates who had established themselves in professional fields or in small businesses.[25] The JACL leadership came from professional backgrounds in terms of economic position. Kido, for instance, began his college education at the University of California, Berkeley, and later entered Hastings College of Law in 1923, where he received his law degree in 1926.[26] He became a member of the State Bar and started a private practice in the San Francisco Bay Area. Yatabe, also a graduate of the University of California, received his D.D.S. in 1918.[27] And Clarence Arai, the last of the "big three" in the National JACL, graduated from the University of Washington in 1924 with a law degree.[28]

As attorneys, both Arai and Kido were active in stimulating second-generation businesses in their respective communities. Arai played the leading role in creating the Associated Businessmen, a young men's business club, to improve the business life of the community which had suffered because of the Depression.[29] Kido played a similar role in San

Francisco by initiating the Second Generation Businessmen's Club in 1930.[30] In Los Angeles and its vicinity, JACL leaders also formed the Nisei Business Bureau during the late 1930s.[31]

At the local level, particularly in the cities, JACL leadership also reflected its middle-class status. In San Francisco, which had one of the major urban chapters (along with Seattle and Los Angeles), board members were generally businessmen and professionals. In 1932, the Board of Directors consisted of T. Domoto, Vice President, North American Mercantile Co.; Akira Horikoshi, Purchasing Agent, N.Y.K. Line; Steward Nakano, Manager, Specialty Division, Mutual Supply Co.; Toshimi Ogawa, Manager, Endo Silk Co.; Takeshi Tsuda, C.P.A.; and Fumi Yonezu, Business Department, Soko Transfer Co.[32] In the Santa Maria area, a Nisei observer stated that all the Nisei backing the JACL were "...established in the big Japanese companies."[33] Another observer noted that in the Sacramento area, the JACL had been dominated by Nisei professionals concerned with their own social status and economic interests.[34]

Thus, from its inception, JACL leadership was not comprised of the "rank and file" Nisei who came of age in the late 1930s. The leaders were much older than most of the second generation and were considered "prominent" young people within the community—that is, promising leaders who would eventually represent the Japanese American community. In an altruistic sense, they were concerned with the welfare of the second generation and the Japanese American community, but at the same time they were deeply concerned about their own economic advancement.

Continuity with Issei Leadership

Despite the severe generational tensions which surfaced in the 1930s, JACL leaders worked closely with the Issei. They embarked not only on cooperative ventures but also established policies that paralleled those of the Japanese Association:

> The policy of the organization was to exert efforts to amend discriminatory laws through legislative activities, to test through lawsuits the constitutionality of various state and federal statutes, and to exercise the right of franchise so as to elect sympathetic public officials. Educational campaigns were launched to inform the American public of the efforts of the JACL to instill the principles of democracy and good citizenship in its members. Nisei were urged to cancel any dual citizenship status.[35]

The emphasis on legal and legislative change and public relations work mirrored the political style of the leaders of the Japanese Association of America. The relationship between the two generations was clearly demonstrated by the resolution that the Citizens League passed at its founding convention: to secure both the repeal of the Cable Act, which "provided that any American-born woman who married a person ineligible for citizenship would automatically lose her United States citizenship," and the right of naturalization for Issei veterans who had fought in World War I.[36] With the backing of the Japanese Association, the JACL and its Washington, D.C. representatives were able to secure favorable legislation.[37] In 1935 the passage of the Nye-Lea bill granted U.S. citizenship to approximately 500 veterans of Asian ancestry. A year later the Cable Act was repealed—the first time that one of America's racist naturalization codes had been successfully challenged. The JACL and the Japanese Association also often joined together to conduct public relations work. In the 1935 Tulare County incident, for example, the JACL and the Association, through arbitration, conciliation, and nonviolence, helped to resolve the community conflict that arose after white agitators had terrorized Japanese residents.[37] Apparently, the "inroads" established by Issei and Nisei farmers in the "pea-growing industry" in Tulare County, California, became the source of "inspired organized white resistance."[38]

The compatibility between the JACL and Issei leaders resulted in part from the nature of U.S.–Japan relations. On the question of Japan's involvement in Manchuria, the JACL adopted a position similar to that of the Japanese Association.[37] In fact, the JACL often became the representative for the Issei who defended Japan's role in the Far East. Before Japan invaded Manchuria, James Sakamoto was clearly sympathetic with Japan's actions on the Asian mainland when he reiterated the claim that Japan functioned to defend Chinese territorial integrity from Russian encroachment.[39] Immediately after the 1931 Manchurian Incident, Sakamoto came to Japan's defense:

> The sooner China becomes aware of the position that Japan is intending to play in the Orient and the sooner she realizes that the security of her neighbor means her security, as well, the better she can come to realize the road of progress and power that lies open to her. The security of Japan and China is interdependent.... Manchuria, as it constitutes the bone of contention between the two nations, must not blind China from this fact.[40]

In taking this line, Sakamoto was following the interpreter ideology articulated by Kawai, although Sakamoto's response might be better characterized in terms of what Tanaka called "dualism."[41] Tanaka was referring to the JACL's twin affinity with the United States and Japan during the crisis-ridden 1930s. Dualism differed from the bridge ideal in that the JACL did not stress playing an intermediary role as part of its policy, although men like Sakamoto adopted that role while simultaneously emphasizing the American ideal.

In response to the 1937 Marco Polo Bridge Incident, Sakamoto once again rushed to Japan's defense. He argued that Japan had preserved law and order in the face of Chinese warlordism and Communist insurgency and had protected Japanese nationals and investments.[42] While the JACL supported Sakamoto's view, other branches expressed their concerns about a proposed boycott on Japanese-made goods following Japan's invasion of China proper. The Northern California District Council of the JACL, for example, recognized that the Japanese in the United States possessed no "responsibility" or "control" over the Sino-Japanese conflict. They expressed concern that a boycott would "seriously jeopardize" the welfare of citizens of Japanese ancestry and their families and passed the following resolution:

> . . . the Northern California District Council of the Japanese American Citizens League appeals to the people of America to refrain from private or organized movement to deprive the American citizens of Japanese ancestry and their families in this country of the means of earning their livelihood, through a boycott of Japanese services, enterprises or goods already in the hands of resident merchants.[43]

While the Northern California groups may have sympathized with Japan, they also perceived the domestic racial implications of Japan's political actions. Consequently, they felt compelled to reject the boycott against Japanese goods. Nisei leaders maintained a tenuous position, given their ties to Issei leaders.

It is understandable why the Nisei Old Guard would show so much continuity with the Issei. For one thing, their generational location suggests greater compatibility with the Issei experience both historically and culturally than with that of their younger peers. The changing economic position of JACL leaders eased generational tensions since Issei leaders represented the interests of the business establishment within the Japanese American community.[44] Finally, like the Issei, the JACL also lacked political resources. Of course, in contrast to the alien status of the Issei, the citizen status of the Nisei gave them an important advantage.

As Robert Blauner has indicated, however, citizenship for racial minorities in American society was often only a legal status that offered little protection from the racial structure that kept them in "their place."[45] The ideology of white supremacy prevailed and set rigid social parameters of operation for groups like the JACL. Thus the legal privilege of citizenship did little to help Nisei integrate into the larger civil society. Relying on whatever sources of support they could muster, therefore, the Old Guard attempted to formulate its own ideological perspective and political strategy.

Enchantment with the American Dream

At the center of JACL ideology was a staunch faith in the capacity of American institutions to promote economic and racial progress. Allegiance to America was given without question. The JACL's optimism also served to mute their criticism of racial contradictions and sustain them through adverse conditions. The thinking of James Sakamoto, one of the key ideologues of the JACL and a national JACL president in 1936, is illustrative. Even though his thinking may have been more developed than that of most Nisei, his ideas bring into sharp focus the basic ideological premises of the JACL. A review of his positions on American enterprise, the Constitution, white patrons, and the Old Left offers concrete examples.

During the late 1930s when domestic labor strife was acute, Sakamoto reaffirmed an adherence to prevailing economic ideals of American democracy when he stated:

> In recent years some politicians have made much of the cry that placed human rights above property rights. Yet, the two cannot be separated. When a man's property is destroyed, his means of subsistence is gone. And in a communistic state he is denied the right of individual pursuit of happiness. ... The public must come to realize their hope for security and happiness lies in a civilization that protects life and property, in government that proceeds along an orderly way; that recognizes the sanctity of the home and the family; that holds fast to the common-sense principles that have been found practical and enduring for many centuries past; and that will not tolerate the agitators who seek to destroy that form of government.[46]

Stressing the connection between human and property rights, Sakamoto avowed his belief in the vitality of "American enterprise" and the therapeutic quality of a thriving economy for the country's ills and against the "evils" of Communism. In the brief preceding passage, he alluded to the classic republican virtues underlying American capitalist society.

In practice, Sakamoto supported Franklin Delano Roosevelt's policy of economic nationalism as a strategic method to rebuild America's beleaguered economy.[47] He viewed Roosevelt's principle of "the greatest good for the greatest number" as the basis for constructing such New Deal programs as the National Recovery Act. Moreover, he supported the notion that economic individualism was no longer functional to the national well-being and that "individual profiteering" must be replaced by "cooperation within the business community."[48] Sakamoto was wary, however, of too much government regulation of the private sector. When taxation on corporate surplus was proposed in 1936, he balked at the trend because he felt it was too great an infringement on the corporate sector.[49] Above all, he thought enhancement of American business was the panacea for economic and social crisis.

Sakamoto's strong faith in American enterprise was also indicative of his belief in the constitutional principles of bourgeois democracy. In an editorial statement in 1939, he praised the American Constitution and its relevance for Japanese Americans during those difficult times. He argued that the Constitution was "based on [the] American theory that government derives its powers from the will of the people," in contrast to the British Constitution which is unwritten and established by custom. Because it was written down, he said the American Constitution guaranteed the rights of all American citizens. Furthermore, he claimed, "[it] protects the rights of the people and demands their constant attention," and thus makes it incumbent upon American citizens to participate in the civil process. To substantiate his position, Sakamoto quoted from an address given by Dr. Aurelia Reinhardt of Mills College to a recent JACL District Council meeting in San Francisco on the subject of the American Constitution:

The builders of the American government, its early founders and its faithful citizens through 150 years have given us a vision of a happy people. They have completed this vision with a practical equipment of government that asks of you and me an intelligent participation.[50]

Sakamoto concluded by calling upon Japanese Americans to uphold the principles of the Constitution during periods of world strife in order to safeguard the future welfare of the country.

An important feature of Sakamoto's editorial was not only his faith in the American Constitution and the governmental process, but also his reference to Dr. Reinhardt, reflecting the tendency of second-generation leaders and intellectuals to rely heavily on white American role models for guidance and direction on such matters as citizenship and political orientation. We can infer that because Dr. Reinhardt was deemed an expert on American government, she was considered best equipped to provide the JACL with the "correct" line on civic participation.

It was common for the second-generation newspaper, the *Japanese American Courier*, as well as English sections of other community newspapers, to call upon their white patrons to advise the second generation on the proper conduct of their affairs in the larger society. Offering a variety of reasons, Sakamoto explained the practice of having "distinguished" contributors such as Elbert D. Thomas (U.S. Senator, Utah), Ray Lyman Wilbur (President, Stanford University), Clarence D. Martin (Governor of Utah), and W. Walter Williams (President, Seattle Chamber of Commerce) featured in the New Year's edition of the *Courier*. According to Sakamoto, these men reflected high attainment and character; their willingness to contribute demonstrated their high regard for "the vehicle of expression and the audience reached"; and they contributed important messages to the young people. "Such expression, and such counsel is rarely ever assembled in one publication, and this no doubt is due to the policy of the *Courier* the past decade in seeking such counsel and advice to pass on to its readers."[51] These VIPs stressed citizenship, American ideals as a foundation for youth, and American democracy.[52] Their messages affirmed the fundamental notions of Americanism that Sakamoto himself promoted so vigorously.

It follows from his belief in American economic and political institutions that Sakamoto would criticize anyone seeking to transform them. His comment about the importance of property rights suggests that he felt that subversion of American institutions was the motive of the "Old Left." He was severely critical of the agitation precipitated by both the labor movement and by Communists, on the grounds that it threatened the democratic way of life. He opposed the 1934 general strike in San Francisco, arguing that this action posed a threat to American institutions and the values they represented.[53] Moreover, he viewed the impending passage of the Wagner Act as promoting "the dictatorship of labor" rather than solving employer-employee problems.[54] He declared, "Cooperation is the key note of the times and it is in a cooperative spirit that labor and employers should get together to attempt to establish some means for settling all future disputes amicably."[54] His emphasis on cooperation and conciliation was clearly in keeping with the political style of the JACL.

Even after the passage of the Wagner Act, he was adamant that favoring labor interests solely violated the principle of justice.[55] He thought that an amendment to the Act was necessary to achieve fairness in labor relations. He also felt that Roosevelt should hear the position of industrial leaders of goodwill to ameliorate tensions between labor and business. The Wagner Act created the National Labor Relations Board, a body which, according to Sakamoto, would set the stage for continued conflict involving labor, employers, and the public. And it was the public, he thought, that suffered as a result of this discord:

> . . . in general labor strife the public suffers largely; possibly more than the other two groups. We do not know of any one more properly placed to look out for public interest under such conditions than the President—unless it be the Congress. There are hopeful signs that something may be done at the coming session.[56]

Sakamoto did not see social movements as a source for inducing change nor did he value agitation as a means of achieving social equality; rather, Sakamoto viewed the state as a mediating mechanism among the interests of labor, management, and the public.

An extension of Sakamoto's anti-labor sentiment was his support for the deportation of Harry Bridges, the longshoreman leader. He was upset because Bridges, although eligible for naturalization, declined to become a U.S. citizen. The allegation that Bridges was a Communist, despite a lack of evidence to support that charge, made Sakamoto wary of Bridges' labor activism. Sakamoto favored deportation because "Bridges was a disturbing element and an undesirable resident."[57] Clearly, Sakamoto had in mind the political ideology of Bridges and his role in the labor movement.

Anything that suggested anti-American behavior aroused Sakamoto's patriotic instincts. Despite public attacks on the Dies Committee (the House Subcommittee on Un-American Activities) for its red-baiting tactics, Sakamoto voiced his support for its work against the Communist Party:

> The exposure and conviction of leaders of the two most active groups in the country charged with being subversive was due to the work of the committee. This alone justifies its continuance.[58]

It is ironic that Sakamoto offered his unqualified support for this committee on the principle of Americanism; Martin Dies, Committee Chairman, eventually played an instrumental role in agitating for the internment of Japanese Americans in 1942.[59] Sakamoto's support for the Dies Committee suggests the extent to which he opposed the Left.

James Sakamoto's perspective was characteristic of the JACL. Before the intense campaign of the Dies Committee even began, the JACL passed a resolution at their 1934 Biennial Convention in San Francisco urging Congress to deport undesirable alien Communists. With the general strike as a backdrop they asserted,

> . . . be it resolved that the Japanese American Citizens League cooperate with and support any organization or governmental agency to expel and deport from the United States such undesirable alien communists who are found guilty of subversive acts toward our nation regardless of race, creed or nationality.[60]

Sakamoto's adherence to the political tenets of the American way and his disdain for the labor movement and radical groups such as the Communist Party reveal the nature of JACL political consciousness.[61] The Nisei leadership's attachment to the dominant economic and political ideals of the times was personified in Sakamoto, who held dear private property, individualism, and free enterprise. His faith in American institutions and his desire that the second generation "lower the anchor" indicate that embracing the ideals of the American Dream was an important strategy among Nisei professionals and small businessmen in confronting racism.

At the same time, in Sakamoto's thought, we find that the struggle for identity was tied to the racial currents of his times. Within the context of increasing tensions between the United States and Japan, Nisei like Sakamoto were restricted by a prevailing ideology which defined them as foreigners rather than as American citizens. Thus, Nisei found themselves in a situation where they had to affirm their identification with American life in order to avoid criticism and rejection. Their participation in electoral politics, therefore, was consistent with the ideological views outlined by Sakamoto.

Nonpartisanship

From the standpoint of policy, the JACL adopted a nonpartisan approach towards electoral politics—that is, exercising one's civic duty as an American citizen by voting in local, state, and national elections. Voting, therefore, was deemed more important than one's party affiliation. As a collective body, the JACL maintained a profile of nonalignment. Candidates' nights sponsored by local chapters typified this nonpartisan approach. Rather than support specific political aspirants, the leaders invited candidates from the major political parties to express their views. In this manner, Nisei voters could assess objectively all sides of the issues in question, weigh the information, and decide individually for whom to vote.

The JACL's emphasis on nonpartisanship stemmed from the liberal criticism that bloc voting, as practiced by some European immigrant groups, was contrary to the American way.[62] American nativist groups such as the California Joint Immigration Committee called bloc voting unpatriotic and voiced their apprehension that the Nisei would engage in this practice.[63] The JACL was quite sensitive to these charges and made a special effort to demonstrate its above-board approach to electoral politics. At the 1930 founding convention, a special round-table discussion devoted to the topic of politics focused on political ethics.[64] Emphasis was placed on the fact that members of JACL should vote independently, not in a bloc. The *Pacific Citizen*, the official organ of the JACL, argued that the JACL should act as a medium for dialogue between political clubs and should function as a clearinghouse for all political candidates.[65] This approach would render important assistance to both its members and political aspirants.[66]

Concurrently, JACL leaders and members could practice partisan politics as individuals. For the Old Guard, "individual" affiliation with the Republican Party was consistent with their middle-class aspirations. The political ambitions of Clarence Arai, one of the first Nisei to run for public office, offer an example of the Old Guard's political inclinations.

Active in the Seattle G.O.P. since the late 1920s, Arai had been chosen as one of the 102 delegates to attend the King County Republican Convention, where he was selected as one of 23 delegates to attend the state convention in 1934. Because he was a Japanese American, his selection was significant. He was part of the delegation from the 37th District, the second largest in the state.[67] He was also vice-president of the 37th District Republican Club.[68] In July 1934, Arai made his bid to become the representative of the 37th district in the State legislature.[68] The two issues on his platform were: 1) fighting artificial price fixing, and 2) returning to the Constitution. Both stands reflected his bias against the New Deal and his conservative Republicanism. Arai rejected the criticism that race was a determinant of good Americanism. In order to allay suspicions about his allegiance he exhorted, "No matter what racial origin we may come from we are Americans."[69] Despite the support of the second generation and the leadership of the Jewish community in the 37th District, Arai finished a dismal fourth place in the primaries. He received a total of 320 votes; the winner received 1,250.[70]

In spite of Arai's defeat at the polls, Sakamoto perceived Arai's participation as a moral victory because it brought recognition to Japanese Americans and demonstrated that they had become "election conscious." Voicing his idealism, Sakamoto praised Arai as a pioneer who fought a "clean and fair fight."[70] Arai ran once again for the representative position in the Republican primaries. This time his issues were support for vegetable growers and limiting government interference in local affairs. Again, he was soundly defeated.[71] As a token gesture, Arai was appointed by the mayor of the city in 1937 to a five-year term on the Library Board in recognition of his civic participation.[72]

The distinction between a policy of nonpartisanship by the JACL as a whole and individual partisanship is intriguing. It reveals how the Old Guard attempted to combat anti-Japanese American propaganda at a collective level while promoting their Republican political ideals in the name of individual participation. Although there is no conclusive evidence at this time, the distinction seems to be an artificial one in that the entire foundation of the JACL, which fixated on American democracy, advanced a Republican ideology. If one were serious about putting into practice the basic principles of Americanism that had been outlined by the Citizens League, embracing the JACL and proclaiming nonpartisanship seemed to be a contradiction.

By the late 1930s, when tensions on the domestic and international fronts were reaching crisis levels, the political strategy of the JACL leadership had clearly evolved. As their position as professionals and small businessmen solidified, JACL leaders echoed the political and economic ideals that prevailed in America at the time and took a nonpartisan approach to politics that reflected their general cautiousness in race relations. This stance brought them into conflict with Nisei and Kibei who considered it too conservative.[73]

Nisei and Kibei Progressives

The participation of some members of the second generation in the Old Left movement suggests that their response to a subordinate status was by no means uniform. Demonstrating a continuity with the early political activism of Issei laborers, Nisei were also involved in the Communist Party, the labor movement, and the Young Democrats—the left wing of the Democratic Party during the 1930s.[74] Nisei in Seattle and the San Francisco Bay Area demonstrated their labor union consciousness through their activity in organizing the Alaskan cannery workers.[75] Within these groups and organizations, there was diversity in perspective and style, ranging from left-liberal to radical approaches to social change. One unifying feature, however, appears to be their self-definition as "progressives." The use of the term progressive appears to have been a strategy to circumvent the intense anti-left bias prevalent in the Japanese immigrant community while presenting a left perspective on domestic, international, and community issues. The best way to comprehend the second-generation progressive style is to consider the experience of one who viewed himself as a progressive.

Kenneth Akazuki has lived in the San Francisco Bay Area for most of his life, except for the war years and the late 1940s, when he and his wife settled for a time in the Midwest.[76] Born in America, but having received the equivalent of a high school education in Japan, Akazuki is considered a Kibei. I interviewed him when he was in his middle sixties and worked as a computer technician. For most of his early life, he was involved with "progressive politics," particularly the trade union movement of the 1940s. He is less politically active now, but is still a member of a labor union.

Akazuki's father immigrated to America at the turn of the century for the explicit purpose of making money. Although his father came from a *samurai* background, the family experienced financial problems, thus forcing Mr. Akazuki to try to make his fortune in America where he worked for many years as a vegetable peddler. After some years, he made a visit to Japan to get married. The Akazuki family eventually prospered and returned to Japan, as did many Japanese immigrants.[77]

As a youth, Ken Akazuki was "strong willed" and rebelled against his father's wish that he attend college in Japan. After he completed high school in Japan, they allowed him to be "independent" and to realize his ambition to return to America for his college education. He was accepted at a university in the San Francisco Bay Area in the early 1930s and studied mathematics. In order to make ends meet as a student, he took part-time jobs. For a time he worked at a cleaners owned and operated by an Issei. He also worked at a nursing home. During summer vacations, he picked fruit on Japanese-operated farms because that was the only work available to him. "Our perspective was that it was only summer work, so it wasn't so bad. We made $100 for a summer; were paid $1.50 a day and 50 cents went for room and board." In retrospect, however, he felt that he had been exploited.

Economic survival was a constant worry for Akazuki. He stated: "I decided not to go back to school because I couldn't make enough money to get through. It didn't make much sense in going because there weren't any jobs." After leaving school, working first as a truck driver and later as a presser at the cleaners, Akazuki's wages were meager. "I made $21 a week." Thinking back, Akazuki thought that state labor laws required that workers be paid a minimum wage of $85 a month and that he made less than the minimum. Like so many Nisei and Kibei, he understood that his alternatives were limited. He realized that since he was excluded from the larger job market and was compelled to take whatever position was available to him within the Issei business community, he should be grateful for the work he did have. Although he possessed the intelligence and the potential to do more complicated and challenging work, no opportunity existed for him.

During this period in his life, Akazuki developed a serious interest in politics. His first exposure to radical thought occurred when he participated in informal discussion groups with some former childhood friends. One university student in particular, a member of Phi Beta Kappa, had a special influence on him. She was a progressive who spoke about politics and socialism. At first Akazuki did a lot of listening and seldom talked. "I absorbed it." At one meeting, when he finally "spoke up," everyone was surprised that he understood what was going on.

The exposure to progressive ideas through group discussion was an important influence in developing Akazuki's political awareness. But equally important was the mood of the 1930s. He reminisced,

. . . the 30s had a different feeling than the 60s. There was a feeling of hope. During the Depression things were bad racially and economically. But there was a spirit, a drive to get involved and get things accomplished. People were much more serious because the consequences were much more grave. People had greater concerns for other people.

The only comparable feeling that he could think of was the spirit among those students in the Civil Rights Movement who "went down South." In California, Akazuki experienced the "changing scene." According to him, many Nisei were interested in going to fight in Spain during the Spanish Civil War. "There was more enthusiasm and more idealism about bringing about changes [in the 1930s] than in the 60s." There was an assumption that things would never get better in the long run if things were simply left alone. "In order to change things, people had to get involved."

In 1939, Akazuki was active in the formation of the Japanese American Young Democrats in Oakland. "It was the only outlet for those [Nisei] who had political interests. At that time, there was nothing in the Japanese community to fill that vacuum, except the JACL." A year earlier, progressive-minded Nisei in the Los Angeles area formed the first chapter of the Young Democratic Club in response to the creation of the Nisei Voters' League, "the Japanese-American branch of the Republican party in Los Angeles."[78] At this time, politically minded Nisei were absorbed in the 1938 local elections. Immediately after the Nisei Young Democrats formed in Los Angeles, Larry Tajiri, liberal journalist for the *Japanese American News*, spearheaded the organization of the Japanese American Democratic Club in San Francisco. Together with some other Young Democrats (YDs) from Los Angeles, Tajiri worked with Nisei in Oakland to form another branch of the Young Democrats.

Ken Akazuki recalled that the Oakland group was the largest, with about 40 members; the Los Angeles branch had about 30 members, and the San Francisco chapter had approximately 20 core members.[79] In contrast to the professional and small business backgrounds of JACL leaders, the economic position of the Oakland YDs was much more working class and student based.[80] About 10 members attended the University of California, Berkeley. The occupations of the men included gardening and produce work; most of the women had clerical jobs. The members of the Los Angeles group had similar backgrounds.

According to Akazuki, YDs were concerned, intensely critical, and vocal about major political issues of the day. Limited life chances and restricted job opportunities sparked much of their interest. Since a college education did not guarantee a career or even a job in a field for which one was trained, Nisei were compelled to take what was available within the Issei ethnic economy. Under these circumstances, radical political thought had a definite appeal to many YDs. In addition, the changing political mood of the 1930s spurred many Nisei to become politically active. As a result, questions of political mobilization and social change were crucial, as their approach to domestic and international issues demonstrates.

Domestic Issues

On the domestic front, progressive groups like the Young Democrats had four priorities. First, they gave full support to the national and state New Deal administration. In conjunction with the parent group, Young Democrats of California, Nisei Young Democrats worked to bring Governor Culbert L. Olson into power, along with local and state and New Deal slates.[81]

Second, they were concerned with raising Nisei political consciousness and getting Nisei to vote in favor of progressive bills that protected the welfare of racial minorities in the state. Political organizing and recruiting among the Nisei were a central facet of their work.[82] In line with this type of organizing, the Young Democrats published their monthly *Nisei Democrat* to promote Nisei political consciousness.[83] Nisei progressives, who predated the current movement in Asian American politics, worked with their Chinese American counterparts to secure more government jobs.[84] In 1939, progressive Nisei circulated a petition seeking 1,000 signatures in support of bills that guaranteed equal rights in employment, housing, and civil liberties to racial minority groups in California.[85]

When necessary, they engaged in confrontational tactics to emphasize racial issues. At the December 1938 state conference of the Young Democrats of California, four Nisei delegates from the Los Angeles club, led by their president Ruth Kurata, issued four demands before the convention: 1) that a bill be introduced at the next session of Congress making any act of discrimination on the basis of race, color, or creed a misdemeanor punishable by law; 2) that a council be established which would "act as a consulting body to the state executive committee of the Young Democrats and which will ferret out all discriminatory legislation and recommend to the executive committee action against such legislation," and that they and other representatives of other racial minorities be placed on that council; 3) that they be given a voice in the state youth commission to be established in the near future; and 4) that the present pro-rate be changed since it was doing more harm than good to the small farmer, "among whom there are many Japanese."[86]

Doho, the progressive bilingual weekly newspaper which directed its attention to the second generation in the late 1930s, reported that all of these demands were accepted by the convention.[86] *Doho* columnist John Kitahara praised the progressives who had been maligned by the Japanese community as alleged "Reds," while criticizing other community organizations in Los Angeles, such as the Japanese Chamber of Commerce, the Nisei Voters League, and the JACL, for refusing to take action on the issues of discrimination and segregation. The Young Democrats were successful, he argued, precisely because they were involved with progressive people. He implied that the conservative tactics of the established community leadership were vacuous.

Although it is difficult to determine if the allegation that the Young Democrats were "Reds" was correct, the important consideration is that the progressives attempted to grapple with the race issue within left circles.

According to Joe Oyama, a member of the Los Angeles Young Democrats, their involvement put them in touch with members of other racial and ethnic groups who faced the same type of discrimination experienced by the Nisei.[87] This interaction broadened their horizons immensely and made them realize that the world did not start and end with "Little Tokyo." Progressive politics brought them into the world, while many of their second-generation peers remained isolated from the larger sphere of social and cultural events.

Third, Nisei progressives supported the labor movement and the tactics of mass action. Akazuki recalled participating in the picketing of the General Motors Plant in Oakland, California, in support of the workers' demands for better wages and improved working conditions. Having been in close touch with CIO organizers, the Young Democrats became conscious of the plight of the auto workers and backed their cause. Joe Oyama also recollected that the Nisei progressives supported the efforts of Nisei produce workers to secure better wages and working conditions through unionization.[88] Overall, the political dynamism of the labor movement, particularly the CIO, captured the imagination of politically conscious Nisei and Kibei like Akazuki and informed a great deal of their political activity.

Fourth, progressives were especially mindful of the repression inherent in American society. Defining the situation as the rise of domestic fascism, they attempted to articulate this threat to their peers. A *Doho* commentary outlined their thoughts on this issue:

> Democracy which is an abstract word to many nisei today may be their sturdy fortress tomorrow when fascism attempts to strike with dramatic swiftness, spurred by peddlers of racial hatred, and fanned by a jingoistic press. . . . Citizenship, in the true sense of the word to nisei, should mean an active participation with the forces of progress and democracy to combat the menace of fascism in this country and not a passive acceptance of the fruits of democracy which [we] are enjoying today. . . . The forces of reaction within our own country are seeking by every open and concealed means to destroy our basic and democratic rights. Suppression of civil rights, attacks on the rights of labor, the promotion of the "red scare," and anti-Semitism, the fomenting of religious and racial hatreds, show the forming of American fascism.[89]

It is interesting to notice the parallel between the philosophy of *Doho* and that of the JACL with regard to democracy and citizenship. Both subscribe to these basic principles of American life. However, progressives perceived attacks on the labor movement, racism, and "red" baiting as basic threats to democracy and viewed citizenship as the practice of defending those rights. In contrast, the JACL defined the labor movement, Communist organizers, and "left" civil rights organizations (such as the Young Democrats) as menaces to democracy, while citizenship to the JACL meant civic participation and the individual exercise of one's voting privilege. In schematic terms, Nisei progressives followed a collective, class-oriented style to domestic political issues, whereas JACL members practiced an individualistic, nonpartisan style.

International Issues

The concern about fascism at home provided Nisei and Kibei progressives with a framework for assessing the international situation. The Young Democrats clearly opposed the rise of militarism in Japan and Germany and openly voiced their fears about fascist threats to world democracy. It was because of Japan's imperialistic ventures in China during the late 1930s, Akazuki said, that "the progressives supported the embargo of war material to Japan."[90]

Moreover, the progressives were cognizant of the negative repercussions Japanese militarism would have for Japanese Americans. *Doho* columnist Kitahara pointed out that the Marco Polo Bridge incident compounded problems of discrimination for the Nisei, who had been viewed by the American public as representatives of the Japanese government:

> There are many today who cannot tell the difference between the government of Japan and the Japanese people, between the arrogant demands of the Japanese militarists and the masses whose main hope is security and peace. These misguided Americans see in every Japanese, though that Japanese may have been brought up in the United States, receiving American education, and completely at home in the traditions of America's great democracy, a potential Japanese soldier or ardent backer of Japanese militarism.[91]

Given these circumstances, he realized that Nisei had become justifiably bitter since their lives had been altered. Yet he cautioned,

> . . . we must remember that the moral protest against savage bombing of cities and the brutalities of war expressed by the American people arises out of the spirit of international justice and their desire to see nations dwell at peace, although such mass expression may find pitfalls....[91]

Kitahara asserted that the key issue was the impact of Japanese propaganda on the Nisei. He cited cases where Japanese fascists deliberately misinterpreted the American boycott of Japanese goods to bias Nisei sentiment against progressive forces in America. As a result, Kitahara argued that Nisei support for Japan was contradictory. If they protested against the military actions of Italian and German fascists, then they should also be critical of Japan's invasion of China. Otherwise, he pointed out, their views and actions would be inconsistent.

Furthermore, progressives warned against blind cultural nationalism.[92] A conceptual attempt was made to distinguish between taking pride in one's ethnic ancestry and allowing cultural nationalism to become a rationalization for supporting militarism. If Nisei were to adopt the latter cause, they would be taking a reactionary position, regardless of their liberal stance on labor, welfare, and civil rights. Nisei progressives realized that the question of Japanese nationalism was complex and that it was important to understand the implications of Japanese militarism.

In contrast to the perspectives of the JACL and of Kazuo Kawai, Nisei and Kibei progressives were extremely critical of Japan's role in China. They linked the rise of Japanese militarism with discrimination against Japanese Americans. Both were fueled by feelings of racial superiority. A racial ideology that merged American citizens of Japanese ancestry with Japanese nationals allowed white Americans to treat the Nisei as though they were part of the enemy race. Progressives thus felt an urgent need to formulate a political perspective on international events that was broader than Kawai's emphasis on cultural exchange, on the one hand, and the JACL's sympathetic response to Japanese militarism, on the other.

Nisei Progressives and the JACL

For the most part, Nisei progressives were critical of the JACL. The tension between them was largely due to differences in their ideological perspectives and in the strategy each favored for improving the position of Japanese Americans. Ken Akazuki's early involvement with the JACL gives us a good sense of this conflict.

Before the formation of the Oakland chapter of the Young Democrats in 1934, Akazuki had helped to organize the Oakland chapter of the JACL at the request of the local Old Guard. He recalled, "Being a Kibei, I could speak Japanese and the JACL leaders thought I could talk with the Issei so they would let their kids join the JACL." But after a short period of activity, he dropped out: "Eventually, I moved away from the JACL; I formed different opinions and went into different directions" because the Old Guard was much too conservative to suit Akazuki's political outlook. "They didn't want to touch anything controversial." Men like Saburo Kido, who were either professionals or small businessmen, formed a "power elite" in the Japanese American community. They had cordial relations with the Japanese Association and the Japanese Chamber of Commerce, the most powerful organizations within the community.[93] Despite their social concerns, they were also seeking "status," just as the Issei leaders who were concerned about their class position and status. This bothered Akazuki. He was also wary of the material preoccupations of the Issei community. "Money made it and if you had money people would listen to you." In his view, the JACL seemed to be heading in this direction also.

Progressives like Akazuki had different values. They were concerned about opportunity and mobility, but they looked at them from the standpoint of collective movement among the rank and file, in contrast to the quest for individual advancement implicit in the ideology of the JACL. Progressives saw the Old Guard as reinforcing the stratification system within the community. This was inconsistent with their more egalitarian concerns.

In addition, Akazuki was very dissatisfied with the "keeping quiet" and the "110% Americanism" strategies dictated by the JACL to handle the problems of racial discrimination. He could understand that "they were unsure of their status and they wanted to hang onto any gains they had made." But the soft-spoken and noncritical approach to the issues of the day did little to improve their subordinate position. If changes were to be made, political mobilization and direct action were necessary, Akazuki believed. To impart this perspective to the JACL, many progressives joined the JACL in the late 1930s with the intention of moving the JACL leftward. With the infusion of some younger leaders, many hoped that the conservatism of the Old Guard could be successfully challenged.[94]

Despite the generational tensions, it is ironic that a tenuous consensus emerged between the progressives and the JACL, due not so much to an agreement over political style but to the crisis created by the impending war with Japan. Generational as well as racial unity became an important source of strength, which temporarily transcended the ideological differences between the two groups. In line with this consensus, *Doho* voiced its support of the JACL in early 1940:

> The annual membership drive is again launched by the Japanese-American Citizens' League. The *Doho*, following the past policy, again urges every eligible nisei voter to join the league to forge the unity of nisei to face the crucial tasks ahead. All nisei rank and file should join to make the JACL a more progressive organization. Join the J.A.C.L.![95]

This call for solidarity suggests that Nisei progressives considered the JACL the most effective organization for mobilizing the Nisei in a time of crisis. They hoped that by working within it, its direction and perspective could be changed. This strategy is understandable since the progressives lacked a strong organizational base of their own. In addition, the restrictions imposed by worsening U.S. and Japan relations and the resultant anti-Japanese propaganda compelled them to temper their political differences for the sake of ethnic unity. Thus the political, racial, and economic situation placed progressives in a subordinate position vis-à-vis the JACL and enabled the latter to assume an important leadership role within the Japanese American community.

Kibei Alienation from American Society

While Nisei were rejected by the larger society, the Kibei had to contend with a dual form of rejection. Besides occupying a racially subordinate position in the larger society as Japanese Americans, they were also rejected by their Nisei peers. This was a difficult and complex situation, especially for Kibei who were sent to Japan during the 1930s. In contrast to older Kibei like Akazuki, who turned to "progressive" politics, the younger Kibei felt alienated from the larger Japanese community, and consequently congregated among themselves and affirmed the "Japanese" side of their experience. This affirmation was perhaps most pronounced during World War II, but its roots certainly seem to be embedded in their prewar experience. The early life of Ty Sasaki, who spent his adolescent years in Japan, provides insight into the Kibei situation. Although he is technically third generation in terms of birth order, he identifies himself as a "Kibei" and shares the experience and the same historical position as his pre–World War II Kibei peers.

Ty Sasaki was born in Oakland, California in November 1924. He is the oldest in a family of eight brothers and two sisters. His father was born in Hawaii but returned to Fukuoka, Japan with his parents when he was about two years old. The elder Sasaki was reared in Japan until he was 10, at which time he went to Seattle with his father, but lived a very transient early life, being sent from place to place when he was young. Sasaki, Senior, worked at various odd jobs after his father returned to Japan. After a brief stay in Wyoming, where he lived with a Caucasian family, Sasaki, Senior, came to San Francisco when he was 15 years old to work in a Japanese-owned hotel. His job was to pick up people coming from Japan at the harbor and take them to the hotel. After a brief stint there, Mr. Sasaki went to Concord, California.

Ty Sasaki's earliest recollections revolve around the movement of his family from place to place and the kind of work his father did. He remembers Concord, California because his father worked for a *hakujin* farmer there and later operated his own tomato farm. A family photo that he has kept reminds him that his family was part of the Issei community, but beyond that Sasaki does not remember much. He does not recall going to school because they moved around so often. The next move was to the Redondo Beach area in Los Angeles where his father became a "haul man." "With his truck, he would go around to the small farms and pick up vegetables and take them to the wholesale market." This was during the Depression, "so times were hard."

Sasaki does not remember many pleasant things about his early childhood. One of the few things that he does remember is his uncle (his mother's brother) whom he admired, apparently because he had the nerve to stand up to his maternal grandfather, of whom Sasaki was afraid as a young boy. Also, he liked baseball and wanted to play when he was a child. Aside from these few recollections, he says that "it's this unpleasant thing that really stands out." His subsequent experience helps us understand why.

Sasaki's mother took him and his three brothers to Japan in 1934 to live with their grandfather, the same one who had lived with the family for a time in Redondo Beach. Sasaki was 10 years old then and he questioned why his parents sent him away. He believes that the economic situation had something to do with his being sent to Japan, as was the case for so many other parents of Kibei who were "too busy working to care for their young children."[96] But he also stated, "One of the reasons I was sent to Japan was because I didn't get along with my parents." He hinted that his dislike for authority might have played a role in this. Giving him an education in Japan was not a consideration for Ty Sasaki's parents as it had been for other parents.[97] But the fact that his parents sent his brothers with him suggests that economic necessity may also have been a key factor.

The adjustment to Japan was difficult. Sasaki and his brothers were the only "foreigners" at the school they attended. He "couldn't speak Japanese" and the fact that he was "an American" did not help him gain acceptance from his peers. Moreover, he felt that he was discriminated against because of his differences. His problems were compounded by family difficulties as well. He said that he and his brothers experienced a lot of hardship because his "grandpa drank all of the money" his Dad sent. As a result, he recounted that "we had very little to eat and it was kinda hard. The youngest one was only seven then. I more or less raised my brothers, from [the time I was] ten to sixteen. I had to feed him and the others. And we had to wash our own clothes." One small consolation was that the villagers were very nice to the Sasaki brothers. But because they lived quite a distance from the village, he and his brothers had little opportunity to befriend them.

Despite the hardships, he felt that he did well in school. "When I was in junior high," he recounted, "I was thirteen years old." But he passed out of the lower grades quickly. To earn admission to the five-year high school program, he had to pass an exam. "And I passed it," he said, expressing pride, "so I guess I did all right." He completed three years of high school before returning home.

For the entire time he was in Japan, "Japan was at war with China," so he was educated in a military manner. "The war started when I was in the second grade in high school." Schooling consisted of military training, with part of each day devoted to drilling with a wooden rifle or spending time on bivouac:

> At first it was one hour [of] training, then it was two hours . . . , three hours. Then by the time I was in third grade, it was half a day [of] training. Then it was in the morning, and in the afternoon. Twice a week we'd stay out all night. I was fourteen or fifteen years old.

Although "everything in school was about the war," he recalled that students also had to learn kendo or judo. Since he was physically bigger than his classmates, his peers recruited him for the judo club. This was something at which he excelled and he managed to make the team for second-year students.

After nearly six years, Sasaki decided to return home because "it got so bad that [he] couldn't take it any more." He intimated that he was no longer willing to put up with his grandfather, so he had his parents send his brothers and him their passports and their fare. Sasaki said that they actually had "to run away from grandpa." It was ironic, according to Sasaki, that he decided to return home just before the war broke out. He heard that "there was going to be a war," but he had not realized that it would break out so soon after they departed. During this time, he also thought about what he would say to his parents when he saw them because he could not understand why they had sent him to live with a grandfather whom they knew he disliked.

Sasaki returned home to Los Angeles in July 1941 and rejoined his family who were now living in North Hollywood. Sasaki was 16 years old at that time and one thing was quite apparent: he was not close to his mother and father, nor was he close to the siblings who had been born in California during his absence. "I didn't know my parents that well, and we always had friction." This was clearly a disappointment to him because he wanted to get closer to his parents. His alienation from his family was something that he carried with him to Manzanar and later to Tule Lake. Sasaki mentioned that many years passed before he mellowed and was able to develop a more intimate relationship with his parents.

Although family relations were strained, Sasaki, along with his brothers, helped his father after school and on Saturdays. While he was away, his father had turned to gardening to provide for the family. During his free time, Sasaki continued to pursue his interest in judo. The bulk of his time, however, was devoted to school. Since he spoke only Japanese, he attended Maryknoll School for a few months where he learned to speak English again. He then transferred to Belmont High School. He was there only a month or so before the war with Japan broke out. As it turned out, the war ended his formal education: five years in the United States and three years in Japan. "Eight is the most education I had. I don't have a high school diploma or nothing." His knowledge and intellect, however, give one the impression that he has spent a lot of time studying on his own.

In general, Sasaki's adjustment to life at home was difficult. His experiences took on a character reminiscent of his early experience in Japan. He said, "And of course when we came back we were treated again like we were treated in Japan at the very beginning, discriminate . . . ." "So no matter where we were . . . , in Japan [we] were discriminated [against] because we were American; come back here and we were Kibeis, and again, there was [discrimination]." As a result of such reception, Sasaki indicated that it was natural "to react to whatever was imposed upon [him]." This led to conflict with Nisei. As a 16-year-old, he had "a lot of hot blood. I was getting in more fights with Nisei." Although his thoughts about being alienated and isolated did not truly crystallize until he was in a concentration camp, he did wonder, "Where do we belong?" He indicated that this feeling of being displaced was one that he shared with his fellow Kibei, particularly those who encountered a lot of problems, including gambling and getting into fights. In retrospect, he found it quite interesting; but at the time, it was certainly something that he pondered constantly.

Although he was just beginning to develop a broader consciousness about the status of the Kibei, he realized that Nisei, like the Kibei, could not get decent jobs either. Because Kibei like himself were already "a certain age," it was very difficult to learn the English language after returning from Japan. Without this skill, he recognized that life would be difficult for them: "Most Kibei felt that they would remain as produce clerks, cleaning lettuce or cleaning celery, kind of thing." Experiences voiced by other Kibei confirm Sasaki's outlook. Evelyn Nakano Glenn found in her study that "among the families ... who had sent some children to Japan and kept others in California, the kibei offspring were less successful occupationally. Kibei siblings were employed in service and blue-collar jobs, while their nisei brothers and sisters worked in white-collar jobs."[98]One Nisei who was interviewed during the "resettlement" phase of evacuation observed that the Kibei were often paid lower wages than the Nisei.[99]

Although Ty Sasaki was one of the younger members of the Kibei cohort at the outbreak of the war, his feelings of rejection and alienation seemed to be quite similar to those of other Kibei with whom he later became acquainted in camp. In fact, it was in camp where he finally met other Kibei like himself and managed to establish friendships and a feeling of community that he had longed for before the war. Similarly, Harry Y. Ueno, an older Kibei, recounted that it was not until he heard a Buddhist reverend talk about the parental problems that other young Kibei experienced that he began to realize that his situation was not unique.[100] Nakano likewise described the experiences of the Kibei women whom she interviewed as follows: "Some had endured the trauma of feeling rejected and experienced difficulty renewing an affectionate relationship with their parents when they returned to the U.S."[101] This lack of closeness also extended to sibling relations. As was true for Sasaki, oftentimes the eldest in the family who had been educated in Japan were strangers to their brothers and sisters who attended American schools and were socialized into American culture.[102]

Clearly, Sasaki was part of the Kibei community that had developed a much stronger cultural identity with Japanese culture and values. Unlike Akazuki who left Japan in the 1920s and missed the entire phase of Japanese militarism that younger Kibei who were sent to Japan in the 1930s encountered, Sasaki was schooled in Japan when militarism was at its height. Within a racial context antithetical to Japanese Americans and a Nisei social milieu that was critical of the Kibei, it is not surprising that Sasaki would affirm his "Japaneseness" by congregating with other Kibei who shared his experiences and values. In contrast, Akazuki and other Kibei like Karl Yoneda had been in Japan during a much more liberal and democratic period. Harry Ueno, another older Kibei who helped to organize kitchen workers in Manzanar, recalled that his experience was quite different from that of the younger Kibei: "I came back [to the United States] in the early 1920s when I was rather young, and some came back just prior to World War II. They had finished high school, and their ages were probably eighteen or twenty, around there. . . . He added, " . . . the militarists had more of a grip on their education, probably. So, they had an altogether different kind of mind. . . ."[103] While we cannot assume that every Kibei who was schooled in Japan during the 1930s embraced Japanese nationalism and militarism, Kibei like Sasaki possessed, in varying degrees, an affinity towards Japanese society and culture.

Because of the differences in their cultural style, as well as the language barrier, Kibei found themselves outside of "Nisei society" and were compelled to form their own groups.[104] Had Sasaki returned home sooner, it is likely that he would have befriended other Kibei. Individuals like Kimiko Tamura who returned to Los Angeles in 1935 "spent her leisure time with other Kibei, joining the Kibei Club, a kind of literary group in which members shared short stories and poetry."[105] This seemed to be one outlet where they could share their unique cultural experiences and express them through the medium of the Japanese language.

Kibei leaders also established special divisions within the JACL. Such a need seemed to derive, in part, from the fact that Kibei did not perceive the JACL to be sensitive to their concerns. *Doho* reported that in the Los Angeles chapter of the JACL, Kibei members considered many of the JACL members to be too "high-hat" and distant from the youth and the community.[106] Perhaps, more importantly, the heightened ultra-Americanism expressed by the JACL as war with Japan became imminent came into conflict with the Japanese nationalism felt by many Kibei.[107] It appears that such differences in political orientation also led Kibei leaders to question their affiliation with the JACL.[108] Not only were such discussions held within the JACL, such groups as the Kibei Citizens Council of San Francisco in northern California, and their counterparts in southern California, held conventions to discuss Americanization programs, relations with the JACL, and the role of Kibei citizens.[109] In this respect, Kibei social clubs and organizational affiliations helped to assuage their marginalization from both the mainstream society and their fellow Nisei.

Evacuation and internment, however, short-circuited the resolution of these social tensions and personal issues for people like Sasaki. Once in camp, Sasaki's feelings of alienation and anger intensified and became part of the reason he rejected American society and his Nisei peers who were "pro-America." In Manzanar, Sasaki openly declared himself to be part of a "pro-Japan" faction. He felt that he had no other choice:

> I got no country now. Even my own country, come back from Japan, come to my own country, come home, and then we're treated like this. So, why belong to America? They don't treat us as loyal. That was a typical feeling amongst the pro-Japan [people]. Since we [were] labeled pro-Japan, I felt that I would show them how a pro-Japan [person] would act.

Responding negatively to Questions 27 and 28, which aimed at gauging the loyalty of Japanese and Japanese American internees, in a survey administered by the War Relocation Authority in March 1943, Sasaki eventually became a "no-no boy," as did so many of his Kibei peers.[110]

Significance of Competing Political Styles

During the socioeconomic crisis of the Depression years, the Japanese American second generation developed different styles of leadership and ideological perspectives in response to racial subordination. In many ways, Mannheim's notion of the generational unit helps us to understand the competing leadership direction that emerged in a period of social and cultural ferment. Kazuo Kawai is representative of one type of generational unit—one that attempted to articulate for the second generation the relevance of the "interpreter ideal." On the other hand, the Old Guard leadership of the JACL—people such as Arai, Kido, and Sakamoto—formed another unit which did not directly compete with Kawai's ideal but urged the Nisei to "lower the anchor" and become loyal Americans.

The notion of Americanism itself, however, became a competing perspective in the late 1930s and the early 1940s when relations between Japan and the United States soured. While the Old Guard did subscribe to such tenets of the "bridge" perspective as promoting mutual understanding between Japan and America, their major ideological emphasis was on embracing American democratic ideals, which resulted in adopting a strategy of legal/legislative change, public relations with the larger society, and conciliation.

In many respects, the JACL style was reminiscent of the accommodationist strategy practiced by Southern blacks in the pre–World War I era. Men like Booker T. Washington were compelled to accept racial segregation, and even to acknowledge the need for separation as a strategy for the advancement of black people. Such encouragement to practice mutual cooperation with white society was epitomized in the speech he delivered at the International Exposition in Atlanta in 1895: "In all things that are purely social we can be as separate as the fingers, yet one as the hand in all things essential to mutual progress."[111]

Although Washington has been severely criticized for his accommodationist political style, his approach seems reasonable, given the social and economic conditions that prevailed in his day. Economically, blacks were excluded from labor unions and the skilled trades.[112] They were incorporated into the labor market as semi-skilled labor to fill the demand for cheap labor required by Southern industry. Their economic subordination was reinforced by a caste structure in which blacks were culturally defined as inferior beings. The ideology that viewed people of color as the "white man's burden" was integral to American imperialist ventures at the turn of the century and interpenetrated with the cultural domination of whites over blacks.[113] During the 1880s and the early 1890s, the lynching of blacks averaged 100 per year.[114] This form of abuse was the physical manifestation of political oppression. The practice of disenfranchisement, the educational policies of separate but equal set down by the Supreme Court in *Plessy v. Ferguson*, and other Jim Crow practices relegated Southern blacks to a subordinate status.

Within this racial context, Booker T. Washington chose a pragmatic approach for achieving racial equality. An emphasis on black self-reliance and economic development apart from white society became central in his strategy. Learning a skill or a trade for the purpose of achieving dignity, self-sufficiency, and social progress became more important than "mere book education." Washington stated that he " . . . learned to love labor, not alone for its financial value, but for labor's own sake and for the independence and self-reliance which the ability to do something which the world wants done brings."[115] Washington's exhortation to blacks to learn "to do a common thing in an uncommon manner" and learn "to produce what others wanted and must have" was similar to the Issei notion of excelling in some special line. In this respect, the development of working skills and small businesses and farms served the dual function of combating a rigid racial structure and improving one's social status. The limits imposed by the racial structure of the pre–World War II United States posed similar institutional limits which compelled individuals like Kawai and JACL leaders to accommodate to their economic and political circumstances.

Accommodation did not mean, however, that Washington eschewed the fight against discrimination and disenfranchisement. There is some evidence to suggest that he contributed his own money to advance black civil rights.[116] He was secretly involved in the court fight against disenfranchisement in Alabama and railroad segregation in Richmond, Virginia. Also, he sought funding from philanthropists to combat the provisions in the Louisiana constitution that excluded black participation in electoral politics. In this way, he was able to use the influence of his public position and image to struggle covertly against the racist practices which he appeared to accept. During Washington's time, the racial structure offered few alternatives. Similarly, the combined efforts of Issei and Nisei leaders to repeal legislation such as the Cable Act were part of the legal strategy to secure racial equality. The JACL's emphasis on a nonpartisan political strategy was designed to neutralize criticism, and was, at the same time, geared to arouse Nisei political awareness.

Thus the political and economic circumstances faced by leaders like Washington and those in the JACL were important in the formation of their respective styles. This is not to say that the conditions or the responses were identical, since there were clear differences in the historical experiences of the two groups. Still, what they had in common was that their political styles were tied to the racial circumstances of their times.

In contrast to Kawai and the Old Guard, Nisei and Kibei progressives, exemplified by the Japanese American Young Democrats, developed a definite competing generational unit. While this unit was similar to the JACL in that it linked the destiny of the second generation with that of the larger American society, its perspective and strategy were "left" oriented and largely critical of the JACL. The Young Democrats supported the labor movement as a pivotal source of social change; they rejected Japan because of its militaristic and fascist direction, and they connected the Japanese American struggle for civil liberties with that of all minorities. In this sense, progressives embraced a more universal approach to the question of race relations, compared to the more particularistic concerns of the Old Guard and Kawai.

The ideals of Kawai and the Old Guard reflected much of the dominant ideology espoused by American political, business, and intellectual elites in the pre–World War II period. Mutual cooperation, conciliation, harmony, and economic interdependence, as well as economic progress, gradualism, and optimism for future social relations were central to the Nisei "establishment." In a correlative sense, these Nisei embraced the prevailing racial and economic order in America and believed that racial advancement would become possible as increased communication and understanding were forged between the races. Given the hegemony of the American cultural order at that time and the limited political and economic resources within the Japanese American community, it is understandable that the more privileged and middle-class-oriented leadership of the Old Guard would adopt this conservative style.

It was within the context of the social unrest created by the labor movement that younger members of the second generation, or those like Akazuki who were isolated from the establishment by their social position, attempted to challenge the Old Guard. These "young bloods" tended primarily to be working class and less privileged than the Old Guard. Their desire for equality exceeded that promised by the slow racial and economic progress of the incrementalist variety. Because many of the progressives came of political age during the national and international crises of the late 1930s, they projected a sense of urgency and commitment to change that has been characteristic of youth movements in general.[117] They articulated the need for immediate changes that would improve not only one's working conditions and wages, but also one's life chances.

In contrast, Kibei youth like Ty Sasaki were situated outside both Nisei and American society. Simultaneously rejected by their peers because they were culturally different and by the larger society because they were racially different, the Kibei had to turn inward and develop a sense of self-reliance and social cohesiveness among themselves. Certainly there were many who were able to cross over into Nisei circles without experiencing major difficulties, but they were few in number. It is unfortunate that the Kibei were subjected to such abuse by their fellow Nisei because they embodied many qualities that the Issei had hoped that the Nisei would retain. Yet, the hegemonic character of the prevailing racial ideology shaped the views of the Nisei with respect to their brethren. In general, Nisei considered the Kibei to be "too Japanesey." The Kibei cultural style served as a reminder to Nisei who were desirous of being accepted as Americans that anything "Japanese" had to be submerged.

Also, Nisei considered the political views of the Kibei to be much too "authoritarian." Socialized to accept American democratic procedures and values, many Nisei youth who came of age in the late 1930s tended to clash sharply with Kibei like Sasaki who were imbued with a strong sense of Japanese nationalism and militarism. Conversely, Nisei rejection resulted in Kibei adhering to their "Japaneseness" all the more. In this respect, the racial and political tenor of the times shaped relations between Nisei and Kibei that would soon lead to direct and open conflict in the internment camps.

Each in its own style, these groups or at least their leaders solicited the rank and file of the Nisei community who were coming of age but who lacked any kind of political awareness. Appealing to the socially isolated and economically disadvantaged Nisei was a difficult task for both the JACL and the progressives. Few Nisei could relate to the lofty ideals and program proposed by the JACL. Because of the class orientation of the Citizens League, many rank and file Nisei viewed its members as "high hat" and more concerned about their own professional and business interests than the community at large. But at the same time, the progressives experienced far greater problems in securing community support than did the JACL due to the overriding fear and suspicion within the Japanese American community that stigmatized them. The progressive brand of Americanism was deemed subversive to democracy and, therefore, far less engaging to the Nisei than the loyalty espoused by the JACL. Except for Kibei like Akazuki who gravitated to the progressive side of the community, most Kibei were marginalized and found the JACL to be at odds with their concerns and needs. In this respect, the progressives seemed to provide a broader umbrella under which Nisei and Kibei were able to come together.

It is evident that not only generational location and the formation of units, but also the social and economic position of the Nisei, were important in the development of diverse political styles in the pre–World War II era.

The strategies of bridging East and West, lowering the anchor, and advancing political progressivism, as well as the resulting alienation, were not so much tastes or preferences as they were reactions to social and political realities that limited the second generation's alternatives. Thus, the generational term, "Nisei," as it has been used in the existing literature, while helpful in sensitizing us to the general experience of the second generation, has also cloaked the intragenerational tensions that derived from the generational units' divergent social and economic positions in American society. The location of its key spokespersons influenced the perspective, strategies, and tactics which a particular unit adopted. As we examine the Nisei response to internment and assess why a particular political style assumed dominance, we must be mindful of the social and economic position of Japanese Americans in the overall racial context of the United States.[118]

Chapter 4

"Constructive Cooperation"

Submersion of Ethnicity and
Rising Significance of Americanization

SHORTLY AFTER THE BOMBING OF PEARL HARBOR AND
the United States' entry into the war with Japan, more than 110,000 persons of Japanese ancestry—American citizens and permanent residents—
were evacuated from the West Coast and placed in internment camps.
Executive Order 9066, issued by President Roosevelt in February 1942,
provided for the imprisonment of Japanese Americans, in direct violation
of their civil rights. Many were compelled to sell their property and material possessions at tremendous losses.[1] Small groups voiced protest, while a
few individuals resisted internment.[2] Despite these scattered valiant efforts
to challenge the order, the vast majority of Japanese Americans complied.
Assuming community leadership during the crisis, the Japanese American
Citizens League (JACL) charted the response of the Japanese American
community when they pledged their full cooperation with the evacuation
decision. The key question, in retrospect, is why a people would affirm
their loyalty to America and emphasize their American identity at a time
when their rights and dignity were being blatantly violated.

In order to understand better the apparently paradoxical reaction of
the Japanese American community to evacuation, we need to divide the
period into two phases: 1) the preinternment crisis, and 2) the actual camp
experience. Both phases involved a conjuncture of racial and cultural factors, and an examination of each phase reveals the restrictive context in
which Japanese Americans acted. During the preinternment crisis, Nisei
obeyed the prevailing law and submerged their ethnicity in order to
demonstrate their loyalty to America and affirm their American identity.
Due to the hegemonic nature of the legal and racial order, Japanese Americans felt that they had few alternatives.[3] This orientation also converged
with the professional and petty entrepreneurial position of JACL leaders
and their "middle-class" aspirations. During the actual camp phase, the

War Relocation Authority discouraged dissent and suppressed protest and resistance. Generational and incipient class differences that gave rise to competing cultural orientations and sparked debate about political strategies within the pre–World War II community were muted. As a result, the Americanization ideal assumed greater significance than it had in the pre–World War II period and the JACL gained a legitimacy that carried over to the post–World War II period.

Preinternment Crisis

As political tensions between the United States heightened in the late 1930s, National JACL leaders became increasingly mindful of the negative repercussions for Japanese Americans. Wanting to deflect discriminatory actions away from the Japanese American community and hoping to educate the American public about the distinction between the Nisei and Japanese nationals, the JACL mounted a campaign to demonstrate to the American public that Japanese Americans were loyal citizens who were essentially no different than other loyal Americans. Placing on the back burner the "self-protective objectives" that had emerged during the 1930s, the JACL pushed to the forefront the theme of "loyalty" at its 1940 Biennial Convention in Portland, Oregon.[4] JACL President Walter Tsukamoto, in his keynote address to the convention, quoted from the JACL Constitution to emphasize the ideals to which the Citizens League had "dedicated" itself.

> We, the American citizens of Japanese ancestry, in order to uphold the Constitution of the United States, to foster and spread the true spirit of Americanism, to build the character of our people morally and spiritually on American ideals, and to promote the welfare and aid in the development of the Americans of Japanese ancestry as an integral part of the national life, do establish this Constitution for the Japanese American Citizens League of the United States of America.[5]

Tsukamoto's address also highlighted the key resolutions that were passed and underscored the JACL's ultrapatriotic posture.[6] According to Togo Tanaka, ". . . the organization went on record, in a dizzy swirl of oratory replete with references to 'Old Glory,' (1) to support universal military conscription whereby 'we call upon every American of Japanese ancestry to offer his life in the defense of his country' and (2) to cooperate with the government in the fingerprinting of their Issei parents under the Alien Registration Act." The JACL leaders suggested that they place less emphasis on discrimination, while acknowledging the law as the basis for securing equality.[7]

After Japan invaded French Indochina and increased military activities in China, the United States terminated commercial relations with Japan in July 1941. War clouds loomed over the two countries. Three months before the bombing of Pearl Harbor, JACL President Saburo Kido called an emergency board meeting and voiced the need to hire a full-time staff person to direct and expand the League's national program.[8] Kido argued that in this time of crisis the JACL required a new style of leadership, to be exercised by someone who was extroverted, aggressive, and innovative, someone who could carry the message of the Nisei to white America. The person he had in mind was Mike Masaoka, who was said to be "cocky, aggressive, bursting with enthusiasm and ideas."[9] Masaoka had been reared in Utah with little contact with Japanese Americans, which explains, in part, why he was so different from other Nisei on the West Coast who had grown up under very different circumstances. Trained in rhetoric and employed as a speech instructor at the University of Utah, Masaoka also had political ties to such influential white men as Utah Senator Elbert Thomas, a fact that Kido deemed essential for a National JACL leader who would be representing the larger Japanese community to the white American public. The appointment of Masaoka in August 1941 marked an escalation in the League's loyalty campaign. As JACL's first full-time worker, Masaoka established a two-point program that became the foundation for what Ichioka has referred to as the JACL's ultra-Americanism perspective: the first was to build the JACL as a national organization; the second was to fight for equal rights for all Japanese Americans.[10] The slogan that Masaoka coined—"Better Americans in a Greater America"—captured the political orientation that the JACL would follow during this time of crisis and thereafter.

Immediately after President Roosevelt issued Executive Order 9066, the JACL adopted a controversial course of action. Chosen by the federal government to be the liaison between the Japanese community and the military, the JACL established policies and made recommendations that would have significance for all Japanese Americans.[11] At their Special National Council Meetings, held March 8–10, 1942 in San Francisco, JACL leaders discussed three possible alternatives: 1) to resist evacuation, 2) to strike a compromise, and 3) to make use of "constructive cooperation."[12] The JACL leaders discarded the first option because they believed that patriotic citizens should not question military authority. Although they believed that they could gain some bargaining leverage by consenting to evacuation and thus secure privileges and concessions, JACL leaders ultimately rejected the second option in favor of cooperation. They believed that cooperation would help the war effort and prove to others that the Nisei were in fact loyal Americans, as well as create a moral obligation on the government to reciprocate similarly. "Constructive cooperation" was the only option that both met military necessity and provided a means for Japanese Americans to retain their dignity, self-respect, and civil rights.

According to Mike Masaoka, the strategy of constructive cooperation did not shelve the issue of the constitutionality of the evacuation process, nor was it an admission of guilt and disloyalty. Furthermore, cooperation did not mean that Japanese Americans were compromising their rights as American citizens. It simply meant that they believed a temporary suspension of their rights would enable them to secure all of their rights in the future. This course of action, according to Masaoka, would be contributing to "the greatest good for the greatest number."

Masaoka's themes of loyalty were shared by other JACL leaders and their supporters. Tokutaro Nishimoto Slocum, an Issei who became a naturalized citizen after serving in the army during World War I, voiced the thoughts of many members when he addressed representatives of the 66 West Coast chapters of the JACL at the three-day emergency session:

> We're dealing with a problem that cannot be solved at a glance, and that we are facing this problem today because of the short-sightedness of the Japanese leaders in America up to the present time. They only thought in terms of Japanese and were not grateful to the land which gave them protection, education and freedom.
>
> In order that we do not repeat the mistake that our fathers made we must break our ties although home ties are hard to break. It is in this time of crisis that we take advantage of the opportunity to test our own mettle.
>
> How we meet this problem will determine the future destiny of Japanese Americans in America as Americans. We must not expect comfort or luxury in time of war.[13]

An American citizen, Slocum criticized Issei leaders who identified strongly with Japan and urged Japanese Americans to demonstrate their loyalty to the United States. At the close of the emergency session, past national officers expressed views that echoed Slocum's sentiments and resonated with JACL's prewar ideology. James Sakamoto articulated these sentiments best when he stated, "let us demonstrate our loyalty to the United States. This evacuation is a defense need and defense effort. Let's be good soldiers by cooperating with the National Officers as well as with the Government."[13] Pledging allegiance to the American flag as the meeting adjourned further reflected their faith in the American way of life.

Some observers of the Japanese American experience have suggested that full cooperation with internment has its roots in the cultural traditions of the Japanese American community.[14] Old World values such as *shikata-ganai*, which means that "it cannot be helped," have been used to explain why the Japanese were willing to endure this adversity in a fatalistic manner. While we cannot deny that traditional cultural values did have an influence on the socialization of the Nisei, we must also be mindful of the racial and political context in which men like Masaoka developed the strategy of constructive cooperation.

Obedience to Law as Loyalty to Nation

Constructive cooperation was closely linked to the fact that Nisei, by and large, respected the law and accepted the existing racial order. In 1941, Masaoka was simply articulating the same ideological orientation that National JACL leaders had preached earlier. Similar to Sakamoto's notion of lowering the anchor, Masaoka emphasized the "American way"— the judicial court system, the legislative process, and a faith in democracy. As the war with Japan approached, the objectives and goals articulated by Masaoka clearly departed from the lingering ambivalence that had characterized the earlier policies of the National JACL. According to Togo Tanaka, the JACL maintained friendly ties with the Japanese Consulate until 1941. Except for the claim of neutrality, JACL had not established a policy regarding the military actions of Japan nor a strategy to deal with the impending political crisis.[15] In an effort to address this issue, Masaoka advocated building up the national organization and fighting for equal rights. Embedded in both these goals was the emphasis on loyalty. Under Masaoka's leadership, the JACL disassociated itself with the Japanese Association and emphasized its members' identification with America. The closing line of "The Japanese American Creed," "Better Americans in a Greater America," which was written by Masaoka, captured the essence of their thinking.[16]

But JACL's notion of loyalty involved more than an expression of patriotism and support for American ideals. It also meant an adherence to the law. By respecting law and order, JACL leaders hoped to deflect criticism and gain public acceptance. This was evident when the National JACL criticized those Nisei who resisted pre-evacuation restrictions. For example, Min Yasui, an attorney from Hood River, Oregon, violated curfew restrictions in order to test the legality of the war emergency measures.[17] James Sakamoto censured Yasui and the others who had challenged the curfew because they felt that doing so abrogated their civil rights. Besides calling them "negligent," Sakamoto stated:

> There is no excuse for them. They knew the rule. Of course, all this reflects on the Japanese generally, but this is not the point. Loyalty is shown by obedience to the laws, and we can best prove our loyalty by obeying the orders of those in authority.[18]

Sakamoto's comments point to his concern for how the Japanese would be perceived by the larger society and what the Japanese could do as a collective body to shape that perception. Thus, rather than supporting protest as a strategy to maintain their rights, he emphasized obedience to the law as a way for Japanese Americans to demonstrate their loyalty to America.

The JACL, however, was not the only segment of the community to support the precepts of law and order. Many Nisei who were interned said that their fellow Nisei generally accepted what Max Weber called legal-rational authority—respecting the validity of legal statutes and rational rules of behavior.[19] Marshall Endo, a Nisei teenager at the time of evacuation, suggested that most Nisei like himself strongly supported the notion of law and order. Commenting on his experience in a rural community in Southern California, he stated, "Before (the war), everybody was a law abiding citizen." He thought that "nobody including whites questioned the 'status quo' and the authority of the FBI and the military." He added that the Nisei perspective was quite different from that of Japanese American activists who questioned institutional authority in the late 1960s. The Nisei in their youth basically supported American institutions.[20]

Many of the Nisei whom Charles Kikuchi interviewed during the resettlement phase of internment also revealed that they maintained a deep respect for the law.[21] A Nisei small businessman in his early thirties at the time of internment described his initial entry into camp in the following way:

> I had been feeling fine, but as I went through the camp gates I suddenly got a very depressed feeling and I felt like a prisoner. There were guards at the gate and it was all fenced in. The barracks all looked dirty and I hated to think of having to live there for any length of time. This was the start of my life in a concentration camp. I could have escaped so easily if I didn't have a family that was waiting for me. There was nothing to prevent me from buying a train ticket out of town to the unrestricted zones. I didn't even think of it though, as I didn't want to break any laws.[22]

This Nisei's reluctance "to break any laws" suggests that prevailing legal sanctions were very powerful and that in this time of crisis Nisei were willing to remain obedient.

Ironically, the Nisei believed in their constitutional rights as American citizens. Although they realized that their Issei parents could be interned as "enemy" aliens, Nisei believed that they would be exempt from evacuation by law. Jim Kawamura, a 32-year-old buyer for a produce commission merchant at the time of the internment, expressed a viewpoint shared by many Nisei:

> Until the last minute I felt that I wouldn't be evacuated. For a while we used to run an apartment house in San Francisco during the

wartime and soldiers used to stay with us; and we were listening over the radio; and all of a sudden it came out that Pearl Harbor was bombed. Then there was talk of evacuation so we figured . . . we were citizens, see . . . So we didn't think that we would have to go. If our folks would have to go, we would help them evacuate. So we took it as we would be able to stay, being American citizens. Then they started to evacuate and to me I thought that they called a voluntary evacuation but you got to go out; and you can't stay; and I found that out when I started traveling in [the] San Francisco area. Every area you go to, there is a sentry there and they will stop you; and you have to have a pass to go from one part of the city to another.

My father-in-law had an apartment house there and he was taken in, because he was active in [the] Japanese Chamber of Commerce and the Nihonjinkai, so they took him first. So I had to take care of his property, but I was living in Japanese town. To go from Japanese town to Chinatown, I had to cross that boundary; I had to have a pass from the military Western Defense Command, so every time I had a pass; and so I thought maybe they won't evacuate me. And finally, they started posting all those signs, evacuation of citizens and all. There was actually nothing we could do.[23]

Although Kawamura was much older than the average Nisei, he shared similar circumstances with them. He was neither a political person nor did he follow closely the events leading up to internment. Economically, he had achieved some level of stability in his life. Because he believed in his rights as an American citizen, forced evacuation surprised Kawamura. Under the circumstances, however, he did not feel that he could protest.

Economic Status

The JACL's strategy of constructive cooperation also reflected their economic and social position. As professionals and small businessmen, it was very much a part of their outlook to view obedience to the law as loyalty to the nation. As Tamotsu Shibutani and Kian Kwan have pointed out about voluntary associations like the JACL, "the more successful members of minority groups" assume leadership roles, and because of the privileged position they occupy within their community, they tend to emulate the dominant way of life practiced by the majority.[24] Men like Kido, Arai, and Sakamoto were the more successful and prominent members among the second generation and, as leaders, had been concerned about improving the social and economic status of the Nisei when they launched the JACL. They believed firmly in developing a strong American identity; and their nonpartisan accommodationist political style was clearly consistent with the ideals and values of the dominant society. In this respect, it is understandable that these men who organized the JACL would adopt a defensive stance during the preinternment crisis.

At the Special National Council Meeting, it was quite apparent that one's economic position within the community determined the possibilities for leadership. Only Nisei who were prominent professionals and small-scale entrepreneurs were selected to serve on the central committee that met with military and government officials.[25] As professionals, farmers, and business-men, these men chaired subcommittees reflecting the key economic inter-ests within the Japanese community. For example, Dr. Yatabe, a dentist, headed the professional committee, while Fred Tayama, a businessman, took charge of the businessmen's committee. Convention delegates were asked to participate in one of the various committees to draft questions and identify concerns which the central committee would convey to the government and military officials who headed the evacuation bureaucracy.

Within the context of the prevailing domestic and international crisis, the JACL accepted the military necessity argument for evacuation although the central committee did not agree completely with the policy of mass evac-uation. Believing that evacuation was almost inevitable and feeling reassured by the good will and cooperation expressed by government bureaucrats who were in charge of the evacuation, the JACL decided to comply.[25]

Despite the fact that Japanese Americans were denied their constitu-tional rights as American citizens, JACL leaders held steadfast to their belief in the ideals of American democracy and fair play. Assessing this sit-uation in retrospect, Masaoka indicated that he believed then that the "principles" of democracy would ultimately prevail. He added that much of the political naiveté reflected in his staunch belief in the American way stemmed from his early education. He mentioned that he had not been taught about the legal barriers preventing the Issei from becoming natural-ized citizens; as a result, he could not understand why the Issei were not American citizens. Rather, he had been "taken in by some of the Yellow Peril propaganda" that the Issei did not want to become citizens.[26] In a 1967 interview, Kido mentioned that he believed so fervently in the Amer-ican way that he thought the constitutional rights of the Nisei would pro-tect them during the wartime crisis. JACL leaders, according to Kido, did not think about going to Washington, D.C. to make their case, nor were they conscious of the impact that mass hysteria would have on the decision to evacuate them.[27]

Economic Kinship Dependency

Another important factor was that most Nisei, even if they disagreed, were not in a position to take political action or to challenge the JACL. Given their dependency on the Issei ethnic economy, the Nisei lacked the autonomy and the political sophistication needed to deal with the political complexities posed by the impending internment. As the 1933 El Monte Berry Strike illustrated, the young Nisei generally complied with the wishes of the Issei on political matters that affected the overall economic welfare of the Japanese American community.[28] In this particular situation, Issei berry growers used Nisei high-school youth and unemployed white workers from the Los Angeles area to break the strike of Mexican laborers who sought higher wages. Though they may have disagreed with JACL's notion of constructive cooperation, most Nisei were certainly in no position to grapple politically with the issue. In contrast to JACL leaders who were older and had developed an economic base for political and civic action, the vast majority of the Nisei were young, economically dependent, and lacked political consciousness and experience. This helps to explain their resigned response to internment. Perhaps the comment of a San Francisco youth who had been drifting from job to job after completing high school in the late 1930s conveys the confused feelings of many Nisei:

> The first thing I thought of when evacuation was announced was to wonder what it was all about. All the guys in my gang were pretty sore about it and we cussed hell out of the government.[29]

For the most part, however, these Nisei could do little else but privately express their anger about the government's actions.

Convergence of the Left and the JACL

If there was going to be an organized effort to protest or resist President Roosevelt's decision to relocate Japanese Americans, we might reasonably expect it to come from the organized left within the Japanese American community. But this was not the case. The left adopted the same cooperative stance that the JACL advocated but for different reasons. While youth and inexperience did play a role in preventing the progressives from organizing against internment, it was political circumstances and the limitations imposed by the state of race relations in the early 1940s that largely shaped their response. As Karl Yoneda, a longshoreman and Communist Party (USA) activist and community organizer in the prewar period, explained in retrospect,

> The left-wingers and progressives, including communists, among the Japanese decided not to fight the evacuation order. Although it was in violation of our constitutional rights, it would be carried through by the use of the armed forces against those who might resist, thereby immobilizing them from the immediate important fight to smash the fascist axis—including the Japanese military clique which was endangering the lives of all mankind.[30]

As expressed by Yoneda, the radical perspective emphasized the fight against fascism and militarism as the primary issue; internment was secondary.[31] This did not mean that they condoned or ignored the violation of the civil rights of Japanese Americans, however. Commenting about the racist nature of the evacuation, Yoneda further stated,

> There can be no choice, the fascists must be defeated now, and talk about the injustice of evacuation later. Because of the malicious racism being spread throughout this land—the "yellow peril" forces have all come out of the woodwork—we are helpless in couping [sic] with the situation. The only way to speed victory over fascism and emperor-militarism is to make every effort to complete the evacuation orderly so that our country can turn her sights—unhampered— against the enemy. Am I wrong in not only pursuing this line of thought, but loudly speaking out? Only history will tell.[32]

Ironically, Yoneda rejected the stand taken by Norman Thomas of the Socialist Party who spoke out against evacuation.[33]

Like Yoneda, progressives such as the Nisei Young Democrats also chose cooperation. A policy statement issued by the Nisei Democratic Club of Oakland shortly after the announcement of Executive Order 9066 indicated the basis for their compliance.[34] The Nisei Democrats protested that the proposed mass evacuation was "inconsistent with the democratic principles in which we believe and for which we fight." They also maintained that evacuation was a moot issue since "saboteurs and spies" could easily be handled by the FBI. However, they reasoned that the wartime crisis "created a disunity which seems to necessitate an order for evacuation by the Army." Thus, "in order to gain national unity . . ." the Nisei Democratic Club pledged their "fullest cooperation toward this end." They were clear in emphasizing, however, that the war was not "racial" but "a war against fascism and for the preservation of democratic ideals." They nonetheless concluded on a critical note: "Suspension now of democratic principles for some may mean permanent loss for all."

In keeping with their prewar political focus, Nisei progressives and radicals focused on the issues of fascism and militarism. In contrast, the JACL's policy of constructive cooperation had a pragmatic orientation. While there was some similarity between the JACL and the Nisei left, both groups were compelled to modify their principles in light of the military exigencies posed by the war with Japan. The JACL's pledge of ultraloyalty placed tremendous faith in the American institutions of government. The left, in comparison, felt that the government was obligated to protect the constitutional rights of individual citizens as well as the welfare of the nation as a whole in a time of crisis.[35] Radicals and progressives rejected the notion that the government policy should be accepted, "right or wrong." Instead, they argued that while the government's actions should be supported under the prevailing conditions, they should be questioned nevertheless.

Tensions between the JACL and the left did not deter them from attempting to form coalitions. Because internment was racially based and affected all classes within the Japanese community, various groups formed to discuss methods of confronting the issue. In the San Francisco Bay Area, several Nisei organizations gathered immediately after the announcement of Executive Order 9066 to discuss the impending evacuation. Diverse organizations—the Nisei Democratic Club of Oakland, the Bay Region Young Buddhist Association, the Nisei Writers and Artists Mobilization for Democracy, the YWCA, YMCA, the staff of the Nisei magazine *Current Life*, University of California Nisei students, and the Catholic Youth Society—came together as a "medium of expression" for groups outside the JACL to voice their "needs and desires."[36] Called the "Sounding Board," this coalition was designed to "work through the Bay Area Coordinating Council of the JACL and cooperate with it on any action that must be taken for the welfare of the Japanese groups."[37]

Federal and military officials worked with the JACL because they deemed the Citizens League the official representative of the Japanese community. But was JACL's recognition as community leader warranted? There is some evidence to suggest that the JACL did receive considerable community support. Both the Buddhist and Christian churches pledged their full cooperation.[38] Reverend K. Kumata, Field Executive of the Buddhist Church of America, announced that 40,000 Buddhists gave their support, while the General Council of the Japanese Christian Federation of North America, and the Northwest, Northern California, and Southern California Young People's Christian Federation also backed the JACL.[39] Even earlier, the *Doho* had headlined in bold print a few days after the bombing of Pearl Harbor, "JACL URGED TO ACT IN CRISIS TO LEAD JAPANESE PEOPLE."[40] Although *Doho* did voice some qualifications about supporting the JACL, it stipulated that it did so because the JACL was in the most strategic position to assume leadership at the time. The JACL also participated in umbrella organizations linking various community interests. In the Los Angeles area, the JACL, Buddhist and Christian churches, fruit and vegetable workers, American Legion Posts, Nisei writers and artists, athletic organizations, and others formed the United Citizens Federation. In addition, the Anti-Axis Committee of the Los Angeles Chapter of the JACL planned meetings to discuss evacuation.[41]

Although the JACL established working relations with other groups, the Citizens League's political philosophy did not go unchallenged. James M. Omura, a Nisei florist and editor of *Current Life* magazine, expressed his opposition to the JACL at the Congressional Tolan Committee Hearings on the Evacuation of the Japanese from the Pacific Coast. He declared that the evacuation of citizens on racial grounds would be not only "an indictment against every racial minority in the United States," but also "a stigma of eternal shame."[42] Omura's opposition continued throughout the internment period. Despite the efforts of Omura and other critics who remained steadfast in demanding their civil rights and who rejected pragmatic or ideological considerations, the vast majority of Japanese Americans went along, however begrudgingly, with the notion of cooperation.

The constructive cooperation of the JACL and what might be termed the "critical cooperation" of the left converged. This was a working consensus influenced by several factors. Besides their youthfulness, the loss of Issei leadership, and political inexperience, the interplay between the economic position of the Nisei and their firm belief in the legitimacy of law and order were the most important. Thus we find that professionals and small businessmen like Kido, Masaoka, and Sakamoto, whose political ideals and beliefs shaped the strategies and recommendations for dealing with Executive Order 9066, played a leading role in the negotiations over evacuation. Remaining obedient to the prevailing order as a way of demonstrating loyalty to the nation seemed to be a logical extension of their economic status and cultural conditioning. This dovetailed consensus helps to explain the absence of widespread protest and the Nisei declaration of loyalty to the nation.

Actual Camp Experience

Loyalty to America as an ideological perspective became even more salient during the actual camp experience. As the War Relocation Authority (WRA) became the "providers" for the Japanese, the Issei lost the economic basis of their leadership and control. Subsequently, Issei authority waned as Nisei assumed the role of leader and decision maker within the family and the community. Once this occurred, the WRA, in conjunction with the JACL, was strategically positioned to promote the ideal of Americanization. This did not mean that Japanese Americans subscribed wholeheartedly to the notion of Americanization. Rather, Japanese Americans found themselves in circumstances where it was difficult to debate such matters as loyalty and Americanism or to grapple with the complexities of ethnicity and culture that had been part of their prewar discourse. A new mindset emerges in camp where ethnicity was submerged as the ideal of Americanization gained ascendancy. This is reflected in four aspects of the camp experience: 1) registration and segregation, 2) resettlement, 3) camp socialization, and 4) the convergence of WRA and JACL politics.

Registration and Segregation

In January 1943, Japanese American internees were compelled to declare their loyalty or disloyalty to the United States through a process initiated by the WRA and the military called registration.[43] The WRA wanted to establish a clearance program that would allow internees to resettle in authorized areas in the interior of the United States. The War Department, meanwhile, had approved the formation of an all-Nisei combat team. The crucial task for both of these agencies was to determine the eligibility of the internees. To expedite the process, the WRA and the War Department jointly conducted a registration program in which all persons 17 years and older were required to complete a questionnaire designed to determine their loyalty. Questions 27 and 28, which caused the greatest consternation, asked: "Are you willing to serve in the armed forces of the United States on combat duty, wherever ordered?" and "Will you swear unqualified allegiance to the United States of America . . . and forswear any form of allegiance or obedience to the Japanese emperor, or any other foreign government, power, or organization?"[44] The ambiguities contained in these two questions and the uncertainty about the consequences of giving affirmative replies created a crisis within each of the 10 internment camps.

Many Issei were troubled by Question 28. They feared that a "yes" answer would make them stateless persons since they were ineligible for American citizenship. Even when the question was reworded to allay their apprehensions, Issei remained frightened and unsure of the proper replies. Other Issei were fearful that answering "yes" to both questions would result in the break-up of their families. They did not want to lose their sons in combat nor to be dispersed once again into what they perceived to be a hostile "outside world."[45] Many Nisei protested answering these questions because their rights as citizens had been violated. Some felt that their rights must be restored before they would respond. In general, Questions 27 and 28 generated resistance to registration, particularly among the Nisei and the Kibei. For example, more than 6,000 Nisei answered "no" to Question 28, while 3,000 either qualified their answers, refused to answer, or refused to register completely.[46] Despite their feelings of loyalty to America, 28 percent of the total male citizen population in all 10 camps who were 17 years or older did not answer "yes-yes" or refused to register.[46] Overall, "approximately 6,700 of the registrants answered 'no' to Question 28; nearly 2,000 qualified their answers in one way or another...."[47]

While it is important to note the protest and resistance to registration as an index of Japanese American resistance to internment in general, it also remains true that the large majority of the Issei and Nisei responded affirmatively to Questions 27 and 28. I say this not to imply that they were docile, compliant, or passive in their acceptance of registration, but rather to affirm Douglas W. Nelson's point that Japanese Americans have been stereotyped "as a people who, either out of patriotism or a peculiar Oriental stoicism, peacefully co-operated in what retrospectively seems a terrible and needless hardship."[48] As Nelson puts it, Japanese Americans were not "moral innocents" who were "culturally predisposed to tolerate unacceptable injustices" and "the conditions of detention."[49] Instead, the negative sanctions placed on resistance to registration and the limiting circumstances of the camps led the majority of the internees to conclude that they had little choice but to state their loyalty.

Despite the expression of personal indignation, suppressed protest, and covert forms of resistance, more overt forms of protest, such as draft resistance and displays of Japanese nationalism, were not alternatives widely practiced within the camps.[50] However, dissidents did gain the tacit support of many internees. In his study of Heart Mountain, Nelson commented on the situation facing the "forces of resistance":

> They existed instead as a kind of underground, meeting in laundry rooms and passing out hand-written or typed petitions and news sheets. Opposition leaders who expressed themselves publicly were harassed and often removed from the center. But despite all this, they continued to thrive and at times seem to have struck a deeper cord of sentiment in a majority of Heart Mountain residents than did the JACL.[51]

Still, the various forms of repression directed at those who challenged or confronted the WRA on such matters as registration created an environment and a political climate that compelled cooperation. A Nisei mechanic from a farming community who was 28 at the time of registration echoed the sentiments of many Nisei:

> There was no use in trying to show our discouraged feelings by answering "no" because that would not have gotten us any place. We wanted to be loyal to this country, but it often looked like the odds were against us and we were distrusted too much. I answered "double yes" myself as I felt that if I didn't I would be shipped out to Japan. I knew that I had nothing to do with the old country and I had no business there. There wasn't anything else for me [to do].[52]

This respondent's remarks suggest the magnitude of the threat of deportation that faced the internees. Deportation was clearly a repressive tactic used by the WRA and the military to coerce internees to obey. The deportation of internees who answered "no-no" to Questions 27 and 28 was the culmination of a series of measures used to punish resistance.

Besides the threat of deportation, the WRA and the War Department used extensive propaganda as one of their subtle coercive techniques to enlist the cooperation of the internees. At Topaz, WRA Director Dillon S. Myer and War Department officials responded quickly to Nisei who protested the discriminatory conditions under which they were asked to volunteer for military duty. Myer and his colleagues announced that the actions of the Nisei would be a "crucial test" of their loyalty and that "mutual confidence and cooperation" were the only means by which their civil rights could be reinstated.[53] At Minidoka, the WRA administration developed a similar line of propaganda. They informed the internees that "the future of the Japanese minority in America" hinged on the success of the volunteer program for military duty. In both cases, the implication was clear: if Japanese Americans did not fully cooperate with registration, their honor, integrity, and loyalty would be discredited.

The threat of indictment under the Espionage Act, or 90 days' imprisonment for violation of WRA regulations, was less subtle. Among those affected by these policies were Kibei dissidents who steadfastly opposed registration. The WRA defined these Kibei as subversive because of their pro-Japan sentiments. Consequently, they were arrested and isolated in detention centers. At Gila River, more than two dozen Issei and Kibei who were suspected of being "subversive" leaders were apprehended. The Issei were placed in the Lordsburg internment camp for enemy aliens, while the Kibei were confined in the WRA Isolation Camp at Moab, Utah.[54] The WRA also exercised more comprehensive forms of repression which affected the entire camp population. One of these was the segregation of the "loyal" from the "disloyal." Internees from each camp found to be "disloyal" were transferred to Tule Lake, the camp designated as the place for the "disloyal" Japanese Americans.[55] "Loyal" Tuleans were parceled out to one of the other nine camps, allowed clearance for permanent leave, or permitted at their own discretion to remain in Tule Lake. According to Dillon Myer, Tule Lake was selected as the major segregation camp for the potentially subversive since it was "a large center . . . and its population included a large number of potential segregants."[56] Forty-two percent of all Tule Lake evacuees 17 years or older had answered "no" to Question 28 or refused to register—the largest proportion of "disloyals" among the 10 internment camps.[57]

The activities of pro-Japan agitators in Tule Lake put them into continual conflict with WRA authorities and created an atmosphere of fear, insecurity, and despair throughout the camp.[58] Continual resistance within the camp was brutally suppressed as protest leaders were imprisoned in "the stockade," a temporary detention area for disrupters that became part of institutional life. For the internees, the stockade symbolized their dissatisfaction over Tule Lake's substandard conditions and their feelings of persecution. Moreover, government interrogation and harassment of protesters over the loyalty issue added to the disruption of day-to-day life. As a result of this untenable situation, many Nisei and Kibei renounced their U.S. citizenship. Dorothy Swaine Thomas and Richard S. Nishimoto summarized this response best when they described the impact of internment on the Nisei protesters:

Their parents had lost their hard-won foothold in the economic structure of America. They, themselves, had been deprived of rights which indoctrination in American schools had led them to believe inviolable. Charged with no offense, but victims of a military misconception, they had suffered confinement behind barbed wire. They had been stigmatized as disloyal on grounds often far removed from any criterion of political allegiance. They had been at the mercy of administrative agencies working at cross-purposes. They had yielded to parental compulsion in order to hold the family intact. They had been intimidated by the ruthless tactics of pressure groups in camp. They had become terrified by reports of the continuing hostility of the American public, and they had finally renounced their irreparably depreciated American citizenship.[59]

After renunciation, Nisei were deported or kept in confinement for the duration of the war. Once the tensions and conflict within Tule Lake had subsided, many renunciants unsuccessfully sought to regain their citizenship.[60] The significance of Tule Lake, however, is found in the discreditation of protest by "criminalization" and deportation. Both stood as reminders to internees of the severe consequences of challenging authority.[61]

The extreme measures taken at Tule Lake to suppress protest were not indicative of the way that protest was treated in the remaining nine camps. Still, the process of registration and separation created a repressive environment in which internees had to pledge their "loyalty" or "disloyalty" under coercion and duress. Although the "loyal" and the "disloyal" each had their reasons for complying with or resisting registration, the prevailing tension did not make their decisions any easier. In many ways, internees were caught in the proverbial double bind, where even declarations of loyalty did not mitigate feelings of frustration, anger, and resentment towards their captors. Ultimately, their choices of "yes" or "no" were nonchoices. A declaration of loyalty to America was oftentimes a calculated strategy to avoid imprisonment or some other form of reprisal. In this way, the WRA in collaboration with the JACL discredited protest and legitimated loyalty.

Even more unfortunate for Japanese Americans, registration and segregation created severe problems that carried over into the postwar period. John Okada's novel, *No-No Boy*, published in 1957, poignantly illustrated the trauma and tragedy of the postwar Nisei experience and the conflicted nature of their consciousness. In the characters of Ichiro and Kenji, Okada depicts the victimization of the Japanese Americans during the war and its aftermath. America had not allowed either man to discover his identity on his own terms. The alternatives of loyalty and resistance (disloyalty) compelled Ichiro and Kenji to make stark choices. As a "no-no" boy, Ichiro could not volunteer to fight for his country and, thus, lost his chance to affirm his American identity. And yet, to declare his loyalty to America would have denied the ethnic experience embodied in his Issei parents who were so much a part of him. Swayed by his mother who clung tenaciously to her Japanese identity, Ichiro became a "disloyal" and served two years in prison. He became confused about his decision and his position in America and longed to trade places with his friend, Kenji, a veteran who had lost a leg in the war. Kenji was the archetypal Nisei who fought in the war to prove his loyalty, even if it meant sacrificing his life. Unlike so many of his peers who served in the armed forces, Kenji sympathized with Ichiro's plight, in part because he understood that Japanese Americans were still "Japs" in the aftermath of the war and that people like Kenji and himself were the same. Through these characters, Okada shows us that both the "loyal" and "disloyal" Nisei were victims who suffered damages and losses. Ichiro sustained a psychological wound marked by the loss of self-respect and dignity, while Kenji sustained a physical wound that eventually took his life.

For Hiroshi Kashiwagi, a "no-no" boy who was in his late teens at the time of registration, community resentment and hostility prevented him from openly discussing his experience. It was only during the changing political climate of the early 1970s that Kashiwagi could finally speak publicly about his reasons for taking a "no-no" stand. Similar stories were recounted by several "no-no" boys at a community forum held in San Francisco in the late 1970s. Like Ichiro, some of these individuals experienced community ostracism and the loss of friends. Their re-entry into and acceptance by the Japanese community was certainly difficult and in some cases impossible. Although these cases did not reflect the experiences of all "no-no" boys, they suggest that the anti-"disloyal" sentiment was pervasive among Japanese Americans and that the notion of loyalty to the nation remained an important part of their political thinking.

Resettlement

If registration and segregation created an environment that compelled loyalty, the selective dispersal of Japanese Americans resumed the Americanization process that the Nisei had begun in their prewar schooling. Assuming that resettlement would improve the moral and overall life situation of Japanese Americans, help reduce the financial burden created by internment, and supplement the wartime demand for labor, the WRA implemented a program that placed internees in areas not designated as strategic military zones.[62] This form of internal migration, which Dorothy Thomas termed the "salvage," occurred between March 1943 and December 1944. Approximately 36,000 evacuees resettled throughout the Midwest and East in areas that were receptive to Japanese Americans. In Chicago, Cleveland, Des Moines, Minneapolis, Milwaukee, and New York, former evacuees were able to resume more or less normal lives. The overwhelming majority who received clearance to resettle were Nisei from nonagricultural, Christian, and college-educated backgrounds. They were the most Americanized of the West Coast Japanese-ancestry population and their social profile sharply contrasted with the "disloyals" who were segregated at Tule Lake, and who were largely Kibei from agricultural, Buddhist, non-college-educated backgrounds.[63] In all, over one-third of the camp population participated in the "salvage." Estimates indicated that many more would have left camp if the WRA had not favored the more Americanized internees.

An integral component of the "salvage" operation was the student relocation program that preceded the resettlement of families and to some degree provided the initial impetus for it. In his study of the college Nisei, Robert W. O'Brien suggested that student relocation, which operated under the auspices of the Student Relocation Council, played a critical role in encouraging Nisei students to leave camp and pursue an education.[64] According to O'Brien, this program was essential in preventing Nisei students from becoming despondent as a result of camp life. He had observed Nisei who had already become apathetic, insecure, and fearful of the hostile reception they might face outside camp. Comprised of educators, religious leaders, and Nisei leaders, the Student Relocation Council found placements for their prospective students in midwestern and eastern colleges so that they could complete their college education and work toward social and economic integration. At the same time, the WRA, liberal supporters and educators, and Nisei leaders themselves expected the Nisei students to be the vanguard in winning public acceptance by educating white Americans about the Japanese American situation.[65]

While the overall resettlement program was designed to benefit the Nisei by structuring their integration into the American mainstream, it also compelled them to accept without question the Americanization process to which they were subjected. This was promoted by placing students in institutions and families in communities where they would be favorably received. Through the assistance of the Student Relocation Council, for example, Monica Sone attended Wendell College, a Presbyterian liberal arts college in southern Indiana. Her college education and her experience living with a white American family helped Sone feel much more integrated into the American way of life. In her book, *Nisei Daughter,* Sone described her experience in the following way:

> In the beginning I worried a great deal about people's reaction to me. Before I left Camp Minidoka, I had been warned over and over again that once I was outside, I must behave as inconspicuously as possible

so as not to offend the sensitive public eye. I made up my mind to make myself scarce and invisible, but I discovered that an Oriental face, being somewhat of a rarity in the Mid-west, made people stop in their tracks, stare, follow and question me.

In spite of the war and the mental tortures we went through, I think the Nisei have attained a clearer understanding of America and its way of life, and we have learned to value her more. Her ideas and ideals of democracy are based essentially on religious principles and her very existence depends on the faith and moral responsibilities of each individual. I used to think of the government as a paternal organization. When it failed me, I felt bitter and sullen. Now I know I'm just as responsible as the men in Washington for its actions. Somehow it all makes me feel much more at home in America.[66]

Her concerns and optimism about America were shared by other Nisei who were part of the resettlement program. Writing from Independence, Missouri, Robert Hosokawa, a former resident of Seattle, reported,

We have settled in a suburban community close to one of the great Midwest cities. We have tried to be honest and diligent. We have tried to carry our loads as Americans, who want foremost to help win the war. We have made friends and have established ourselves fairly well.... There were times when we began to lose faith in ourselves and our ability to take it. Life in the camps was not easy. It was inadequate and morale-killing. But never in those months did we lose faith in America.[67]

Another Nisei stated his perspective about the new opportunities offered by resettlement this way:

The Nisei . . . are ahead of their first generation parents in American ways and thought and speech. And even in wartime America, the Nisei face more favorable public opinion than their parents did three decades ago, as far as the country east of the Sierras is concerned. So long as the Nisei did not attempt to entrench themselves economically in conspicuous fashion, they will avoid the treacherous attacks of jealous reactionary groups. The Nisei thus must forge ahead as individuals rather that as a group so that they will be assimilated into the mainstream of American society—continuing to offer whatever cultural gifts and understanding they can transmit from the Oriental to the Occidental civilization.[68]

In many ways, resettlement enabled the Nisei to win acceptance and to find new places for themselves in the Midwest and the East Coast. Once they overcame their fear and anxiety about adjusting to a new part of the country, Nisei resettlers were able to integrate themselves into white communities, an inconceivable reality on the West Coast in the prewar period. Commenting about this new situation, one Nisei stated, "You begin to forget that you are of Japanese ancestry, or any other ancestry, and remember only that you are an American."[69]

At the same time, these Nisei were compelled to submerge their ethnicity as the ideals of loyalty and the American way of life became more salient in their consciousness. The experience of Chizu Iiyama, a Nisei who was 21 when she left camp to pursue graduate studies, provides an example of what occurred. A college graduate and a staunch supporter of "loyalty," Iiyama easily qualified for student relocation. Just before she and her fellow students left camp, the camp director briefed them about how they were expected to behave. In assessing that experience, Iiyama talked about feelings that she could not articulate then:

> The director told us, "Don't get into groups, don't bring attention to yourselves, don't speak Japanese; on your shoulders rests the success of the relocation movement." We were young kids at the time and his talk had an impact on us because we believed that we might jeopardize the chances of others if we did not do what the director said.
>
> This is how the Nisei were influenced to take the approach of "don't make waves" because it creates problems. This was the kind of brainwashing that the government practiced which made Nisei fearful and very self-conscious about themselves.[70]

With this experience still very clear in her mind, Iiyama reminisced that student relocation had been a heavy burden to bear and that the suppression of the ethnic part of herself and the avoidance of other Japanese was a consequence of the times. She felt that the WRA did not act out of malice, but was concerned about the best interests of the Nisei. Still, Iiyama declared quite candidly, "I bought that stuff about creating problems. I'm not bitter about it. I can understand why it happened. Our concern was to win acceptance." Like many other Nisei whom I interviewed, Iiyama mentioned that she and her peers were ignorant about politics and race relations when they were young. She spoke for many Nisei when she said, "If we knew what we know now, we wouldn't have done the same kind of things."[70]

Internment Socialization

The Americanization process that Nisei resettlers experienced appears to have been part of a similar process that evacuees experienced in the camps. As Alexander Leighton observed about the internees' sentiments in Poston, "they were disillusioned with the Americanism taught in school and felt that democratic principles and the ideals for which the war was being fought had failed to prove a reality."[71] This was certainly true for those who protested against registration. But at the same time, Japanese Americans were confined behind barbed wire and subjected to an Americanization program developed by the WRA and supported by Nisei leaders, particularly those affiliated with the JACL. Whether or not such programs were effective is difficult to determine. There is some evidence to suggest that Americanization assumed greater significance within the confines of the camp, and that opportunities to come to grips with the issue of ethnic identity were severely limited.

In literature produced in the camps, Nisei writers articulated a faith and optimism in American society; they did not raise critical issues about internment. *Trek*, the literary magazine from Topaz (Utah), contained the work of writers like Toshio Mori. Mori's short stories were a celebration of American life, rather than a critique of the society. In one story, "Topaz Station," Mori expressed "hope in the American way of life," and said that Japanese Americans needed to be "better Americans in a greater America." These sentiments were nearly identical to those of Mike Masaoka in his call for constructive cooperation.

Camp newspapers likewise emphasized certain ideals such as loyalty, citizenship, and the American way of life. In the assembly center at Tanforan (San Bruno, California), the *Tanforan Totalizer* apprised internees on their arrival to show their patriotism: "An informant tells us that the first barrack to unfurl an American flag overhead is No. 22. A good example to set, say we, particularly since this is Citizenship week."[72] On Memorial Day, the *Totalizer* emphasized American citizenship.

> Exercise and cherish the rights of American citizenship in every way open to us, keeping in mind that those who would deny them to us are in the minority and speak not for the heart of America. To oppose those elements by our right of franchise, by our access to the forums of public opinion and by the sense of justice in our hearts and minds—this is to be American.[73]

The concerns expressed by the *Totalizer* were reiterated by individuals in other assembly centers. Mary Oyama, a Nisei writer and observer of the assembly center at Santa Anita, articulated her feelings of loyalty through the words of someone she overheard:

> Across the street I could see a door ajar revealing an American flag on the wall, just about the size of my own flag at "Valley Forge." I had

mine sent in by a friend on the "outside" after I had heard a Nisei girl say, "You know, every unit in every barrack should have an American flag in it so that the Nisei and especially the very young children will always know this is America—so they will not forget what their flag looks like. Locked up in here with nothing but Japanese and cut off from American contacts, we might lose something. We mustn't ever forget that we're Americans."[74]

Even after Japanese Americans were moved into internment camps, many camp newspapers continued to affirm themes such as loyalty and Americanism. The *Heart Mountain Sentinel*, under the editorship of Bill Hosokawa, was an example of this practice. In his New Year editorial of 1943, Hosokawa reflected on the hardships of the preceding year. Regarding evacuation, he stated that "we do not revive the issue of evacuation. No American can resist the edicts of military necessity and call himself an American. Military necessity was the official reason for evacuation, and that was our sacrifice and contribution to national unity and safety." The *Sentinel* approached other key issues similarly. When the matter of military service arose, Nisei were encouraged to enlist.[75] On the question of segregating the "disloyals" at Tule Lake, Hosokawa declared: "Loyal residents of Heart Mountain will welcome the WRA's decision to segregate the 'loyal' from the 'disloyal' in the centers as a necessary and overdue measure."[76] To circumvent the myriad problems posed by confinement, Hosokawa advised internees to resume their normal lives by taking part in the WRA's resettlement program.

Besides newspapers, educational programs were also geared to promote Americanization. Americanization classes were offered as part of the Adult Education Program.[77] At Topaz, for example, such classes were designed to inform the internees about American life. Guest speakers were brought in on a regular basis to lecture on American law, American history, American foreign policy, and the American West.[78] English classes were also given and were especially popular among Issei women who wanted to communicate better with their Nisei children. These Americanization classes were similar in scope to those that had been offered at the various assembly centers. For example, at Tanforan, numerous Issei and Kibei studied subjects which included "etiquette, social graces, letter writing, conversation, phonetics, vocabulary building, reading, writing and business English."[79]

Primary and secondary schooling in the camps was patterned after "community oriented" schools and administered by the WRA. The schools provided a "progressive" curriculum, which was developed at Stanford University, to enable students to enhance their traditional learning by drawing from their so-called community life experiences.[80] The curriculum included vocational education and a "core class that combined English and Social

Studies to teach common ideals of democratic citizenship."[81] At Topaz, for example, the high school curriculum consisted of vocational classes such as industrial arts and home economics, as well as the core course and "a limited college preparatory program."[82]

Taught by white and Japanese American teachers, Nisei students were imbued with the principles of the American democratic way of life, even as they were confined in concentration camps. We should consider the message of Project Director L.T. Hoffman to Topaz students, which appeared in the 1945 school yearbook, *Topaz Ramblings:*

> In a new and very real sense you are the leaders of tomorrow, not only for a particular group of people, but for all people who look forward to the future with hope, faith and confidence that the principles of freedom and tolerance will be available to all.

It is ironic that the ideals of freedom and tolerance were emphasized in a situation in which justice and fair play were so clearly absent. While students were conscious of this paradox, there is some evidence that suggests many young Nisei took these teachings to heart. Charles Kikuchi, a reporter on life at Tanforan, made an interesting observation about the behavior of the third graders:

> This morning the third grade held their class in the Buddhist Church up at the end of our barracks. Could hear them singing "God Bless America" at the top of their voices. It was interesting to hear one Issei say something about his little daughter was in there because she was an American while he was a Japanese.[83]

The purpose of education for older students was to promote their integration and their future success. One student commented on the relevance of education to the Nisei in the following way:

> In resisting the many challenges of the war, the most vital and pressing to Topaz residents is the education of the nisei. To continue to educate them for the "American way of life," and at the same time to prepare them to face the future with courage is the vision to which the residents, as a part of the Japanese in America, must adhere. . . .
>
> True, the unnatural and drastically-changed schooling conditions are not conducive to the highest efforts of students here, but the existence and survival of a truly vigorous spirit towards education absorption by the Topaz youth element is wholly desirable.
>
> Training in living with others, full participation in the community life of the school, individual attention to special needs, excellent

preparation for college or a more general education for those not col-
lege-minded ... the Topaz school promises these attainments, if the
student rises to the challenge of relocation, and turns disadvantages
to advantages.[84]

Nisei social life also reflected American patterns. The formation of
organizations for the youth was encouraged—Girl Scouts, Boy Scouts,
YWCA, YMCA.[85] Football, basketball, and baseball—the major American
pastimes—became important activities for young and old alike. As participation increased, teams were formed and leagues were established. Dancing also became an important social activity among the Nisei. In Heart
Mountain, for example, a swing band was formed and it played for dances
in the camp gym.[86] The culture absorbed by the Nisei differed very little
from that of young Americans outside camp. The movies, magazines, and
radio programs were American in focus and contrasted sharply with Issei
culture. While Japanese art forms (e.g., tea ceremony, calligraphy, *kabuki,*
and poetry) and language instruction were offered and generated interest
among the older internees, the younger Nisei who remained in the camps
after resettlement overwhelming favored American culture.[87]

WRA/JACL Politics

Another aspect of internment socialization was the WRA's attempt to
structure camp politics in accordance with American democratic ideals.
Within each camp, the WRA established a formal political structure
designed to promote what they termed "self-government."[88] The Community Council, which was comprised of representatives from each block, was
designated the central self-governing body and formed the basic political
unit within the camp.[89] Even prior to their removal from the assembly
centers to the internment camps, the concept of "self-government" had
been implemented in those areas of confinement. In the case of Tanforan,
for example, political campaigns were patterned after the American electoral process.[90] In anticipation of the first general election, the *Tanforan
Totalizer* stressed the significance of Japanese Americans exercising their
franchise:

> Tanforan's general election this coming week will be a significant
> event from more than one standpoint. It will be, first of all, a concrete
> reaffirmation of the whole principle of democratic franchise. In going
> to the polls here we will be in direct touch with the same tradition
> which has animated the elective processes of American civic life since
> the days of the founding fathers.

But our election will be significant from another and special standpoint. For the issei parent generation it will be their first opportunity to participate on an equal footing with their citizen offspring in a balloting. For them, an initiation; for us, a renewal of a cherished and accustomed American practice.[91]

Although the Issei were allowed to vote, only American citizens who were 25 years or older were eligible for office.[92] Tanforan was divided into five precincts. The top vote-getter in each precinct was elected to the Council.[92] Tanforan also had a Legislative Congress comprised of representatives from each precinct.[93] On the ratio of 200 residents to one Congressman, the number of representatives varied from 6 to 11. Formal rules and regulations were specified to ensure that balloting was properly carried out. Although there was an 80 percent and 69 percent turnout of eligible voters for the Council and Congressional elections, respectively, the *Totalizer* reported that a general apathy pervaded the elections, since there seemed to be a lack of "genuinely-felt interest in the balloting."[94] Given the unjust circumstances surrounding internment, the high turnout of eligible voters is surprising. Perhaps, some internees were simply obeying instructions while others were demonstrating their loyalty and their belief in American democracy.

For many Japanese Americans, the process of "self-government" was the first exposure to electoral politics, but the criterion that only citizens were eligible to hold office restricted the participation of the Issei and relegated them to inferior political status.[95] At Poston, the first Community Council was made up of Nisei who averaged 31 years of age, but who had little or no political experience.[95] This did not make for effective "self-government."

Within the camp structure, the privileged position of the Nisei was strengthened by emphasizing English as the primary means of communication with the WRA. Consequently, the Issei had to rely on the Nisei to interpret their political concerns. Also, the mess hall system of feeding undermined what Daisuke Kitagawa called the "family table," a family institution that reinforced Issei authority over their children.[96] As the WRA became the "providers" for the Nisei, the Issei family head lost an important source of control and respect. And when the Nisei found work within camp or through resettlement, the Issei could no longer exercise at all the authority they had prior to evacuation. Kikuchi noted this problem in the case of his own father:

Mom and Pop went up to interview for the barber shop, but Greene told Pop that he was a little too old. Pop protested that age did not make any difference because he was a "first class" barber. Greene told Mom that she could work if she wanted to on the girls' hair, but she did not want to do it alone. Besides, she felt that she had too much to do at home. We told Pop that he could concentrate on his English lessons now. For the past few days he has not taken out his razors to sharpen them. We bring a few fellows home for haircuts occasionally just to keep him in practice. He took it surprisingly well; perhaps he is not saying what he must really feel. Being cast aside is not easy to take.[97]

In general, the Issei were not accorded proper recognition by the WRA, either because of policy, or, as Leighton pointed out, because of the administration's bias against people "whose language and cultural values they could not understand."[98] The Issei, however, did not remain totally passive. Through demonstrations, strikes, or protests, Issei gained some voice in camp operations and secured access to the political process that had been primarily reserved for the Nisei.[99] Advisory Boards were created, allowing them to advise the Council and the Project Director on community affairs. Within the blocks, Issei secured the position of Block Manager which gave them the authority to monitor the day-to-day activities of the evacuees. However, the inclusion of the Issei in the formal political structure occurred only after the registration and segregation crises had been quelled, and resettlement was well under way. Ironically, their participation seemingly helped to maintain the ensuing equilibrium. Although minor tensions existed between internees and the WRA, and among the internees themselves, camp politics, at this juncture, was relatively calm.

In essence, the internal political process had little significance in terms of shaping camp directives. Although Council Committees played some role in uncovering corruption in the distribution of food and services, and subsequently stimulated the administration to investigate and make improvements, the Council was not taken seriously. Leighton summed up the position of the Community Council nicely when he said, ". . . the Council was suspended between the Administration and the people, both of whom were skeptically waiting to see what it would be capable of doing before giving their support."[100] Self-government within the camp was more of an exercise, somewhat similar to student government, where the ultimate decisions rested with a higher authority.

In contrast to the ineffectual formal structure of "self-government" established by the WRA, informal political interaction between JACL leaders and the WRA was important. The JACL appears to have been influential in suggesting and implementing policies that had long-range impact on Japanese Americans. For example, the JACL recommended that the "loyal" be separated from the pro-Japan factions. Masaoka stated, "We thought if we could get the two groups separated, it would be easier to get the Nisei into the mainstream of American life."[101] The JACL also supported the Americanization concept.[102] Writing to Milton Eisenhower, the first director of the WRA, Masaoka outlined several recommendations which focused on the JACL's concern for integration and assimilation: 1) the WRA should be designed to create better Americans; 2) the WRA should promote as much interaction as possible with whites in order to prevent the formation of "little Tokyos" within the camps; 3) no Japanese language classes should be conducted; 4) self-government should be established to enable the Nisei to learn about democratic procedures, since they were at an impressionable age; and 5) WRA assistance was requested by the JACL in conducting their affairs.[103] These recommendations, in essence, reflected the level to which the idea of Americanization had been elevated during the internment crisis.

How truly influential the JACL was in affecting WRA policy is difficult to determine, though the two were certainly symbiotic. The JACL's recommendations were compatible with WRA policy and stood as an endorsement of WRA actions. In turn, the WRA enhanced the position of the JACL by sanctioning its leadership at a time when it was severely criticized by the internees. The JACL was able to maintain an organizational base in Salt Lake City; it was allowed to publish the *Pacific Citizen*, the Citizens League's ideological organ; it was permitted to discuss with the WRA administrators camp policies that had far reaching significance for Japanese Americans in general.

Although the JACL did not receive widespread support among the internees, its influence was significant. In general, the Nisei were compelled to prove their loyalty through public declarations and behavior. Having had to counter malicious attacks on their loyalty, the Nisei were never in a strategic position to protest their unfair treatment.[104] Thus internment sanctioned the primary dissemination of JACL ideology and discouraged alternative viewpoints. If the manifest function of the WRA's actions was to promote the interests of Japanese Americans by expediting their Americanization, its latent function was to legitimize JACL leadership and to establish conditions that demanded Americanization. While interned, Japanese Americans faced formidable limitations and were prevented from deciding their own course of action. Consequently, it is not surprising that JACL's ideology and leadership style eventually predominated within the Japanese American community.

Subjugation and Leadership Formation

The pattern of racial subjugation and leadership formation which evolved during the internmant phase is similar to the rise of important leadership units within other racial communities. For example, the organizing of the National Association for the Advancement of Colored People (NAACP) was supported financially and influenced initially by white liberals. Although the NAACP secured widespread support from the black middle class, its initial authority had been legitimated by prominent white civil rights activists who played key roles in the organization's development in the early 1900s.[105] A similar situation prevailed among Chicanos in which whites were instrumental in finding Chicano leaders who were "acceptable" to white society, rather than allowing Chicanos to select their own leaders from their community.[106]

In the Japanese American case we find leaders who identified with the lifestyle, culture, and political ideals of America—an orientation shaped primarily by the hegemony of American culture. Their political style became not only a buffer against radical political activism, but a vehicle that promoted a faith in American institutions. Thus cooperation and loyalty to the nation as key responses to internment were not as paradoxical as they may appear to be. The rising significance of Americanization for the Nisei and the submersion of their ethnicity dovetailed directly with the racial context in which they came of age. It is understandable, therefore, that as Japanese Americans resume their lives in the post-World War II period, we witness the rise of a cautious and pragmatic political orientation that reaffirmed Americanization.

Chapter 5

"Making Do"

Reentry to American Life

AFTER WORLD WAR II ENDED, MOST JAPANESE AMERICANS returned to the Pacific Coast and resumed their lives with great uncertainty and concern about their place in the larger society.[1] Adjusting to the myriad changes that had taken place while they were interned was certainly difficult and required considerable courage. As one Nisei put it, "We had to make do with what was available to us."[2] He was referring to their limited economic prospects that were so closely tied to their racially subordinate position. Within a relatively short time, however, Japanese Americans, particularly the Nisei, experienced a significant shift in their economic position. During the 1950s, they slowly left manual labor and petty entrepreneurship and found jobs in clerical and technical fields. By the 1960s, they were entering the professional ranks and finding economic opportunities that had been closed to them before the war. This chapter discusses the reasons for this change and the strategies used to circumvent racial barriers.

Post–World War II Transition

Immediately after the WRA allowed those who were still in the camps to leave, the majority of Japanese Americans returned to the Pacific Coast, to a racial situation that had been shaped by the war. The animosity directed at Japan spilled over to Japanese Americans. Most white Americans failed to distinguish between Japanese Americans and Japanese nationals and thus defined returning Issei, Nisei, and Sansei as Japanese rather than as fellow Americans. Consequently, the returnees were not readily accepted back into their former neighborhoods. The anti-Japanese backlash they encountered between 1945 and 1946 was strong.[3] This was particularly true for Japanese Americans who returned to the Central Val-

113

ley.[4] Outright violence, social ostracism, social harassment, "bureaucratic sabotage," and economic boycotts greeted them.

One of the more noteworthy forms of anti-Japanese activity was the escheat proceedings in California. "Between 1944 and 1948 some eighty escheat cases were filed against Issei by the state of California in which the state took land and money worth about a quarter of a million dollars from a score of Issei-headed families."[5] Also, the limited restitution for wartime losses under the Evacuee Claims Law reflected the national racial climate. Japanese Americans had hoped that the government would compensate them for their wrongful imprisonment.[6] But rather than helping internees recoup their losses, the federal government actually made it virtually impossible for them to reclaim fully their property losses.

After the initial hostility to their return subsided, Japanese Americans still had to contend with differential treatment. Although some Nisei did not encounter prejudice and discrimination, Japanese Americans, as a whole, were not accorded their civil rights. My informants reported that they were treated as second class citizens in the public sphere. When it came to buying homes or renting apartments, their choices were limited.[7] Most white neighborhoods were off limits. Not all public services would assist them, nor could they simply go to any restaurant or hotel and be served.[8]

Moreover, the struggle to reestablish themselves did not simply involve a return to their prewar livelihood. Finding work, seeking new careers, or salvaging the businesses and farms they had not operated for nearly four years posed formidable challenges. These issues were particularly pressing for the older Nisei, those born soon after the turn of the century. Many were married, had families, and assumed the responsibility for taking care of their parents who by this time were ready for retirement. For those returnees who had completed their formal schooling just before evacuation or during the resettlement phase of camp life, there was an urgency to begin new careers and get on with their lives. Those who were younger had to decide whether they would pursue a college education.

In general, Japanese Americans found that their life chances were still as limited as they had been in the prewar period and the future was uncertain. No longer could they rely on a thriving ethnic economy to circumvent the racial boundaries that had prevented them from participating fully in the economic mainstream. Many Issei small farmers and businessmen had lost their property or access to the land they had worked as lease tenants. Many also lost their savings and were unable to start their businesses now that they were older and less resilient. In Los Angeles, for example, Issei were unable to reestablish themselves in agriculture and the production and distribution of fresh produce.[9] They regained only a small proportion of their prewar holdings and only a few managed to reconstitute their wholesale and retail produce businesses.

Significant changes had occurred in those occupational areas that had been mainstays for Japanese Americans in the prewar ethnic economy. Between 1940 and 1950, the number of Japanese American male farmers and farm managers in California decreased slightly from 18.2 percent to 17.1 percent of the gainfully employed, while Japanese American males employed as managers, officials, and proprietors outside of farming dropped from 12.1 percent to 8.6 percent.[10] Correspondingly, the decline in farm laborers who were unpaid family workers, previously an important source of employment for the Nisei, dovetailed with the decline in the Issei economy. Between 1940 and 1950, this source of work dropped from 5.8 percent to 2.5 percent for men and from 21.3 percent to 7.4 percent for women.[10] Although this decrease can be explained partly by the fact that the Nisei were getting older and were seeking outside sources of employment, it also points to the fact that independent businesses were no longer viable sources of employment for younger Nisei as they had been in the prewar period.[11] Moreover, the alternative of taking over family businesses lessened as many Nisei recognized that small businesses, especially merchandising shops, were declining in profitability and, therefore, were unsound ventures. The development of chain stores and the ensuing competition created additional problems for Japanese American businesses.[12]

Since Japanese Americans could not simply pick up where they had left off, they had to rely on alternative sources of livelihood. In part, this quest was aided by a changing labor market. Nisei, in particular, found partial access to new fields of work. In contrast to the prewar period, they now could find jobs in semi-skilled and skilled occupations as the wartime expansion and postwar industrial demand for workers generated new opportunities outside of the ethnic community. In California, for example, the percentage of Japanese American males employed as laborers (outside farming and mining) increased from 11.5 percent to 17.9 percent of the gainfully employed between 1940 and 1950. Despite these changes, many fields of employment were still restricted. Unions, the more lucrative trades, and many professions continued to deny access to Japanese Americans. Japanese American males and females in California experienced about a 2 percent increase in the professional category in the 1940 to 1950 decade.[13]

As a result, Japanese Americans were compelled to "make do." Many had to seek employment that relied on white patronage. For example, domestic work, a specialty for Japanese American women before the war, again became an important occupation.[14] In 1950, 17 percent of working Japanese American women in California were in domestic service, compared to 20 percent in 1940. Japanese Americans also took up flower farming and nurseries once again because of the demand for these specialty skills.[15] Although many returned to produce work, it no longer retained the same significance it had in the prewar period. In Los Angeles, for example, about one third as many were involved in this occupation as compared to the prewar period.[16]

One of the most important specialty occupations for returnees was contract gardening. In Los Angeles, this occupation absorbed many of the displaced agricultural and produce workers.[17] Although it was a form of service work, it was nevertheless an independent enterprise that not only provided an income, but status and dignity as well. Needing neither a high level of capital investment nor hired labor to be profitable, a gardener required only a truck and a few tools to become operational. One simply entered into a business agreement with a client who sought his skill and expertise. Leonard Broom and Ruth Riemer estimated that by 1948, a minimum of 30 percent of the Japanese American male workers in Los Angeles were gardeners.[18]

Several informants indicated that gardening was an important transitional occupation in the San Francisco Bay Area, particularly in suburban areas such as Berkeley, Oakland, San Mateo, and Palo Alto, where there was a heavy demand for yardwork. When Jim Kawamura returned to the Bay Area towards the close of the war, he applied for his old job as a commission merchant at the local produce market. His former white employers turned him down, because they were unsure about hiring Japanese Americans while the war was still in progress. Since the only types of work available then were menial positions such as "taking care of gardens," he started working as a gardener until "things opened up" in the job market. His friends also followed this course and some have continued as gardeners "to this day." For Kawamura, however, gardening was a transitional job that he held until he found an opportunity to do something else.

Economic Incorporation

The racial situation in the postwar decade, however, was not so restrictive that Japanese Americans remained completely isolated from the dramatic transformations occurring in the U.S. political economy, a change affecting the lives of all people on the West Coast. In particular, the prosperity generated by the American involvement in the Korean War had a dramatic impact on Japanese Americans on the Pacific Coast during the 1950s. Nisei college graduates began to establish careers in fields for which they had been trained in the prewar years and during the period of student resettlement. Older Nisei like Jim Kawamura found opportunities to leave their transitional jobs to take up new lines of work that were more satisfying and better paying. The 1950 and 1960 census figures for California illustrate these changes. In 1950, a large proportion of Japanese men were gainfully employed as farmers and farm managers (17.1 percent), while

Japanese women were clustered in the following occupational categories: clerical and sales (25.2 percent), operatives (18.5 percent), private household (17.4 percent), and farm labor (11.0 percent). Japanese Americans had not yet made much headway into the professional and technical fields (4.4 percent for males and 5.3 percent for females) and the crafts (5.2 percent for males and 0.5 percent for females). By 1960, the patterns were noticeably altered. While men actually increased their participation as farmers and farm managers (21.3 percent), they were also located in professional and technical jobs (15 percent), clerical and sales work (12.7 percent), and the crafts (10.4 percent). Fewer were involved in the work force as laborers (5.9 percent) or farm laborers (9.2 percent). Even more women worked in the clerical and sales field (36.8 percent); they had also increased their participation in the professional and technical areas (10.1 percent) as their employment as operatives (16.4 percent), private household workers (11.6 percent), and farm laborers (6.9 percent) decreased. In very broad terms, Japanese Americans were less represented in the manual occupations, and correspondingly more concentrated in nonmanual pursuits, than the general population.[19]

The shift towards "clean work"—professional and technical, and clerical and sales—was especially noticeable in urban areas as Japanese Americans continued their post–World War II move to the cities and suburbs. Between 1950 and 1960, their urban residence nationwide grew from 71 percent to 82 percent compared to an increase from 64 percent to 70 percent in the general population. On the West Coast these residential changes were commensurate with the national pattern: the Japanese American urban population increased from 68 percent to 83 percent.[20] During this period, the 25- to 44-age cohort showed dramatic occupational changes.[21] For example, the growth in the number of urban Japanese American male professionals (from 9.5 percent in 1950 to 28.3 percent in 1960) exceeded the increase for white males (from 14.0 percent to 20.5 percent) in the Los Angeles and San Francisco standard metropolitan statistical areas (SMSA). Urban Japanese American women also showed an increase in professional work (from 8.4 percent in 1950 to 13.5 percent in 1960), but did not surpass white women of the same age, education, and geographical location (from 15.2 percent versus 15.8 percent). Similarly, the percentage of clerical and sales workers among Japanese American women increased dramatically (from 34.2 percent to 46.7 percent), though it, too, did not surpass the percentage of white women in this field (49.2 percent versus 50.8 percent). Furthermore, there was a large reduction in the percentage of Japanese American men employed as laborers (from 23.7 percent to 6.4 percent), although they remained more concentrated in this occupation compared to whites (5.1 percent versus 3.8 percent). Japanese American reliance on proprietorship also decreased compared to whites. In

1950 there were proportionally more Japanese American (15.6 percent) than white proprietors (14.5 percent), while in 1960, there were more white (13.2 percent) than Japanese American proprietors (11.6 percent). This drop was again consistent with the overall shift of this ethnic group towards professional and technical occupations.

The changing economic position of Japanese Americans has led to some interesting discussion and debate about their postwar racial status. Because of the dramatic changes in their socioeconomic position, Japanese Americans have been deemed a "model minority."[22] While their changing economic standing can not be denied, their racial status still remains an issue. Some scholars have shown that Japanese Americans, in particular, and Asian Americans, in general, have remained segmented in the lower tiers of their occupational classifications and, as a result, still face extensive employment discrimination.[23] Also, the persistence of racial violence and the spillover of anti-Japanese attitudes from tense U.S.–Japan trade relations continue to affect Japanese Americans as many Americans still fail to distinguish between Japanese Americans and Japanese nationals. What is missing from this discussion, however, is an assessment of how Japanese Americans themselves have experienced both mobility and differential treatment concurrently. A brief examination of the broader economic and political changes occurring in American society helps us understand how and why Japanese Americans developed new political styles and strategies to advance themselves as individuals and as a group.

Japanese Americans and the Postwar Economic Order

In the immediate post–World War II period, the American economy experienced a period of prolonged prosperity and rapid industrial growth.[24] This meant new jobs, higher income, better services, and increased access to commodities that had been scarce during wartime. New cars, radios, and the like became more commonplace to the average American until the recessions of 1947 and 1948 placed a temporary damper on the postwar economic boom. In 1950 the Korean War brought another substantial boost to the economy, due to the increase in military spending and the emphasis on technology and cybernation in America's new economic order.[25]

After the Korean War, the United States became the world's largest military spender as military outlays accounted for about 10 percent of U.S. national income. This new economic thrust was largely justified in terms of promoting technical progress and containing the perceived threat of Communism.[26] The defense industries boosted technological development. Within the electronics industry, military demand accounted for an estimated 70 percent of the total output of this $14 billion per year industry in the early 1960s.[27] This was a direct reversal of the market situation in 1950: at that time military needs had been only 20 percent, while consumer products accounted for 60 percent. In the 1950s, major electronics firms became increasingly dependent on military contracts. Military diversification became the basis for research and development in the space, chemicals, plastics, glass products, and automotive engineering industries. In essence, military spending became a central component of the postwar economy.

This form of sustained economic growth and expansion stemmed from the coordination and commensurate growth of state and corporate bureaucracies, or what Franz Schurmann has called "the techno-organizational structure."[28] Two major sectors comprised this structure; Shurmann called them "techno-economic and organizational-political." In general, the techno-economic sector grew out of the dynamic intersection of the world market economy, the multinational corporations, and America's modern technology. The smooth operation of the techno-economic structure, however, was dependent on the organizational-political structure, that overarching bureaucratic edifice directing the "American Empire." As a crucial development of the post–World War II economic order, this structure was responsible for the growth in important economic sectors, including defense, communications, welfare, and social services. Its organizational form was the state bureaucracy, which commanded a myriad of subordinate bureaucracies employing over 12 million people in local, state, and federal government.[29] While Schurmann's conception of the intricate system that combines corporate and state sectors of American society may be debated, what is important is that a new "techno-organizational" structure did emerge in the postwar period and that it generated immense prosperity in terms of jobs and wealth. With the emergence of these new administrative and employment structures, technologies, and forms of planned production and distribution, all of which were designed to maximize profits in expanding global markets, small entrepreneurs and independent craftsmen found it increasingly difficult to survive. Instead, a demand arose for nonmanual workers to fill the jobs required for the effective functioning of such public and private bureaucracies, new technologies, consumer services, and the new specialization in the labor market. This development was a significant departure from the 1930s and early 1940s.

These changes were particularly relevant to Japanese Americans who possessed or were acquiring the educational and technical prerequisites for the changing labor market. In light of the shift towards the professions and clerical fields that were central to the emerging political economy between 1950 and 1970, we can easily understand the broad shifts and the changing occupational strategies Japanese Americans have adopted (see Table 2). Until 1950, they were underrepresented in the professional/technical, sales/clerical fields compared to the larger U.S. population. By 1960, however, they had begun to show a slight overrepresentation in these two occupational categories at a time when professional/technical and clerical/sales workers became crucial to the techno-organizational structure of American society. By 1970, Japanese Americans were relying on professional and clerical occupations as economic vehicles to secure social and economic mobility and became proportionally overrepresented in these fields compared to the larger population.

The dramatic economic changes experienced by Japanese Americans resulted, according to ethnicity-based theorists, directly from the compatibility between white middle-class values and traditional Japanese values that have persisted within the Japanese community.[30] Of particular importance was the value placed on education.[31] Because the Issei stressed education, the Nisei studied diligently and used their educational attainments to penetrate the labor market. However, while culture certainly played an important role in the post–World War II mobility of Japanese Americans, it does not explain the absence of Nisei mobility in the pre–World War II period, when they had also attended college and earned degrees in proportionally larger numbers than their white counterparts. Traditional family and community values as reflected in the desire for higher education were actually more salient in the prewar years. Rather than relying on one-

Table 2.   Changing Professional/Technical and Clerical/Sales Employment Patterns for Male and Female Japanese Americans, and Total United States Population Between 1940 and 1970

	1940	1950	1960	1970
Professional/technical				
Japanese American	3.2%	6.7%	13.6%	18.9%
Total U.S.	7.5%	8.6%	11.1%	14.4%
Clerical/sales				
Japanese American	11.0%	15.2%	21.9%	26.7%
Total U.S.	16.3%	19.3%	21.2%	23.6%
Number of males and females in labor force				
Japanese American	54,899	63,600	192,537	265,570
Total U.S.	51,742,000	58,999,000	66,681,000	78,408,000

Sources: U.S. Bureau of the Census, *Sixteenth U.S. Census of Population: 1940, Population,* Characteristics of the Nonwhite Population by Race (Washington, D.C., 1943), Table 8, 47; U.S. Bureau of the Census, *U.S. Census of Population: 1950,* Vol. 4, *Special Reports,* Part 3, Chapter B, Nonwhite Population by Race (Washington, D.C., 1953), Table 11, 37; U.S. Bureau of the Census, *U.S. Census of Population: 1960, Subject Reports,* Nonwhite Population by Race, Final Report PC(2)-1C (Washington, D.C., 1963), Table 34, 108; U.S. Bureau of the Census, *Census of Population: 1970, Subject Reports,* Final Report PC(2)-1G, Japanese, Chinese, and Filipinos in the United States (Washington, D.C., 1973), Table 7, 31; U.S. Census data as reported in Magali Sarfatti Larson, *The Rise of Professionalism* (Berkeley: University of California Press, 1977), Table 5, 250.

dimensional explanations, we must examine how structural changes produced a situation in which Japanese Americans decided to rely more heavily on certain cultural strategies and old world values than on others.[32] Such an analysis would clarify how the interplay between cultural and structural influences resulted in similar, and yet very different, political styles and strategies in the pre– and post–World War II periods.

Education as a Special Line

As mentioned earlier, many immigrants viewed education both as a source of economic survival and a method for overcoming the handicaps posed by racial exclusion in the labor market. This view was predicated on the assumption that such alternatives as farming and small businesses were not the most secure methods of making a living, especially since many Issei small entrepreneurs recognized that their businesses were not in the expanding sector of the economy. Thus they hoped that education would offer an important avenue for upward mobility. By the onset of the Depression, it had also become clear that the ethnic economy was in trouble and that new blood would be needed to revive the failing fortunes of Issei small business.[33] To provide fresh stimuli, new commercial techniques and business practices were required. According to several Nisei informants, older Nisei who were able to inherit family businesses felt they needed to study "commerce" or the "latest" agricultural techniques to improve the productivity of the family business or farm. Nisei who were not going to apply their commercial training to their own family enterprises could use it to find employment with a Japanese corporation either in Japan or the mainland.[34] Thus education was considered an important mechanism either for securing stability or for expanding economic options.

Unlike blacks and Chicanos, Japanese Americans had not been excluded from higher education. Although Nisei faced the problem of segregation in their primary schooling at various times and in various regions, formal institutionalized segregation had not developed except in several small towns in the Sacramento Delta as it had for blacks.[35] This is not to discount the discriminatory problems that Nisei faced in school during their formative years. The second generation did have access, however, to higher education on the Pacific Coast at major schools such as the University of California, University of Washington, and Stanford University. Before them, some Issei had also been able to secure a college education.

By the time most Nisei reached college age, institutional access was not problematical. Japanese Americans were no longer perceived as an economic threat. Exclusion laws had been enacted to prevent the influx of "cheap labor" that had angered organized labor. Also, politicians had little reason to make Japanese Americans a political issue after the 1924 Immigration Act cut their further entry into the United States. More importantly, the Japanese were no longer a central source of labor to the Pacific Coast economy and, therefore, not subject to the kind of regulation and control that had been vital in the domination of black communities in the North and South where blacks remained an important source of labor. Ideologically, the Japanese were not viewed as intellectual incompetents who were incapable of pursuing higher education.[36] Sympathetic professors within the university community encouraged the Nisei to get an education and become "interpreters." But despite their level of educational attainment, the prewar racial order did not allow Nisei access to the larger labor market.

Thus, given the character of the labor market and its technical demands, it made little difference whether the Nisei were educated and qualified or not. There was neither an "affirmative action" policy nor a meritocratic predisposition within the larger society that considered the disparity between educational achievement and occupational position to be a social inequity. Even college administrators who were sympathetic to the Nisei thought that the responsibility for solving the employment problems of the second generation rested with the Nisei themselves, and not on white employers who could exclude the Nisei because it was considered ideologically defensible and legitimate to do so. As a result, there was no need to deny Nisei access to higher education. Status and social mobility had also been important considerations among Nisei in the prewar era. In contrast to the Issei, who pursued economic independence and autonomy as a means of attaining prestige and security, the Nisei generally sought white-collar work.[37] For them, "clean" work was an important source of status and recognition, and they saw a college education as a prerequisite for its attainment. This concern for social mobility came from both the Issei and from American culture, both of which also placed great stock in achieving prominence, success, and social position. Many second-generation ethnic minority youth have been socialized to embrace a desire for social status and mobility through the cultural orientation embodied in the "Protestant ethic."[38]

As a result, many of the older Nisei attended college and achieved a great deal of community acclaim for their scholastic endeavors in the pre–World War II period. They were also cognizant, however, of the need to choose fields of study that had practical applicability: commerce, the physical sciences, agricultural science, and pre-professional training.[39] In the 1930s, few pursued education, teaching, the social sciences, and the humanities, because such pursuits would not have led directly to jobs or careers. Nisei were strongly discouraged from going into fields that placed them in competition with whites.[40]

In contrast, the generation of Japanese Americans who came of age in the postwar period faced a different set of circumstances. The destruction of the Issei economy had virtually ended the option of taking over the "family store." Without farms, businesses, or other sources of capital, Nisei were compelled to find "new solutions."[41] Some of them did turn to independent enterprises. They were primarily the older Nisei who had some business experience or some access to small businesses, and those independent professionals who had established dental, medical, and optometry practices that catered largely to the Japanese community.[42] But for most Nisei of college age, the immediate postwar period was a difficult time. Many were unsure of their future course of action and experienced a period that University of California Professor Paul Takagi, a Nisei college student then, referred to as "drift."[43] Education became both a means to some "vague" end and a means of postponing the hard reality of confronting an uncertain future.

This dilemma was exemplified in the experience of Henry Wakayama.[44] Returning to the Bay Area with his family after camp, Wakayama completed his last year of high school in his former hometown. Despite the lack of "real interests" and concerns about his future, he ended up at the University of California, Berkeley, with many other Nisei like himself. Unlike those Nisei who returned to school to take advantage of their G.I. Bill benefits, or those who had some sense of why they were completing college, Wakayama declared, "I went to college because my parents wanted me to go." He was miserable since he really did not know why he was there. He often asked himself, "What about a job? . . . How you gonna get a job, what are you doing there (at school)? . . . So you went to college for four years and got out. . . . Well, the feeling was the same." Although he almost dropped out, Wakayama "stuck it out" because he did not want to disgrace his family: it would have been too "shameful and embarrassing to the family" if he had dropped out. It was a difficult time not only because he was unsure about his future, but also because the camp experience was still so close: "We were just out of camp and just out of high school, and we still had the camp syndrome." The Nisei were self-conscious and had difficulties associating with "a white man." Although he did not encounter any explicit forms of racism, he still felt uncomfortable on campus and recalled that "the Orientals ate together and stuck to themselves."

After a few years at the University of California, Berkeley, Wakayama developed an interest in bacteriology and studied in the School of Public Health. Bacteriology was a difficult major, so he considered other possibilities. Eventually he chose public health because he thought it was "easier" and would allow him to get out "into the community." Despite the discovery of a suitable way to render service, Wakayama still pondered the question of a job. The Nisei had to consider seriously the possibility of being denied work in a white world. For example, he wondered how white people were going to "accept a Japanese health inspector right after the war." He wondered about the consequences of a Japanese American "telling a white man that their place was dirty and they were going to have to close it up." Fortunately, Wakayama's public health professor was quite supportive of Nisei students and advised him not to worry about whites but to use his judgment and to be fair.

In many respects, Wakayama had been affected by conflicting influences. Parental values that emphasized higher education and his sense of shame and obligation to the family compelled him to finish college, but he felt uncomfortable at the university for "racial" reasons: the camp experience made him exceedingly self-conscious about his "Japaneseness." The two sets of pressures created a great deal of confusion. By searching for alternatives and eventually coming to terms with the college environment, Wakayama managed to stumble across a line of work that was satisfactory and eventually launched him into a meaningful career. After graduation, Wakayama took a job in central California as a health inspector. After completing a year in the field, he returned to the University of California for his Master's degree to specialize further in the areas of public health education and "community involvement."

Henry Wakayama's experience tells us that he was not solely prompted by cultural values. In his case, such values functioned as "negative" incentives to keep him in college. And by taking the time to finish school, he found a field of study that enabled him to develop a meaningful career. His path was not the rational means–ends situation that ethnicity theorists have used to explain the educational "success" of Japanese Americans. His educational career involved a complex process through which he assessed his situation and eventually aligned his interest with a professional field that he felt was "opening up" in the postwar period.

Occupational Specialization

The 1970 census shows that the increase in the median educational level for Japanese Americans parallels their shift towards professional and technical, as well as other nonmanual jobs such as clerical and sales work. It is reasonable to argue that as the labor market changed and access increased for technically trained workers, Japanese Americans and other Asian Americans developed a specialized occupational strategy. If we break down the occupational distribution of the Japanese in the United States into age cohorts, we can see that even among the Nisei there has been a steady increase towards employment in the professions and clerical work. This pattern corresponds to shifts in the larger labor market. Thus, in 1970, the 45–64 age cohort that represents the older Nisei shows only 13.5 percent of the men and 10.4 percent of the women in the professions, compared to 5.0 percent of the men and 1.2 percent of the women working as farmers, an important prewar occupation. The 35–44 age cohort, representing the younger Nisei who attended college during the postwar period and entered the labor market during an expanding phase of the economy, shows a larger percentage in the professions (28.4% men, 13.9% women) and a smaller percentage in farming. In the 25–34 age cohort that entered college during an intense period of technological development, an even larger portion was in the professions for both men (35.4%) and women (29.8%), with a significantly smaller percentage in farming. Of course, the 1970 data show that the entire Japanese American population had substantially increased its proportion of gainfully employed workers in nonmanual occupations since the prewar period. The central point, however, is that the occupational shifts for each of the historical generations within the Japanese community, as well as for units within the Nisei generation, parallel major shifts in the larger economy. Moreover, the median educational level for each cohort correlates with its occupational distribution. Higher education, along with the changing economy and racial climate, all made it possible for Japanese Americans to secure professional and technical employment.[45]

Instead of displaying a wider variety of educational endeavors and career choices, the generation that came of age during the early 1960s tended to be more concentrated in professional and technical fields than the general U.S. population. Two surveys of the majors chosen by Asian American students at U.C. Berkeley affirmed this tendency towards specialization. One study revealed that between 1961 and 1968, 61.2 percent of the Japanese American males chose engineering or the physical sciences.[46] A second study conducted in the early 1970s disclosed a tendency for Chinese and Japanese American males to be overrepresented in engineering and underrepresented in the social sciences.[47] These findings are consistent with the Nisei tendency to eschew the humanities and liberal arts in favor of business administration, optometry, dentistry, and engineering, a pattern that continues to persist.[48] This clustering suggests that Japanese American educational and occupational strategies developed in response to a changing economy when technological and science-oriented fields increased tremendously in importance.

Immediate Postwar Political Style: Mike Masaoka and the JACL

While Japanese Americans were undergoing this gradual process of economic incorporation, the JACL became the major community organization to deal with the racial discrimination and differential treatment they confronted as they busily engaged in the day-to-day demands of postwar life.[49] By this time, Issei organizations such as the Japanese Association of America had been dismantled and were unable to regain their prewar status. As Miyamoto observed in the Seattle Japanese American community, the *kenjinkai* (prefectoral organizations) and other cultural groups such as poetry clubs were reconstituted, but their numbers were reduced and their functions became more limited.[50] The transition from Issei to Nisei leadership was due, in part, to the aging of the Issei and the maturation of the Nisei, but the more important reason was the destruction of the Issei economy and the consequent loss of Issei authority.[51]

In addition, the Nisei political styles and strategies that emerged before World War II no longer seemed to be viable, although many Nisei participated in mainstream politics either through ethnically based political clubs that were affiliated with the Democratic and Republican parties or through individual membership in one of these political groups. In San Francisco, for example, Nisei formed the Nisei Democratic Club to voice their concerns and express their opinions on relevant issues, but for the most part, these clubs had a very local focus.

Within this context, the JACL positioned itself as the main source of leadership and as the key advocate for Japanese American equality. Confronted by the limits posed by postwar race relations, the JACL continued to practice a legal and legislative oriented political style—a carry-over from the JACL's wartime campaign to test the constitutionality of the evacuation and the authority of the WRA.[52] One of JACL's first initiatives was the formation of the Anti-Discrimination Committee (ADC), an entity that became its legal arm, and the establishment of an office for a Washington, D.C. representative, a position assumed by Mike Masaoka.[53] Operating on the assumption that the postwar political climate permitted Japanese Americans to voice their concerns more openly than in the prewar period, the ADC and Masaoka, between 1945 and 1950, played a significant role in securing several legal concessions: 1) the partial awarding of some evacuation claims; 2) the repeal of the California ban against Japanese fishermen; and 3) the overturn of escheat cases based on the California Alien Land Laws, thereby establishing the precedent to rescind the land laws themselves.[54]

In keeping with its legal orientation, the JACL had broadened its platform for action under the assumption that justice through the courts would prevail.[55] Immediate welfare goals such as the return of property held in government custody and status goals such as achieving social equality became central issues.[56] By their 1950 Biennial Convention, JACL leaders had become increasingly convinced that the legal and legislative strategy for the gradual reclamation of their rights was the proper course of action.[57] They also expanded their public relations program to inform the American public about issues facing Japanese Americans.

One of the most important issues taken on by the JACL was the quest for the right of naturalization for the Issei. Although this issue did not become a top priority for the JACL until the late 1940s, community mobilization around the issue had begun a few years earlier.[58] Through the efforts of the ADC, Japanese community support, and the lobbying of Mike Masaoka, the 1952 McCarran-Walter Immigration Act granted Issei the right of naturalization.[59] The attitude of the JACL towards this piece of legislation is revealing because it showed the pragmatic political focus of the Japanese community in the postwar decade. The testimony given by Mike Masaoka at the 1951 Congressional hearings on immigration, naturalization, and nationality laws exemplified the JACL's outlook. A loyal American who volunteered from behind barbed wire to serve in the armed forces as a member of the all-Nisei 442d Regimental Combat team, Masaoka stressed American fair play and equal justice:

> I think that we persons of Japanese ancestry who served in the Army, both in the Pacific and in Europe, did so because we had faith in the long-time and ultimate triumph of fair play and justice in the American way, and so we saw beyond the watchtowers of our own concentration camps and we saw the kind of America that we have got to have, and we saw the kind of world that we have got to have. And so, the sacrifices of the men who died were not in vain, and I think our record is pretty well known. No other unit in American military history, for its size and length of combat, won as many decorations or suffered as many casualties.[60]

His emphasis on the "ultimate triumph of fair play and justice in the American way" was crucial because it established the basic framework for his position on the immigration question, particularly the relationship between Asian immigration and communism. Masaoka argued that it was improper that the Japanese "to whom we look as a bulwark of democracy and freedom" in East Asia and the people of Asia who are fighting communism are denied the right to immigrate to the United States. Masaoka expressed his view in the following way:

> The Korean is ineligible to enter the United States. The Japanese, to whom we look as a bulwark of our democracy and freedom in the coming years, is denied this right. The people of southeast Asia, who today are also battling the Communists on the Asian front, are denied this right. In other words, the last remaining barriers barring certain people of Asia, hit directly at those that we are today seeking as our friends.
>
> It is difficult to convince these people of the sincerity of the American intentions and of the real faith of American democracy, when we say to them that "while we think certain Asiatics are good enough to enter this country, you are not."

This means much, I think, in terms of international relations of our country; and, speaking as an American, and not as a person of Japanese ancestry but as an American, I think as Congressman Judd pointed out, the passage of this kind of legislation at this time would dramatically emphasize our position of friendship and good will to these peoples, and would be worth 50 divisions, I think in his words, in our fight against communism.[61]

Masaoka's rejection of communism and support for making Japan a bastion of democracy in East Asia was, to some extent, a revival of the "interpreter" role:

Throughout the years, and particularly since the end of the war, the Members of Congress have been in the forefront of the American people who wanted to give a measure of justice and fair play to the persons of Japanese ancestry; and I think, as a member of the Japanese race, if you will, knowing how the people of Japanese ancestry feel about America and her democratic ways, as an American realizing how we need the ninety-odd-million Japanese in Japan to serve as our friends and bulwark in the coming trying days, I urge urgently that this joint committee as speedily as possible enact this legislation.[62]

Furthermore, Masaoka's anti-communist stance in foreign affairs paralleled his concern for domestic security and the need to safeguard democracy:

In these days of threats to our way of life, both from within and without, we join with our fellow Americans in our concern for the internal security of our nation. We in the JACL believe that appropriate safeguards are necessary and proper to prevent the entry into the United States of aliens who advocate undemocratic ideologies and to forbid the naturalization of those immigrants whose real allegiance is to a foreign power.

At the same time, we urge that such safeguards be adopted only after careful study and consideration and always in keeping with the concepts of justice and freedom of a living democracy.[63]

It is clear in these passages that internal security and the need to protect the American way of life were consistent with Masaoka's prewar emphasis on loyalty. Just as constructive cooperation helped to demonstrate the loyalty of Japanese Americans in the wartime crisis, an emphasis on anti-communism and the preservation of democracy at home and abroad reflected their allegiance in the postwar period.

Although it is conceivable that Masaoka's testimony was simply a ploy to win the support of the Congressional Committee, his continuing emphasis on the American way indicated a steadfast belief in American institutions. Mas Tamura, a staunch JACL supporter who worked closely with Masaoka, believes that Masaoka's optimism in the American way of life was real and his faith was an inspiration to those who looked to him for leadership.[64] Moreover, Masaoka's position on the 1952 McCarran-Walter Naturalization and Immigration Act underscored his commitment to the ideals outlined in his testimony.

Political liberals within the Japanese community, on the other hand, argued that the 1952 Immigration Act was in fact a compromised piece of legislation that retained the National Origins principle of 1924.[65] This meant that new immigration would be based, not on the 1950 census, but on the 1920 figures. More importantly, the grounds for excluding Asians in 1924 remained intact.[66] Aside from the racist aspects of this bill, some Nisei liberals thought that the JACL did not represent a broad spectrum of the community and, therefore, should not force its view on the whole. Their discontent was compounded by the fact that the JACL was viewed as working with "racists and bigots," such as the American Legion, which had agitated for exclusion in 1924. According to Mich Kunitani, a Nisei civil rights advocate, some Japanese Americans rejected the overly pragmatic approach of the JACL as a violation of liberal political principles.[67]

In defense of the bill, Mike Masaoka indicated that it had been "the best possible vehicle."[68] He argued that the bill's citizenship provision would negate both the exclusion laws and the land laws that had been based on the alien status of the Issei. Furthermore, he claimed that "latent anti-Asianism in Congress and in the country at large" would have defeated a proposal for a larger immigration quota, regardless of the existing statutes. While he recognized the undesirable facets of the bill, he believed that the more immediate concern for Issei naturalization superseded the liberal objections to the Act's conservative character.

Masaoka's willingness to compromise and accept the best possible alternative is reminiscent of the JACL's response to internment. The pragmatic aspects of legislative compromise paralleled the practical thrust of constructive cooperation. While the JACL can be criticized for its acceptance of the McCarran-Walter Act in much the same way that it had been censured for cooperating with internment, it is clear that the prevailing political and economic situation influenced the thinking of Japanese Americans like Masaoka who felt compelled to make concessions in order to bring about any change at all.

Masaoka's testimony reflected the Cold War ideology of the 1950s.[69] His references to the threat of communism in Asia and Europe, the need to cultivate Japan's friendship as an important international ally, and the threat of domestic communist subversion reflected the conservative climate accompanying the rise of the United States to the status of the paramount international leader of the postwar capitalist order.[70] The ideology of communist "containment" was integral, technically and militaristically, to America's postwar economic development and mirrored a political climate in which strict loyalty was demanded. Within these political parameters, the ADC, under the direction of Masaoka, had carved out its strategy for Issei naturalization.

Given the nature of race relations in the postwar decade, Masaoka recognized the importance of working with other groups. At this time, white racial privilege was still an enduring feature of institutional life, and the civil rights movement, which gained momentum after the 1954 Supreme Court desegregation decision, was still in its incipient stages. The possibilities for protest and militant action were thus limited. Through the American Council of Race Relations (ACRR), however, Masaoka had an opportunity to network with other ethnic leaders. A national organization formed in 1944 and based in Chicago, the ACRR promoted "intergroup relations" and the achievement of racial equality for all minorities in America.[71] ACRR's programs designed to secure full human rights for all American citizens included: 1) the formation of a permanent Commission on Civil Rights; 2) federal protection against lynching; 3) better protection of the right to vote; 4) the creation of a Fair Employment Practice Commission; 5) statehood for Hawaii and Alaska; 6) equal opportunity for naturalization for U.S. residents; and 7) the settlement of Japanese American evacuation claims.[72]

Of these concerns, in 1948 only a bill to settle Japanese American evacuation claims was passed. Despite the allowance for partial reparations and the later passage of the 1952 McCarran-Walter Act, the lack of Congressional response to President Truman's civil rights program reflected a rigid racial order. Japanese Americans were still denied full institutional participation, a situation aggravated by lingering anti-Japanese sentiment. Resistance to the formation of a Fair Employment Practice Commission and equal access to educational facilities also underscored the persistence of differential treatment practices and a labor market where racial minorities occupied less desirable jobs than whites.[73]

Within black communities throughout the country, organizations such as the NAACP were likewise playing a leading role in the struggle for racial integration. Although returning black veterans who were enraged by the racial conditions in the United States voiced their dissent, and activists like Paul Robeson agitated for civil rights, black leaders in the late 1940s and the early 1950s used conventional political strategies and tactics that were directed at the inclusion of racial minorities into American institutions.[74]

Similarly, JACL leaders like Masaoka approached civil rights cautiously. Through the ACRR, the JACL interacted with the NAACP, the League for United Latin American Citizens (LULAC), and the American Jewish Congress. In the late 1940s, Masaoka served on ACRR's Board of Directors.[75] In the 1950s, ACRR coordinated "intergroup" action in the areas of fair employment practices, fair housing, equal access to education, and equal participation in the government process.[76] To implement its objectives, ACRR worked with organizations at the local level. On the Pacific Coast, ACRR sponsored the development of the California Federation for Civic Unity, an organization that assisted community-based groups such as JACL.

Within the racial and political context of the post–World War II period, Masaoka and the JACL exercised caution and relied heavily on a legal and legislative strategy in their quest for eqality. The legal and legislative concessions that they won bound them to this style of politics until the 1970s. A remaining issue is the extent to which the JACL mirrored the political views and orientation of the Japanese American community, especially the younger Nisei who were coming of age during this period of political and economic transformation.

More Than "Conservative"

Postwar Political Styles

THE NISEI RESPONSE TO THEIR RACIAL AND ECONOMIC situation in the postwar period was not as uniform as it has been depicted in the literature on Japanese Americans. Most accounts suggest that the political style of the JACL was coterminous with the political style of the Nisei in general.[1] Certainly, the JACL and leaders like Mike Masaoka were the most visible and received the most notice because the Citizens League had emerged from the wartime experience as the major Nisei organization within the Japanese American community. Other groups of Nisei who came of age after the war did develop, however, different political styles as they experienced the economic and racial changes taking place in post–World War II American society. To explore this issue, we will focus on the experiences of two Nisei who came of age during the early 1940s. Because they, like the majority of the Nisei, were in a formative period of their lives during and immediately after the war, their experiences can sensitize us to the ways that Japanese Americans negotiated the social and economic currents of the times, as well as their racially subordinate position. Their situations pose a contrast to the conditions faced by the JACL leaders and the older Nisei who had attained some degree of economic stability before the war and were eager to reestablish themselves. By examining the lives of Marshall Endo and Michi Nakada, we can better understand the complexities of their political thinking and the extent to which their political styles and strategies were shaped by the 1950s. We will also see that their formative years influenced their political positioning and feelings about racial matters in the late 1960s.

More Than a Conservative

Marshall Endo is a resident of a suburb in the San Francisco Bay Area. A 55-year-old small businessman when I interviewed him, Endo considers himself to be very "atypical" of most Nisei. On objective grounds, however, he could be viewed as a "model minority" citizen. He has a family and, with a master's degree, is well educated. A registered Democrat, he has been active in local electoral politics, often crossing party lines to work for Republican candidates. Endo is active with the Chamber of Commerce and encourages other Nisei businessmen to get involved. In addition, he is active in the Japanese community. Working with the youth in his community has been a long-time pursuit and he takes pride in those youth who have made "successes" of themselves. From time to time, he has taken a leadership role in the local JACL, oftentimes adopting a critical posture toward his contemporaries who ignore community involvement. Marshall Endo is outspoken about his beliefs; in this respect, he is "atypical." Although he openly acknowledges the fact that he has become more politically "conservative" in the last 10 years or so, there is more to his political style than that. His approach to race relations is quite complex and is reflective not only of his present social and economic circumstances but of his historical experiences as well. Thus, in spite of his "atypical" traits, Endo's life is suggestive of many others who have had similar experiences and occupy a similar social location.

Marshall Endo grew up in a small farming community in southern California. During those early years he socialized mainly with whites and seldom associated with other Japanese Americans. In high school, he said, "I hung around with *hakujin* or those Japanese who hung with *hakujin*," even though one-third of the students in his school were Japanese Americans.[2] An average student, he was deeply involved in extracurricular activities that included band, varsity tennis, and the school yearbook. He participated in student government and was a class officer. Endo has fond memories of his youth. The way he spoke about his experience gave me the impression that he might have gone to an integrated suburban high school during the 1950s where active Japanese American students were quite popular among white students.

Because he associated mostly with *hakujin*, he was not viewed by other Nisei as being very friendly. He attributed the response of his peers to their petty jealousies, a reaction that he felt was typical within the Japanese community. Social distance from the Japanese community and the Nisei, however, was no loss to Endo. He disliked other Nisei for their intense competitiveness in all phases of life. In his view, competition was acute for grades, in sports, and even over women. Endo's reaction to all of this was "life is too short to deal with that petty bullshit." Because he did not encounter the same intense jealousies, competitiveness, and concerns for status among the white students, he felt more comfortable with them.

It is interesting to hear Endo's early attitudes toward Japanese Americans and whites in light of his family's social position. His father operated two packing sheds and farmed 2,000 acres of leased land. This business provided a lucrative income and enabled the Endos to live comfortably and to send the eldest child to medical school at a prestigious university. His father, John, had also been a "big shot" in the Japanese community. John Endo previously had been active with the Japanese Association in northern California before moving to southern California, where he worked with the Japanese consulate and had been part of the Issei leadership that fought against the exclusion movement. Having received a college education at a midwestern university, John Endo spoke fluent English and, as a result, could work closely with white attorneys who represented the Japanese Association. John Endo's language skills also enabled him to carry on public relations work on behalf of Issei businesses with the white community. In terms of race relations, John Endo believed that the Japanese should become integrated into the white community, so the Endo family lived in the white section of town instead of in the Japanese community. Endo greatly respected his father's ideas and achievements and acknowledged their important influence in his early life.

Shortly after Marshall Endo graduated from high school, the Japanese were evacuated and the Endo family was interned at Poston. He experienced tremendous shock because he was thrown in the midst of so many Japanese. He exclaimed, "It was the first time I'd seen so many Buddha-heads!"[3] He was definitely uneasy about this new racial situation. Endo survived by making friends with other "Nisei who saw things the way I did," those who were assimilationist in their orientation. This idea of being an American and the desire to be eventually absorbed into the mainstream was clearly demonstrated in Endo's stand on the loyalty issue. Although he was not pro-JACL, he felt no qualms about indicating his loyalty to America. As he put it, "Hell, I don't know those people over there, I'm an American." While he understood, in retrospect, that having to answer a loyalty questionnaire in confinement was wrong, he elected not to take issue with it at the time. Endo recalled that he was ready to volunteer for the Army to demonstrate his loyalty until his mother talked him out of it. After clearances were issued for resettlement, the Endo family moved to Salt Lake City, Utah, where Endo's older brother planned to continue medical school. When selective service was reopened to the Nisei, Endo was drafted in 1944 and sent to language school to improve his Japanese and to become an interpreter. He served with the military intelligence branch of the Army and was discharged in 1946.

When he returned to Salt Lake City, he married and considered his career options. Initially, he collected unemployment, then accepted odd jobs in a cannery and a brickyard to support his wife. But Endo viewed these jobs as temporary because he planned to attend college. He considered optometry because he learned that a friend in the San Francisco Bay Area had "a hell of a business going" there. At the same time, he was torn by family pressures. Endo declared, "My brother wanted me to go into medicine; my mother wanted me to be an ambassador; and my father wanted me to go into law. I was one confused kid." Yet, he knew he wanted to make money. Since he heard that dentists were "making it," he considered that field, too.

When Marshall Endo came to the Bay Area, he had some vague ideas about a career. He soon found out, however, that college was difficult. He admitted that he "never acquired good study habits." The fact that he preferred to be a "good time Charley" as he had been in high school did not help his academic performance. After some experimentation with various courses, he tried public health, primarily because he heard that "it was easy." Marshall and a fellow Nisei were "the first Buddhaheads to graduate in sanitary engineering (later referred to as environmental health)." After graduation he passed the civil service examination. Although he did not do well on the written portion, his oral performance was good enough to get him a job in a city nearby. By the early 1950s, Marshall Endo was in an enviable position: he had a good job in a field where few Nisei had the chance to work.

After a few years on the job, his boss encouraged him to return to school for a master's degree. Endo believed that his chances of acceptance into graduate school were good because "his boss had some pull" with a local university and his recommendation would almost guarantee Endo admission. After completing his M.A., Endo found a new job with a health research agency in the East Bay. By 1960, he was earning $1,000 a month.

Although Endo was earning good money at his job, he decided after 13 years to change his line of work. He wanted something more challenging and more satisfying, something that would allow him greater independence. He decided to go into business for himself, despite the fact that such a change meant a severe drop in pay, at least initially. Although it took a few years to get the business started, he is now doing quite well, not only financially but also in terms of his sense of personal achievement. He reasoned that being in business was much like being in social services. Both fields were oriented towards contact with people. He liked interpersonal interaction and the chance to get to know all types of people. His most important reason for changing jobs was the potential to "make it" on his own merit. Being independent and relying on his own abilities have been important goals for Endo; going into business for himself has enabled him to realize them. His present economic circumstances are especially significant because they have affected his political consciousness.

"Take Discrimination with a Grain of Salt"

Marshall Endo acknowledges that racism and discrimination have been a central part of his experience. He recalls that when he arrived in the Bay Area just after the war to attend college, Nisei faced widespread discrimination in all phases of life. Even before this, he had already understood the racist nature of internment and its impact: his father had lost his farm and his business because of it. Before returning to school in California, he was apprehensive about the racial situation on the West Coast. In part, this anticipation had been prompted by various incidents he had experienced while living in Salt Lake City. He recounted one incident in particular that made him wonder whether the racial climate on the West Coast would be safe. While dancing with his wife at a public club, he had been "elbowed in the head" a number of times and heard his tormentor curse at him, "goddamned Japs." Endo thought that if it were this bad in Utah, "what the hell is it going to be like in California?" At the first barber shop he went to when he arrived in California, he said that he got the "no Japs allowed" treatment.

Marshall Endo was angered by these forms of what he called "Jap-crow." But his response was "screw'em." He said that he could not do much under the circumstances and he did not intend to let "racism" defeat him. His approach was to "take discrimination with a grain of salt." Rather than take up the "hue and cry of racism," which he felt that many Nisei did because they faced problems getting jobs, getting into medical school, or finding housing, Endo believed that this type of reaction was merely a "crutch." In his view, it only "exonerated" one's shortcomings. Also, the reason that Japanese Americans were not surmounting the problems of discrimination was that they were not assessing themselves honestly. They were not evaluating their actions in light of their capabilities. If one had personal deficiencies, then it was the responsibility of that person to make self-improvements.

Underlying Marshall Endo's ideological outlook is the assumption that individualism and personal initiative are the keys to getting ahead in this world. For him, racial discrimination is not a structural problem that keeps people disadvantaged or restricted in their life chances; rather, it is simply a matter of attitude. If there is something "negative" about Japanese Americans, then they should do something about it so that they can improve their situation. Thus, in Endo's view, coping with and circumventing racism is an individual matter. This perspective comes through clearly on his opinions regarding issues such as affirmative action. In the case of law school or medical school admissions, Endo is against the use of quotas or preferential treatment for minorities. The real question for Endo is "competence." "When I go to a doctor, I want to feel this guy knows his medicine and that he can give the best treatment possible." He does not want affirmative action programs because he feels that they will allow less competent people to practice medicine. In short, he believes that admissions must be based on standard criteria, "either you have it or don't have it." What is necessary to correct the selections problems raised by the Bakke case, according to Endo, is to have numbers rather than names listed on professional school applications.[4] Then, applications can be judged objectively in the review process. He added, "then there'll be no squawks anywhere."

Despite his anti-affirmative action perspective, Marshall Endo is sympathetic to the notion that some people are historically disadvantaged. He agrees that blacks have been victims of poverty and poor education. He understands that many of them lack the opportunities available to the more privileged classes in our society. Thus, he says, "When you go into their historical background, sure, blacks have had it really tough. I feel that it is *the* situation when it comes to discrimination or whatever it is." Yet, he does not feel that government programs are the remedy for improving their condition. He declares, "I believe a person has to pay something for what he gets. If everything is handed out like (the government) started doing (in the 1960s), there's no appreciation for it; they take it, run, and expect more. Make them pay something for it."

Endo's critical viewpoint of government spending also applies to black politicians. Now that they have been elected to office, he feels that they should bear the responsibility for improving the status of blacks; if the politicians do not, it is their own fault. Thus, he states, "There are more blacks in Congress than Orientals. There are more blacks becoming mayors and whatever. They're getting up there in high echelons of government, and hell, they're not really doing anything. So if blacks are getting into office, they are doing all right; and if they don't do anything for their people, well, that is their problem."

Marshall Endo's perspective on those people who are reaping the benefits of social reform spending is also critical, but tempered by an implicit theory that poverty and deprivation will generate a reaction. He says,

The ones who are screaming the loudest are the ones who don't got nothing and don't give a damn whether they get it or not; they're going to scream. And so, I can't listen to a lot of that, see. Those who make noise make use of the adage, "the squeaking wheel gets the oil"; and the louder the squeak, the more oil. If ten persons get together and yell, it's a louder squeak. And I think this has something to do with mob psychology. Individually they wouldn't do anything on their own. But when the bandwagon gets moving it is difficult to stop.

What Endo hears, as far as demands and rhetoric go, is distasteful to him. But this does not mean that some of the grievances are not legitimate in his view. He does have feelings for those who experience racism. Yet, Endo is torn when it comes to taking action on these problems. If it came to a vote to decide whether to institute reforms or not, Endo would be "undecided." He would rather maintain a "middle" position, because he is sympathetic to the condition of those who suffer from discrimination, but at the same time he is not sympathetic to their style of pressing for their demands.

"You Have to Be Selective"

Marshall Endo is willing, however, to make some concessions on affirmative action hiring in the job market if employers are "selective" in their hiring of racial minorities. He emphasizes *selective* because he feels that many who are brought in do not know how to live with "their success." Once they get a job, according to Endo, they feel that "you owe them that job." Then, he says, "their production starts to sag because they feel that they are entitled to the job without having to put out." For Endo, this creates a major problem in the case of blacks because, "you can't fire them—you could a *hakujin*, you can't a black. . . . Attempt to give these guys parity, they abuse it; you want to get rid of him to bring in another black, but you can't fire that guy." What the issue comes down to, according to Endo, is whether or not a person is capable: "If we don't have the proper screening processes along the way to see if he is of managerial capacity and capability, then forget him. Just because he is black, don't do it. If we lose sight of this, then we come to the point of leaning too far backwards." In essence, hiring "just by virtue of race . . . is reverse racism."

A closer look shows that Marshall Endo's image of blacks is not as simple as it appears. Before the war he had very limited contact with blacks. After the war this changed to some degree. In the late 1940s he patronized black bars without giving it a second thought. He explained that he "wasn't intimidated in those days" by blacks. Today he is intimidated by their physical size, numbers, and "the fear of the unknown." Here, Endo is talking about blacks who live in ghettos and who are supposed to be "bad actors." Yet, his impressions are quite different when he speaks about blacks who are professionals and politicians with whom he has had extensive contact through business and politics. Thus, when he discusses affirmative action for blacks, he is referring to lower-class blacks whom he feels will benefit even when they are not competent. This is what bothers him. If the black underclass were hardworking and competent like his "middleclass" black friends, then affirmative action would be acceptable because "reliable people" would be getting jobs; therefore, production would not decline and quality would be preserved.

Marshall Endo's concerns about affirmative action and lower-class blacks derive from his dissatisfaction with a trend toward "liberalism" which he says was ushered in during the late 1960s. He has been robbed six times and he is definitely outraged. In his eyes, nothing is being done to correct these problems. He asks, "What are the alternatives? In order to shoot a robber he must be on your property." Also, he is angry that rapists are allowed to "get off in two years." "Bull shit," says Endo, "too much liberalization is working against society." He used to be more liberal in his views. However, since he has been in business for himself he says that he has become more of "a law and order conservative." This leads him to remark, "My equations are based on conservatism more than ever before."

"... a Buddhahead Could Have Made It Earlier ..."

On the question of politics, Marshall Endo believes that there is a need for Japanese Americans to become more active in the political arena. He is pleased to see that more Asian Americans have "tossed their hat in the ring." He is also pleased to see that Japanese Americans are being elected to political positions, including a Nisei elected as Mayor of Gardena, and Nisei serving on various city councils. The election of Congressman Norman Mineta from San Jose is a particular source of pride for Endo. But he believes that in a lot of cities on the Pacific Coast, "a Buddhahead could have made it earlier, if they had been articulate and had some interest in politics." Thus Endo sees political access for Japanese Americans as an individual issue rather than a structural one. His emphasis on personal characteristics and qualities is part of the same logic that he uses to criticize affirmative action for underclass blacks. There is a paradox, however, in his thinking about politics. On the one hand, he identifies individual initiative as a key prerequisite for a successful political candidate. On the other hand, he implicitly advocates collective political action. He refers to the political campaign initiated by Japanese Americans to repeal Title II of the Internal Security Act of 1950 as part of a significant trend towards improving the social and economic position of all Japanese Americans. Referring to the campaign's success, he declares, "Things weren't resolving in our favor until we got politically active." Thus Endo is not always consistent in whether individual or collective strategies are more efficacious for social reform. What is consistent, however, is his emphasis on the need for Japanese American institutional participation.

In this respect, Marshall Endo praises young Japanese Americans who became activists in the late 1960s and early 1970s because they began to "recognize the need for politics." But he is skeptical of the kind of community organizing that became the central focus of many of these young activists. Although he believes it is important for them to get involved in the community because of the previous lack of interest in things like service programs for the elderly Issei, Endo thinks that their activism should not stop there. Community involvement, rather, should become the basis for getting "into the majority society." He argues, "If it is not a tool to gain access to the majority" and "remains a source of isolation from the larger society, then it is limiting." Younger people, in his estimation, have to fit themselves into the niches of the larger society. If they are willing to try, they will find that "it is not that mysterious a thing." This applies particularly to politics. Endo's assumption is that Japanese Americans are reluctant to try their hand in the world of electoral politics and that many youth tend to remain within the confines of the Japanese American community because it is a source of security. For Endo, this is regressive because they are not making any impact on the broader population. He would like Japanese American political activism to promote integration and assimilation. For him, assimilation is progressive, and he encourages youth to move in that direction. Thus he sees his own involvement in the Japanese community as an active member of the local JACL as only a stepping stone into the larger community. Community involvement and electoral politics, he feels, should ultimately contribute to the assimilation of Japanese Americans. For Endo, that should be the most important development in race relations.

Significance of Marshall Endo

By the general standards of this society, Marshall Endo may be considered a "success." Those who wish to use the term model minority can point to Endo as a clear example. He is a family man; he is civic minded and involved with the affairs of both the Japanese and the larger community; he is educated. Through his own initiative, he has moved from a good paying position in the field of health services to success as an independent small businessman. He has done all of this after facing discrimination and internment. His attitudes towards overcoming individual weaknesses, building personal strengths, and learning to live in a white society have been important in sustaining himself through hard times. But there is another side to the experience of Endo who has struggled for social mobility in the postwar period like so many other Japanese Americans: his achievements were made possible by the changing political and economic conditions. His social location has influenced his political perspective. Neither reality can be separated from his personal experience.

The significance of the interaction between the larger institutional changes and Marshall Endo's views becomes clearer if we refer back to his college experience. Recall that he had considered a number of career possibilities when he entered college, but chose public health because he thought it was "easy." Whether it was indeed easy in comparison to majors such as engineering, chemistry, or biology is something we cannot determine. From Endo's standpoint, however, he believes he managed to get through because public health was less demanding. Consequently, he became one of the first Japanese Americans to graduate in that field. Despite his failure to score well on the written examination for his first job, his communication skills, an important feature of public service work, enabled him to land the job.

Marshall Endo's access to the professional field of health science was quite propitious in the 1950s. Service professions were an expanding sector of the economy in the postwar period and many Asian Americans who acquired "the values and skills that uniquely suited them for lower-echelon white-collar jobs" capitalized on this type of expansion, just as they did in the areas of technology and the physical sciences.[5] The 1950s marked an important boom era not only for the emergence of a technostructure in the new American postwar political economy, but also for opportunities in the service sector of the economy. Fields such as the health sciences, social welfare, and education in general were supported by the prosperity generated by the Korean War and the economic growth within American society.

Endo's merits certainly cannot be overlooked or underplayed; yet, we cannot ignore the fact that entry-level positions in the professions for people like Endo had been made possible by the larger political and economic developments of the 1950s. If he were to apply his current standards regarding competence and ability to his own performance in the 1950s, when he was a "good time Charley" who had very poor study habits and who was not too sure about a future career, he would be compelled to reject students like himself. This is not meant to denigrate his competence: he became quite competent once he entered college. The point, rather, is that higher education opened new possibilities for Japanese Americans like Endo because they entered new fields that were opening up in a time of economic expansion.[6] Criteria of competence were different then because there was a demand for professionals in all sectors of the economy.

Students like Marshall Endo had opportunities to try various majors and to choose those that seemed to suit their situation precisely because professional fields were more accessible for university graduates then, compared to the highly competitive situation for medical and law school admission that exists now. Nearly 40 years have elapsed since Endo was a student seeking a master's degree, largely at the encouragement of a supervisor who saw Endo's potential and had influence in getting him into graduate school. This was the beginning of a meaningful career that lasted for about 13 years. In today's educational and labor markets, similar opportunities may still exist for struggling minority students, but they are undoubtedly fewer. For young and aspiring social service professionals in

California, the present may be one of the worst times to graduate, given the drastic government cutbacks in social service spending. This is the context in which affirmative action and the ideals of competence and universality in the selection processes of professional schools have become such explosive issues.[7]

Marshall Endo stated that he had once been more liberal—in contrast to his growing conservatism—on race issues. He attributes this to his own economic interests. This is not so unusual for people in petty bourgeois positions, as the study of "middle-class" political perspectives suggests. In many respects, the political views of Marshall Endo parallel the convictions held by Dick Wilson, the subject of a sociological portrait of white racism constructed by David Wellman.[8] Wilson was economically successful and, like Endo, had made it on his own. Dick Wilson experienced poverty as a youth and was highly motivated to make something of himself. Through his own unique abilities in dealing with people, Wilson achieved a successful career in business as an assistant district manager for a large food processing corporation in northern California. He believes that blacks—and by implication other minorities—can also achieve what he has done if they would only develop pride in themselves and have the ambition to get ahead. A staunch critic of the kind of militance and racial politics symbolized by the slogan "Black Power," Dick Wilson is firmly committed to the idea that social change will come through the legal system.

Wellman has illustrated through his portrait of Dick Wilson how middle-class whites have racist beliefs about blacks. Wellman's explanation for this perspective is that white racism is a defense of racial privilege. Regardless of their class position, whites have developed ideological perspectives that justify the advantages they derive from a racially stratified society. But Wellman does not let the matter rest with the notion of white racial privilege. Racial privilege is embedded in the class structure of society. The ideological orientation of men like Dick Wilson "justifies policies and institutional priorities that perpetuate racial inequality" and explains away "the inability of blacks ... to compete with whites on equal terms."[9] This happens because the position of whites in the class and racial structures of this society prevents them from recognizing any other alternatives or ways of seeing what is going on.

Wellman's portrait of Dick Wilson and his discussion of racial privilege and America's class structure is relevant to our discussion of Marshall Endo, because Endo has also constructed a racial ideology that justifies and helps to defend the privileges he has acquired through years of struggle. In his career change from being a health service professional to being a petty entrepreneur, Endo has experienced significant social and economic mobility within a shifting postwar economic and political order. He has worked for and earned what he has achieved. But the opportunities and the conditions enabling him to take advantage of them were, in large measure, structural. Competence, the need for hard work on the part of blacks, and the need for law and order are his solutions to the social problems facing disadvantaged minorities. He does not recognize that racial inequality is connected to the racial order and the system of class hierarchy that serves to perpetuate it. Marshall Endo and Dick Wilson would probably agree that blacks can best get ahead by taking stock of themselves and understanding their abilities and shortcomings.

But in contrast to people like Dick Wilson, Marshall Endo has experienced racism and discrimination. This is what complicates his situation. He is cognizant of the discrimination that Asian Americans have faced and continue to face. But his understanding has been tempered not only by his own experience but by the "successes" of his peers who have benefited from the changing postwar political economy. From where Endo is located in his own private business establishment, there is only "so much he can see," to use Wellman's phrase. From his vantage point, racism is something that is correctable. He faced it but he has been able to make the necessary corrections through his own individual efforts. Thus, seeing blacks entering political office leads him to believe that racism is not structural. Rather, he thinks it has to do with the inability of individual blacks to advance or with those politicians who are not doing anything to help their constituencies. Endo adheres to what Stokely Carmichael and Charles V. Hamilton refer to as equating "visibility for equality."[10]

Ironically, Marshall Endo's conception of racism and discrimination derives from his own experience with racism and discrimination and the way he has handled it. While he is sympathetic to the reality that blacks are oppressed and have suffered their share of problems historically, Endo also accepts the prevailing racial ideology that justifies the institutional practices that perpetuate racial inequality. For example, he emphasizes individual merit and competence—laissez-faire Republican virtues that were also integral to the thought of the JACL leadership. From this perspective, people must take charge of their own lives, because it is only through individual initiative that they can benefit themselves. Consequently, according to his line of thinking, racial advancement is inhibited not by institutional limits, but by individual and character deficiencies.

By taking this stance towards race, Endo is backed into a position that cannot address adequately the subtle persistence of racism faced by Japanese Americans in contemporary American life. Whether racism manifests itself as a lack of advanced mobility among college-educated youth who cannot find work in fields for which they had been trained, or the institutionalized tracking of Japanese American women into clerical positions, Endo can only address these issues as he does for blacks: in terms of individual capabilities. In the case of Japanese Americans today, however, the question is not access to professional schools. Rather, it is the lack of job openings in certain fields—particularly the social sciences and humanities. At one time, Endo may have attributed this lack of access to their lack of "acculturation" or communication skills. Today, Japanese Americans have the social skills and are much better positioned to "integrate" into the economic mainstream. Yet, there remain barriers to advancement for them.

As a result, Marshall Endo finds himself straddling the fence on most issues. He is sympathetic to efforts to eradicate racial inequality and to the collective efforts of Japanese American youth to become involved in activities within their own communities. But his perspective seals him off from progressive approaches to social change within his own community. Community activism, for Endo, must lead to integration in the larger society or else it is merely the parochial politics that he considers as an undesirable feature of his own generation's political style. Consequently, he is locked into a "middle of the roadism" that compels "buying into the larger society on its own terms." One may desire a pluralist alternative that allows greater ethnic identity and cultural diversity. From Endo's position, however, this is not a possibility. In order to resolve the tension between his own experience with racism and his social and economic mobility, he chooses to embrace a more conservative ideological orientation and uses it as a yardstick for evaluating other racial groups.

A Different Point of View

Not all Japanese Americans became part of the occupational drift towards professional and technical fields. A good number remained in the occupations they took up in the immediate postinternment period. Many made modest gains within clerical, sales, semi-skilled, and social service occupations. My discussions with those Japanese Americans who were skilled workers, paraprofessionals (teachers' aides, legal aides, and community-service educational specialists), social workers, and teachers indicated that they had some very different ideas about racial issues compared to people like Marshall Endo. A good example of someone who reflects these differences is Michi Nakada.

A second-generation Japanese American, Michi Nakada was 57 years old when I interviewed her. She is married and has two children. Her husband, formerly a contract gardener, worked on the maintenance crew at the local city park. Although she has held various jobs, Nakada devotes most of her time to working with preschool children. She is not professionally trained to teach, but her 10 years of experience with pre- and elementary schooling are sound credentials. Preschool education is very satisfying for Nakada, not only because of her interest in children, but also because her work puts her in touch with people. Through her work, she has become involved in many political issues that include busing, multicultural education, and school board elections. When it comes to the question of equal access to quality education, Nakada is outspoken and tough-minded because she is committed to making it a reality for all minority children. Thus, when she speaks about her community work, one can sense her vigor and energy as well as her sincerity. In summing up her community involvement, she says,

> I find that I am very satisfied with myself and with the things I get involved with. Some may work out and some may not work out, but as long as I go ahead and speak out for certain issues that I believe should be corrected, then I will. And I don't ordinarily get bothered by the reaction of some people [in the community].

Being outspoken and willing to raise issues publicly, Nakada has been criticized by certain members of the community for "rocking the boat." Despite the negative reactions to her style, she is comfortable with the fact that people in her community consider her to be "an activist." She has participated in community affairs and local politics since she returned to the Bay Area after the war. Her dedication to the achievement of equal education and civil rights may be understood both in terms of Nakada's past experience and her social circumstances.

". . . Being Poor Was Nothing to Be Ashamed of . . ."

Michi Nakada grew up before the war in what was formerly a farming community in the East Bay. The Depression was a difficult period for her entire family. Her parents were sharecroppers who farmed about five to seven acres, or what was called "a half-share." They specialized in strawberries and vegetables. The entire family picked berries. The kids went door to door to sell them because they could not afford the cost of shipping them to market. Nakada recalled, "We had a terrible time. From the time of the third grade, I was delegated the job of writing to the commission merchants to get loans." Apparently she was effective, because her family did get the money. Because they were continually "at the mercy of the commission merchants," her parents shifted to lease tenancy. Unfortunately for the Nakadas, farming did not improve their finances until just before the war, when all five children in the family became old enough to work. Everyday the children would work before and after school. Aside from family picnics, there was not much recreation. This "constant thing of working" sticks in her mind to this day.

Being the oldest, Michi Nakada learned very early about her family's economic status. She remembers her mother telling her that "being poor was nothing to be ashamed of." What was important to the Nakada family was education. Nakada vividly recalls her mother saying that "education is something that stays with you." So education was a "very high priority." Her parents insisted, as poor as they were, on paying the tuition for Japanese-language school so that she could become bilingual and bicultural. Because of this training, she learned such traditional Japanese values as obedience and respect for her parents. As a result, Nakada feels that *shushin* (morals training) is still an important part of her thinking. Rather than rejecting this type of schooling, she sees it as an important "value reference." Nakada concludes that her experience with poverty and her education provided a rich foundation that made her a "stronger person."

Besides her early schooling, the evacuation experience had a definite impact on her life. For nearly two years, she worked in Topaz as a grade-school teacher. Because of the teacher shortage, she took over a second-grade class without formal training after observing for a short time how a first-grade class operated. An opportunity to pursue her interest in Buddhist studies, however, enabled her to resettle in New York in July 1944, where she went to work for a Buddhist church. She also took on additional jobs as a lapidary assistant and lingerie factory worker to supplement her income. But it was her experience working in a child care center that introduced her to the line of work that she has pursued ever since.

"My Thinking Was Way Ahead of Time . . ."

After the war, she returned to the Pacific Coast to rejoin her family. They resettled on the San Francisco peninsula because her family was not allowed to sharecrop on their old farm. After two more trips to New York to pursue a program in Buddhist studies, Nakada discontinued her educational plans when she became engaged in 1948. After marriage, she worked between 1950 and 1961 at a cooperative nursery school. Through contacts with co-workers who were married to activists in the local Democratic Party, Nakada began her political involvement. She worked to get endorsements for Democratic Party candidates in the Japanese American community by holding coffee hours in her home. At the same time, she and her husband became active in the Council for Civil Unity, a national civil rights group that worked quite closely with the local JACL immediately after the war.

Since the 1950s, Michi Nakada has maintained her community involvement. One of her major concerns is racial inequality in the local school system. She believes that the role of education is to promote racial equality for all racial groups by giving them the knowledge and the skills they need to achieve social and economic well-being. Moreover, Nakada likes to act on her beliefs. She recalls that even before the "Third World" student strikes took place at San Francisco State and U.C. Berkeley, she had already worked with the Asian and black parents in her community to secure better educational opportunities for their children. These parents saw that white children from the more exclusive sections of the city were given the option of attending the schools of their choice, while their own children were restricted to *de facto* segregated schools. As taxpayers, they believed that minority families should not have to bear the cost of the privileges extended to white children. Through the local Human Relations Commission, Nakada helped to organize a coalition of minority parents who objected to this form of differential treatment. As a spokesperson for this group, Nakada urged the school board trustees to implement a busing program to achieve integrated schooling. Commenting on the role that certain Asian parents played in applying pressure on the school board, she said, "That was the first time the Board realized that the Orientals can be strong." Through the work of the coalition, busing was instituted in 1965. Nakada takes pride in that accomplishment because her city "was recorded as one of the most peacefully integrated busing programs."

In addition to her concern for inequality in the schools, Michi Nakada would like the Japanese community to take action to improve their neighborhoods. In the late 1950s, Nakada was a board member of the local JACL. One of her co-board members, a small businessman, advocated the idea of having the city, with the assistance of a local bank, adopt a sister city in Japan. Criticizing the proposal, she offered an alternative plan: "The JACL should go on record as recommending that the city adopt the 'East Side' as a sister city." The East Side was comprised of blacks, Asians, and working-class whites, and was viewed by middle-class whites as a ghetto. Nakada argued that before the city considered adopting cities from another country, it should acquaint itself with the citizens of their own city who had been long ignored. The JACL Board rejected her proposal and supported the sister city plan. She thinks the social concerns she raised were ignored because many of the board members had business and public relations interests in a sister city program. Shortly thereafter, she discontinued her participation as a board member because she disagreed with those whom she felt were using the organization to promote their own interests in the name of improving race relations. Her sole concern was the development of programs to assist the "disadvantaged" in her community. For this reason, she commented, "My thinking was way ahead of time in those days, especially coming from a female; that made it even worse."

Interracial Relations

Having lived and worked in a multiracial environment, Michi Nakada does not have the fears about blacks that Marshall Endo has. Through her work in the city schools, she has had contact with black people since the time she and other activists worked to get a busing program started. Her participation in human relations programs has kept her in constant interaction with black as well as white school teachers and administrators. Her family lives in a racially mixed neighborhood that is predominantly black. Several years ago, the Japanese American community was faced with the grave problem of having the elderly Issei attacked and robbed by black youths. This created a negative reaction against blacks within the community and a concern over the violence inflicted by blacks on Japanese Americans. Many Japanese American families contemplated moving out of the neighborhood because they felt that these incidents marked the deterioration of their community. In response, community leaders like Nakada worked with black leaders to alleviate the fears felt by Japanese Americans for their safety. These leaders pointed out that robberies were not strictly a "black problem," but rather a problem of youths stealing to buy drugs. They tried to make clear that these incidents were also of grave concern to black families who likewise feared for their own safety. Nakada felt the need for more effective police protection for the entire neighborhood. As far as she was concerned, violence and crime were not endemic to the black community; social differences existed within the black community just as they did within the Japanese American community.

Activism Versus Militance and Protest

As a person who is involved with political and civic affairs, Michi Nakada respects the institutional process. She favors going through the proper channels in order to express one's interests or grievances. During the late 1960s, one of Nakada's daughters attended the local community college and was involved with a Third World student group. Much racial unrest prevailed on campus and these students were planning to demonstrate to protest the lack of relevant minority programs and faculty of color who were sensitive to the needs of students of color. Through her daughter, Nakada met one of the key leaders of the Asian American students' group and talked to him at length about his ideas. Just prior to the demonstration, she voiced her disagreement with his approach to the problem. She said that she could understand "how blacks are doing things," but she believed that Japanese Americans had "a little different background" and that they could "rise above" the need for demonstration and protest. She told him, "You need to approach it from communication, the dialogue point of view; if that doesn't succeed then go to the demonstration." Nakada offered to arrange a meeting with those college board members whom she knew so that he could express the concerns of Asian American students. She emphasized that he should do this "first." Although the young activist agreed with Nakada, he participated in the demonstration the next day. Later, Nakada talked with him again and asked why he did not let her arrange a meeting. Responding to his claim that "he had to stand up for his black brothers," she contended that he did not have "to do what they're doing." She scolded: "You completely bypassed the route you should take to cover all the processes you should go through before you make your final protest." This was part of her style of "following the channels" and "covering your steps."

Unlike Marshall Endo, however, Michi Nakada is not against demonstrations and protest. Rather, she is against sidestepping procedures. She subscribes to the idea that one must exhaust all available channels of communication before taking up alternative courses of action. She places value on following procedures or the formal institutional guidelines for political exchange between groups. Her adherence to these guidelines suggests a belief in the process of negotiation. She thinks she has good reason to do so, because these techniques have worked successfully in the past on crucial issues such as busing.

Nakada can understand why blacks would resort to demonstrations and protest in the 1960s because their experiences and traditions in dealing with discrimination have been different from those of Japanese Americans. In her view, just because negotiations may not have worked for blacks, it does not mean that it cannot work for Japanese Americans. Thus, she criticized the young activist who supported his black brothers on the grounds that the education system was institutionally racist and could not be dealt with through negotiation. What appears to have been at issue is an ideological difference over the way institutions operate. Nakada believed that the issue could be resolved by negotiation, while the student activist did not. Nakada had developed a working relationship with people in the educational system, whereas the student had not. Nakada was relying on her past experience and her working style within institutions; the student was taking a Third World perspective and looking at the college as part of a racist system. Although Nakada may accept to some degree the notion of institutional racism, she does not think that the elimination of racism in the school system requires structural transformation. For Nakada, communication and the exchange of ideas can lead to social change. She stated, "If we had evacuation again, there's a good possibility that 90 percent of the people would be willing to accept what happens to them. . . ."

Compared to other members of her community, Michi Nakada is not typical. She has developed a political consciousness and is aware that her views separate her from her contemporaries. This appears to have been the case since the postinternment period. Comparing herself to other Japanese Americans, she recalls, "In those days the political awareness was very low and it is still very low." When I ask her why these differences in consciousness that entail a willingness to get involved in community affairs and civil rights activities exist, she could only conjecture:

Maybe it's the kind of work they're doing, they're not as exposed to people; for example, if you're working in an office, depending on the kind of office, your exposure is very narrow—the kind of people you work with, they themselves might not be very politically aware; so you don't get the stimulation and interest. But if you're working in a school district, there is a certain amount of political movement within the school district; you're aware of the CTA [California Teachers Association] and that kind of thing, which would help you become a little more aware . . . you would want to find out a little bit more.

At first glance, Nakada's explanation for the development of political awareness appears to be connected to one's occupation: those who are involved in fields that offer exposure to political issues are more likely to develop their awareness. At one point she stated, "There are a lot of Nisei who are doing domestic work and gardening and so their exposure is different. Everyday they go out and do their thing; but they don't have a chance to associate with people who would like to stop and talk about political issues; and their relationship with their employers is that of an employee; it's not on a peer level." She presumes that Japanese Americans, when cut off from the mainstream and denied contact with a wide range of people, develop narrow thinking and a lack of interest in "what is going on." Thus Nakada seems to be suggesting that the work situation influences one's social relations which, in turn, affect one's potential to develop political awareness.

At the same time, Michi Nakada has a cultural explanation for political consciousness. Her belief that 90 percent of the people would go along with evacuation if it happened again is based on the traditional Japanese *"shikataganai* [it cannot be helped] feeling."[11] "They're not willing to stand up and fight, even if it involves their own children." According to Nakada, this attitude affects their view of racial issues. They tend not to think about racism. They accept the present racial situation and ignore such problems as job discrimination and the need for affirmative action.

Another facet of her cultural explanation is her emphasis on "ideas." When differences arise over community programs and strategies of implementation, Nakada attributes them to conflicting ways of thinking. For example, when the local JACL Board was dominated by small businessmen, their ideas were at odds with hers, as in the sister city incident. As a result, she withdrew from the organization. Now that a new and younger leadership has shown more concern over issues such as affirmative action, the development of a community service center, and programs for the elderly, she has again taken an active role in the local JACL.

Of the explanations she has given for differences in political awareness, the cultural and ideological seem to be the most important in her thinking. Although she alludes to variables such as occupation and opportunities for exposure to political issues, Nakada stresses the importance of hearing new ideas. In her view, so long as a gardener can be exposed to new issues or ways of thinking about his life, he, too, can develop political awareness.

Significance of Michi Nakada

Michi Nakada does not exhibit the political characteristics sociologists generally assign to Japanese Americans. While she accepts many traditional Japanese values, she has not been restrained by them. She is vocal, politically involved, and a community leader. Nakada possesses a multiracial consciousness. A mother and a working person, she has been and continues to participate in the struggle for civil rights because racial inequality exists in her life. Although she and her husband have been able to achieve a modest level of economic stability and security, they do not fit the "success" story image to the degree that Marshall Endo does. For Nakada, success would not necessarily be measured by material achievements, but rather by such accomplishments as the busing program.

Due to differences in their economic position, Michi Nakada and Marshall Endo would not agree on many issues nor would their perspectives coincide. Affirmative action would be an important civil rights victory for Nakada, but not for Endo. He stresses individualism and personal achievement as a source of social mobility, whereas Nakada emphasizes collective approaches such as community organizing and multiracial unity to attain equality. Thus Nakada works with blacks in her community whom Endo may consider to be members of the underclass or incompetent. While she encourages youths to become involved in order to enhance their community's well being and to become active members, he prompts them to assimilate.

Both of them would agree, however, that it is important to adhere to the laws and the rules of the prevailing social order. They would concur that racial equality can be attained within the existing institutional structures. Though they are not always active in the local JACL, they do participate occasionally on the assumption that this organization has the potential to accomplish objectives that they deem important. In this respect, the legitimacy of the American political process is a salient part of their thinking. This is what separates Nakada from the radicals.

Since the late 1960s, however, Michi Nakada has been able to articulate her concerns and find supporters for her ideas because the civil rights movement has given legitimacy to the concepts of community and Third World unity. Also, the women's movement has established a basis for women to assume leadership roles. Before the 1960s, political conditions were quite different. In contrast to the bulk of Japanese Americans who chose not to "rock the boat," people like Michi Nakada were ahead of their time. She has been committed to the attainment of racial equality and is representative of those who have been politically active since the internment. Unlike a majority of the Japanese Americans who stressed the need to maintain a low political profile, Nakada and others like her have been activists. She, therefore, has been rather unique among members of her generation in the Japanese American community.

Concluding Remarks

In the post–World War II period, the professionalization of Japanese Americans took place within the context of the technical and organizational transformation in American society. The rise of cybernation, defense, and welfare spending generated a demand for technically skilled and professionally trained workers. These developments were particularly important in establishing the social and economic parameters within which Japanese Americans struggled to find jobs and establish careers. In this emerging context, Japanese Americans have relied heavily on education as a strategic adaptation to American racial and economic patterns since the early 1900s.

The impact of these processes and patterns at work in American society were illustrated in the life experiences of Marshall Endo and Michi Nakada. The interaction between their changing socioeconomic positions and the institutional dynamics of American society provided the context in which they developed their political consciousness and styles of dealing with racial issues. As a professional who became a small businessman, Marshall Endo represents a political style that might be regarded as "conservative." He supports law and order, rejects affirmative action, and advocates individual advancement. In Marshall Endo, we find a consciousness and perspective on race issues that is shared by a majority of the professionals and small businessmen to whom I have talked. Whether or not they are representative of all professionals and petty entrepreneurs is difficult to say. Individuals like Endo do not fit the popular conception of Japanese Americans as nonpolitical or apolitical. Their perspective, which emphasizes competence and hard work, reflects their changing economic position and values. This orientation, according to interviewees, is quite typical among so-called "middle-class" Japanese Americans.

In contrast, Michi Nakada represents a political style that might be called "progressive." She supports community organizing to achieve racial equality in the schools, she favors multiracial unity, and she opposes community leaders who develop programs that primarily enhance their business interests. Although there are many individuals like Nakada who share her social and economic circumstances, it is difficult to determine whether they would be as vocal or as committed to social reform as she has been. Her own observations and experiences indicate that most Japanese Americans have lacked political awareness and thus avoided political involvement. Other informants and my own experience and observations also indicate that the progressive style exemplified by Nakada was not typical of the Nisei generation. The conservative style seems far more dominant. Still, Michi Nakada's case is striking because she does stand for those Nisei who have struggled for racial equality.

Although there are Nisei who have maintained their prewar radicalism, various informants indicate that they are few in number. If individuals like Nakada had problems securing a forum for their ideas, we can surmise that Nisei radicals, within the context of the Cold War and the anti-Communist campaign of the 1950s, would have had even greater difficulty advancing their ideology and strategies for social change. According to one Nisei informant, several prewar radicals have tempered their views and modified their political behavior as their social and economic circumstances improved. As they began families and careers, political activism became a lesser priority, although they have tried to integrate their ideals into their personal lives. A number of younger Nisei did develop a radical perspective within the political context of the Civil Rights Movement. Coming mainly from academic and social service occupational backgrounds, many of these radicals participated in the development of the Asian American movement as leaders, ideologues, or supporters. Relative to progressives like Michi Nakada, Nisei radicals have been fewer in number and have played only a minor role in Japanese American community affairs. They have been able, however, to align themselves with various Asian American service organizations and academic programs with a progressive ideological focus.

Despite the presence of Nisei radicals and progressives like Michi Nakada, the predominant Nisei political style tends to be some variation of that exemplified by Marshall Endo and the pragmatic and legalistic orientation of the JACL. Many Nisei who were nonaligned joined the JACL by default since it was "the only game in town." This did not mean, however, that they always agreed with the political style of the JACL or its views. At times, the leaders and members of a local JACL chapter had separate agendas and strategies for advancing their respective interests that differed from those of the national headquarters. As we saw in the case of Michi Nakada, some Nisei were quite independent and pursued different paths. In this respect, the Nisei were not at all homogeneous in their political thinking or in their approaches to racial matters during this period of major social and economic transition. The political style demonstrated by Michi Nakada took a "back seat" to the political styles of people like Marshall Endo and members of the JACL until the late 1960s, when large numbers of Japanese American youth began coming of age, many of whom yearned to explore new possibilities for racial change.

Chapter 7

"Divided by Color"

Changing Racial Context

SANSEI, THIRD-GENERATION JAPANESE AMERICANS, COM-
ing of age during the 1960s, a decade of cultural and political turbulence,
sought professional/technical careers and middle-class futures.[1] Their
choice of conventional career paths tended to conform closely to the ones
chosen by the second generation, despite the criticism of the materialism of
American society which was prevalent among the general youth population at that time. They adopted a moderate view or a "low political profile"
on the question of race relations and did not choose political action as a
means of confronting discrimination and institutional racism. Those who
were politically minded and had developed social concerns generally
adopted a political style of reform and gradualism, much like the strategy
practiced by JACL leaders. The rest followed a path of educational achievement and conventional work roles.

At the same time, however, a significant number of Japanese Americans did not follow the path pursued by most of their contemporaries.
These individuals forged a new political orientation during this time of cultural transformation and racial unrest. Besides dealing with the issues of
racial identity and the social and economic welfare of their communities,
Japanese American youth questioned and challenged the legitimacy of
their community's leaders and the authority of American social institutions
as well. Unlike the Nisei who submerged their ethnic and racial identity,
the Sansei's consciousness took on a definite racial tone as they defined
themselves as a racially oppressed group and linked themselves to broader
movements for racial change. The involvement of Japanese American students in Third World strikes on San Francisco Bay Area college campuses is
one illustration of this political change.[2] As part of their overall political
practice, they also engaged in building alternative community institutions.

At first glance, Sansei political activism might appear to be rather paradoxical because the Nisei generation had just begun to carve out a place in American society by the 1960s. But many Sansei rejected the political style that their parents' generation had used to secure the advances that the latter had made. Somehow, a reliance on hard work, the legal system, and incremental change did not resonate with the sensibilities of Sansei activists.

Efforts to explain the changes in political orientation and ethnic consciousness have largely focused on identity and culture.[3] Some have attributed the rise of "yellow militancy" to the efforts of Sansei activists to resolve an identity crisis.[4] A second explanation, based upon Hansen's generational hypothesis, suggests that militant Sansei, like other third generational groups, sought to recover the ethnic heritage that the second generation tried to discard.[5] Some empirical evidence and theoretical considerations challenge the validity of these explanations. The identity crisis thesis suffers from a lack of historical specificity and places far too much emphasis on culture and personality conflict. It overlooks the dynamics of racial change and the changing social position of Japanese Americans within the broader context of American society. Similarly, the recovery thesis poses problems because it also tends to be ahistorical and skirts the centrality of time and place. One could speculate, for example, whether it would have happened had the third generation come of age in the 1930s or the 1950s. From a comparative standpoint, Sansei in Hawaii seem to have had less of an identity crisis than their counterparts on the mainland; they exhibited very little generational protest in the late 1960s. If the recovery thesis were correct, we would have expected greater ethnic consciousness among Hawaiian Sansei as well.

To understand why many Sansei forged a different political orientation as they came of age, we need to examine not only their changing cultural patterns, but also the changing social position of Japanese Americans as they entered the decade of the 1970s, and how their position converged with the major social movements of the times.[6] Despite significant improvements in the economic status of Japanese Americans overall, many Sansei still wondered whether they could participate fully in the social and economic life of the larger society. Having encountered various forms of differential treatment in the postwar years and having had to cope with the legacy of internment, many Sansei felt estranged from the social mainstream despite a desire and an effort to become a part of it.[7] The conjuncture of multiple social movements in the late 1960s and what Omi and Winant refer to as the "disorganization of the dominant racial ideology" captured their attention and prompted them to rearticulate their identity and their relationship to the larger society.[8] This situation gave rise to a new generational group whose political thinking and strategy resonated with the radical and militant style of the times.

An Ambiguous Social and Economic Position

As Japanese Americans entered the decade of the 1970s, they ranked fourth in size among other racial groups—behind blacks, Chicanos, and Native Americans.[9] However, they were the largest among the four Asian ethnic groups—Japanese, Chinese, Filipino, and Korean—in the United States that composed the Asian American category at that time.[10] Between 1960 and 1970, the Japanese American population increased by 27 percent, bringing their total number to 591,290.[11] Immigration from Japan had averaged about only 4,000 per year since 1960 and the large-scale immigration of other Asians, permitted by the 1965 Immigration Act, had just begun.[12] The demographic growth among Japanese Americans came mainly from births, rather than new immigrants. Because the composition of the new immigrants was predominantly female, many of whom were warbrides, the median age of Japanese Americans by 1970 was 29.6 years for males and 34.3 years for females.[13] Lastly, Japanese Americans remained concentrated in the Pacific Coast and Hawaii, as they had been in the pre–World War II period.[14]

Besides experiencing demographic growth, Japanese Americans encountered expanded economic opportunities and greater access to areas of institutional life that had been closed only a decade ago. In contrast to their occupational position in the pre– and immediate post–World War II periods, Japanese American males now earned their living chiefly as professional, technical, and managerial workers (31 percent) and craftsmen and operatives (33 percent), with fewer employed as clerical and sales workers (15 percent).[15] Japanese American women clustered in the clerical and sales (47 percent) and the professional and technical fields (21 percent), with fewer now earning their living in domestic and service work (19 percent).[16] Also, the increased proportion of Japanese American women in the labor force (44 percent in 1960 to 50 percent in 1970) was particularly dramatic for married women whose participation rose from 12 percent in 1960 to 51 percent in 1970.[17] Since 1960, the continued growth of urban Japanese Americans (89 percent in 1970) mirrored their declining numbers in agriculture (from 14.2 percent in 1960 to 7.4 percent in 1970).[18] Whereas agriculture had been one of the economic mainstays for the group as a whole, Japanese Americans now worked in a much more diverse set of occupations that included such professions as engineering and accounting.[19] At the same time, ethnic enterprise continued to be a source of economic activity for Japanese Americans.[20]

Commensurate with their occupational changes, Japanese Americans improved their standing in other realms of institutional life. By 1970, they had one of the highest educational levels of any ethnic group in the country, with a median of 12.4 years of schooling.[21] Nearly 16 percent of those who were 25 years or older had completed four or more years of college compared to 11 percent of the U.S. population as a whole.[22] They had also increased their earning power. The median income of Japanese American families ($12,515) was higher than the national median ($9,596), and Japanese American men and women had higher median incomes than white men and women, respectively.[23] In part, their changing economic position led scholars and journalists to cast Japanese Americans as a "model minority" that had overcome the obstacles of discrimination and oppression.[24]

Despite their so-called "success," there is evidence to suggest that the status of Japanese Americans was a mixed reality in the 1970s. A U.S. Commission on Civil Rights study entitled "Social Indicators of Equality for Minorities and Women" was quite revealing in this regard.[25] Examining the position of American Indians/Alaskan Natives, blacks, Mexican Americans, Chinese Americans, Pilipino Americans, Puerto Ricans, and Japanese Americans in relation to the majority white male population, the Commission analyzed "the Nation's progress toward achieving equality."[26] Their task was to determine the level of equality reached by minority groups in such key areas as education, occupational distribution, employment, income, poverty, and housing.[27] Despite their higher levels of education, income, and employment relative to other minority groups, Japanese Americans were still not at parity with whites. In fact, there were discrepancies that raised interesting questions about their social and economic standing.

In terms of educational attainment, the Commission reported that 53 percent of Japanese American males and 35 percent of Japanese American females who were 25 to 29 years old completed at least four years of college as compared to 34 percent of majority males in the same age cohort. Despite their educational achievement, Japanese American males having four or more years of college earned less than their majority counterparts: $14,253 versus $15,165.[28] Japanese American males and females earned 94 and 55 percent, respectively, of the average that majority males with the same educational level made. This education-to-income ratio suggests that a higher education, at this particular historical juncture, was still not the great equalizer. Disparities such as these led the Commission to conclude:

> In 1976, Japanese, Chinese, and Pilipino Americans were much more likely to have completed a college education than majority males but, as college graduates, they earned far less than majority males. Clearly

the continuing severe disparity between the earnings of women and men at the same educational levels indicates the necessity for more vigorous efforts to ensure equal opportunity in employment.[29]

The Commission also uncovered interesting information about the earnings of Japanese Americans. Although the mean incomes of Japanese American males and females were higher compared to white males and females nationally, the Commission uncovered some startling differences when comparing regional income averages. When the Commission adjusted for state of residence, in addition to such variables as occupational prestige, age, education, and weeks worked, they found that Japanese American males and females earned only 88 and 58 percent, respectively, of the income earned by majority males.[30] This again demonstrated that this ethnic group was lagging in its efforts to secure racial equality.

The Commission found similar disparities when it analyzed the occupational and employment status of the various racial minorities. In line with previous studies that found employment segregation and underrepresentation in such categories as business executives, administrators in policy-making positions, trade unions, and media and entertainment, the Commission stated:

> . . . although minorities and women changed occupations, they still did not move proportionately into the types of employment held by the majority male population. In 1976, five of the seven minority male groups exhibited greater dissimilarities than in either 1960 or 1970. Mexican American, Japanese American, Chinese American, Pilipino American, and Puerto Rican males all share this characteristic of having their greatest segregation at the most recent time—indicating that things clearly are not getting better.[31]

For Japanese Americans, this meant that about 41 percent of the males and 72 percent of the females would have to change their occupations in order to achieve the same occupational distribution as white males.[32]

Since Japanese Americans tended to cluster in professional and technical fields more than majority males, one could argue that such occupational dissimilarity could actually be a favorable trend if these occupational changes were "to better jobs concentrated in a single industry."[31] Anticipating this line of reasoning, the Commission argued that while "a group may become highly overrepresented among doctors and nurses," the real issue was "restricted free choice."[31] Minorities were being rewarded only within a restricted range of occupations and, thus, were limited in their job options. From the Commission's viewpoint, this was not equality. The Commission's findings certainly brought into question the labeling of Japanese Americans as a model minority.

Although they had made some gains relative to other racial groups and experienced considerable social mobility in the 1960s, Japanese Americans had yet to participate fully in the larger society even by the 1970s.

Changing Racial Context and the Asian American Movement

More important than the changes in the social and economic position of Japanese Americans was the cultural and political turmoil of the late 1960s that provided a social space in which Sansei encountered new cultural and political possibilities, options that were quite different than the choices open to their parents' generation. The emergence of the Black Power, anti-war, and women's movements challenged the prevailing social and racial order, as well as the dominant racial ideology. Within this changing racial and political context, young Japanese American activists, in collaboration with other Asian American youth, began to rearticulate their notion of identity and politics. Nowhere was this more evident than in the formation of the Asian American movement.

The coming together of various Asian American youth in a collective undertaking to promote social change was a major development. Although individuals from various Asian communities were interacting fairly extensively in various social settings (such as dances and athletic activities) and occasionally on political issues, they had not yet forged common political bonds based on their social position and shared racial experience. According to Yen Le Espiritu, the formation of a pan-Asian identity and movement had not been possible earlier because Asian groups had previously often engaged in "ethnic disidentification," a practice that set them apart and reaffirmed their social and political differences.[33] Each Asian group's distinctive social, cultural, and political differences that had been rooted in their early life experiences had limited opportunities for collective political action. The camp experience and the political climate of the postwar period also foreclosed the possibilities of progressive Nisei resuming their prewar efforts of working with other Asian Americans.

Those who were politically active prior to the emergence of the Asian American movement seemed to have devoted their attention to social and civil rights issues. For example, individual Sansei men and women who became active in the development of Asian American studies at colleges in the San Francisco Bay Area, participated in such organizations as the Student Nonviolent Coordinating Committee (SNCC) and the Peace Corps. This made sense, as Paul Wong observed, because integration was the dominant ideal at that time:

> As long as the integrationist ideology of the civil rights movement was unchallenged, there was no apparent contradiction in submerging one's own ethnicity for a utopian melting pot.[34]

This submersion took various forms as Japanese American youth attempted to establish a place for themselves in the larger society. Evelyn Yoshimura characterized her experience in the following way:

> I grew up in the Crenshaw district of southwest L.A. in the 1950 and 60s. When my family first tried to buy a house there, many people still didn't want to sell to "Japs."
>
> Like most children of color at that time, I grew up feeling pretty alienated from the society at-large. There were none of us on TV, and the "Leave It to Beaver" type life portrayed there was far different from the drugs, fighting and alienation I experienced. My Asian girlfriends and I would put scotch tape on our eyes to look less Asian, while our black sisters spent many a painful night pressing and burning the African out of their hair.[35]

Yoshimura's comments reveal the kind of social and racial consciousness characteristic of so many Sansei and dramatize the way that ideals of Anglo-conformity permeated their lives.

However, as a result of a common language and a set of shared experiences that sprang from a common social location during the 1950s and 1960s, members of different Asian American groups were better situated to interact and establish a common identity as Asian Americans in the late 1960s. Crucial to this shift were the social and economic changes of the post–World War II period that resulted in the suburbanization of Asian American groups and the incipient breakdown in patterns of residential and community segregation that had prevailed in the pre–World War II era. "Multigroup urban centers also emerged," where members of different Asian ethnic groups had an opportunity to interact socially and to develop a wider range of meaningful relations.[36]

Against this backdrop of social and political turmoil, "personal problems" became the focus of collective discussion and political interaction as the life paths of Asian American youth intersected with a variety of social movements. These developments made it much easier for Asian Americans to mobilize around a common set of issues. Espiritu best described this situation:

> Prompted by broader political struggles and internal demographic changes, college students of Asian ancestry spearheaded the Asian American movement. Critical to its development was the mobilization of American blacks. Besides offering tactical lessons, the civil rights and the Black Power movements had a profound impact on the consciousness of Asian Americans, sensitizing them to racial issues. The anticolonial nationalist movements in Asia also stirred racial and cultural pride and provided a context for the emergence of the Yellow

Power movement. Influenced by these broader political struggles, Americans of Asian ancestry united to denounce racist institutional structures, demand new or unattended rights, and assert their cultural and racial distinctiveness. Normal urban issues such as housing, education, and social welfare began to take on ethnic coloration.[37]

The rise of multiple social and political movements within the context of major international and domestic upheavals created a space for certain Japanese American youth, together with their Chinese, Filipino, and Korean American counterparts, to rearticulate their sense of identity and devise new political strategies that resonated with the times.[38] These individuals were part of a small number of core activists who attempted to mobilize others around the key political issues of the day. In the Los Angeles area, according to one strategically located informant, there were about 100 or so Sansei who were involved, but only about 25 to 30 core people. In the San Francisco Bay Area, a similar situation prevailed. These activists mostly came from middle-class backgrounds, although street youth in large cities such as Los Angeles and San Francisco played an important role in the community sector of the movement.

As the labor movement of the 1930s captured the attention of the progressive Nisei, the early civil rights movement and the other social movements of the 1960s and 1970s were an important catalyst for those Sansei who were vitally concerned about racial equality and social justice.[39] The Black Power movement, in particular, had an especially profound impact on activist Japanese American youth because it illuminated the racial contradictions that were operating in the larger society and in their own lives in ways that the civil rights movement did not.[40] The emergence of leaders like Malcolm X and Stokely Carmichael and groups like the Black Panther Party posed a sharp contrast to such civil rights leaders as Martin Luther King Jr. and their integrationist orientation.[41] The Black Power movement's emphasis on "liberation," "self-determination," "community control," and unity with all Third World people definitely resonated with Sansei activists who began to develop their political consciousness at this time.[42] Alan Nishio, a student at U.C. Berkeley in the 1960s, recalled that:

> It was while I was in college that I became politically involved in the movement for social change. During my first year in college, I was involved in the Free Speech Movement (FSM) at UC Berkeley. The FSM challenged the right of the college administration to determine what could be said on campuses. Today, much of this freedom of expression is taken for granted. This was largely a result of students organizing a campus-wide strike to shut down the campus until con-

cessions were granted. This was my first experience in understanding the power and potential of people acting together in a common effort.

While my identity as a student was affected by the Free Speech Movement, it was the movement of Blacks and other Third World people for equality and justice that affected my identity as an Asian American. What began as a movement for civil rights in the South quickly spread throughout the nation with demands of political power and self-determination for oppressed nationalities. The urban revolts of the '60s and the fight for justice brought home the fact of institutional racism and that the U.S. was a society where the benefits and privileges were divided by color.[43]

Nationalism was another key "political current" that influenced the Asian American movement, particularly its "rejection of the assimilationist and integrationist tendencies associated with the movement moderates."[44] An integral feature of Black Power, nationalism became a strategic facet of the Asian American movement and was expressed on its own terms. According to Omi and Winant:

> Asian American nationalism, for the most part, centered on community control issues. In many cities Asian Americans fought to prevent commercial transformation or obliteration of their communities. In many urban areas, such as San Francisco, Manilatowns and Japantowns have been destroyed by urban renewal schemes which have dispersed residents. Always a popular attraction, Chinatowns have been the site of continual political battles over low-cost housing versus commercial development. Within this context, Asian Americans sought to build alternative institutions which would more adequately address the needs of community residents than could the state or the existing conservative community leadership.[45]

While the Black Power movement served to heighten Asian American racial consciousness and ethnic identity and informed the incipient political strategy and tactics of many Asian American activists, the antiwar movement became a key focal point that drew Asian Americans together.[46] At the Berkeley campus of the University of California, the Asian American Political Alliance (AAPA) began as a result of the need for an organization with which Asians could identify and express their concerns about the war and other political issues.[47] The need for such an organization was a key concern of Asian Americans who had already been active in the civil rights movement and had developed some political consciousness about the inequities of race, class, and gender relations in the United States. Not only did AAPA draw Asian Americans who shared concerns about the Vietnam War and the anti-war movement's focus on the racial nature of U.S. imperialism, it also attracted many Asian Americans who were coming to terms with their ethnic identity.[48]

Asian American activists tended to view the war in Vietnam as a racial war and the efforts of the North Vietnamese as a struggle for national liberation against imperialism and its corollary, white racism.[49] In this respect, Asian Americans challenged the U.S. involvement in the war on racial as well as political grounds. When the U.S. bombing of Cambodia became public in May 1970, Asian American students escalated their organizing efforts in conjunction with the larger anti-war movement. At UCLA, the Asian Strike Committee led a general student protest against the bombing of Cambodia and subsequent events that included the shootings of student protestors at Kent State and Jackson State universities.[50] Similar activities transpired at the University of California, Berkeley, where Asian American activists conducted an anti-war protest and march in the wake of the Cambodian Invasion.[51] Among them were Sansei activists who also brought their concerns to their communities. For example, student organizers from the University of California, Berkeley, and San Francisco State University, in conjunction with the San Francisco Japanese Community Youth Council and other community groups, organized a "teach-in" in San Francisco Japantown on "US involvement in Southeast Asian countries."[52] Many other individuals, both Nisei and Sansei, and a wide cross section of community organizations and campus groups from the larger Bay Area supported the activists' efforts to enable the community to "become more knowledgeable" about the war in Southeast Asia.[53]

Another key dimension of the Asian American movement was the efforts of Asian American students to address issues of institutionalized racism in higher education and the need for educational access, affirmative action, and educational relevance.[54] The demand to establish Ethnic Studies programs was especially indicative of these concerns and in many ways symbolized the multifaceted efforts of students to challenge American cultural hegemony and bring about institutional change. The initial struggles to institute Ethnic Studies programs at San Francisco State and the University of California, Berkeley, provided the impetus for students and sympathetic faculty at other campuses across the country to demand similar programs.[55]

Using the metaphor of decolonization, these activists raised questions about the need for self-determination in the planning and execution of community research. They called for a curriculum that addressed their history and the formation of their communities from an Asian American perspective. This undertaking was especially important because it prefigured the development of an Asian American historiography that would address both the unique and the common features of each Asian group's experience. Of particular interest to Japanese American students was the study of the World War II interment camp experience and its impact.

Campus activism and the establishment of Ethnic Studies simultaneously became a foundation for community activism. Students linked up with community activists and other youth to establish "alternative community institutions" and programs that served needs that had been ignored by mainstream agencies and overlooked by traditional community organizations and leaders. In fact, one of the founding notions of Asian American Studies was that it should be an agency for community service and social change.[56]

Equally significant, the development of the Asian American women's movement became an important source of mobilizing within the Asian American movement.[57] Initially, internal contradictions within the movement brought women together to address various manifestations of gender inequity and male chauvinism. These included sexual norms that privileged men; not allowing women a voice in political matters; treating women abusively; and assigning women such menial tasks as "making coffee, typing, answering phones, and handling the mail."[58] Within the context of the movement, Asian American women began challenging Asian American sexism and expressing their feminist concerns. Through "rap sessions," Asian American Studies courses on women, and study groups, women shared their problems in a supportive environment, developed a deeper understanding of their subordinate status, and discussed alternatives to the cultural norms and roles that constrained them.[59]

These issues did not, however, serve to separate Asian American women from the Asian American movement. According to Yen Le Espiritu:

> because "their ethnic identity was a critical component of their feminism," Asian American feminists refused to advocate a non-Asian alliance—despite the fact that white feminists could offer important resources and shared similar concerns. Distancing themselves from the general feminist movement, Asian American women organized their own movement. For Asian American women activists, the ideology of feminism had to be incorporated into the larger identity of being Asian American.[60]

Much of this had to do with the fact that the women's movement tended to be composed of "middle-class and white dominated organizations" that were not always receptive to the needs and concerns of Asian American women and other women of color.[61] Although Asian American women received some inspiration from the general women's movement, they preferred to affiliate with other women of color who shared similar concerns and circumstances. Asian American women felt that the dynamics of race resulted in very different experiences that called for a very different perspective on how they defined their situation. Thus they articulated "the 'triple oppression' concept: their gender was inextricably linked to their race and class."[62]

Not content simply to discuss gender equity issues and problems of oppression in ideological or intellectual terms, Asian American women established their own organizations and networks to enhance the overall status of Asian American women and to promote change in the larger society.[63] Some activists pursued their work within the context of the Asian American community, while others aligned themselves with political groups whose ideological orientation was informed by Marxist-Leninist-Maoist thought. These activities added an international dimension to their work as leaders came in touch with women who were involved in revolutionary struggles in China, Vietnam, and elsewhere.

Although each movement had its particular impact, their influences clearly dovetailed. At the University of California, Berkeley, for example, Asian American student activists who went on strike after the U.S. bombing of Cambodia fused "their anti-war activities with campaigns to strengthen Bay Area Asian communities."[64] At the personal level, these social forces were powerful. The reflections of Evelyn Yoshimura show how influences from the various movements merged to affect her political consciousness. Recounting an Asian student gathering that she attended in Los Angeles, she mentioned the significance of the Asian American Political Alliance speakers who had been involved in the Third World Liberation Front at San Francisco State University:

> They talked about the need to unite with other Third World people; about the need to demand Ethnic Studies that would serve Third World communities. And they talked about how the Vietnam War was not just killing American soldiers, but it was an unjust and racist war; and about the inspiration of Asian people in Vietnam, fighting for self-determination and freedom.[65]

Alan Nishio likewise recounted his experience during this period of campus activism as follows:

> The student movement, Third World movement, and anti-war movement all helped to crystallize for me the need for a fundamental and basic change within the society. There is a need to change a society that valued profits over people, material goods over human life, and elitism over equality.

From my initial involvement in the struggles of the '60s came the realization of the need for organization. Thus, many of us worked together to form the Asian American Political Alliance (AAPA). The purpose of AAPA was to form an organization that would take progressive stands within the Asian American community—stands in support of other Third World movements, stands against the war in Viet Nam, and stands in favor of developing unity amongst Asian Americans.[66]

With the prevalence of these movements, notions of liberation, self-determination, community control, and educational relevance captured the Sansei imagination and provided them with new concepts to rearticulate their experience as well as guide their political actions.[67] As Yoshimura put it:

I was coming to the conclusion, as did many of my generation, that in order to end racism and the many other injustices in this society, it would take a very deep and fundamental change. And this would only come about with the organization and mobilization of the many in America who were suffering in hundreds of different ways.[68]

Concluding Remarks

For Japanese American youth, the intersection between their parents' changing economic position, their generational location, and the political, cultural, and racial dynamics of the larger society actually made it possible to establish a social and political space in which they could traverse a very different life trajectory. Through the social movements of the day that, in part, contributed to a very different *zeitgeist*, Sansei activists confronted a wide range of issues that centered on their identity, culture, and politics. Many had to come to terms with their ethnic identity. Some had a need for community and a desire for moral cohesiveness that were missing in their lives. The kind of material well being pursued by their parents' generation was not enough. Some rejected the Nisei political style and sought an alternative, something more vibrant and meaningful. Others had personal problems that they felt could be addressed within the Asian American movement. Still, in the process of dealing with these various concerns, they formed very different sensibilities about themselves as a minority group and devised new avenues for dealing with their racial position.

Although the entire generation did not become activists, the formation of a new Sansei generational unit, like their Nisei counterparts in the 1930s, gave rise to a very different set of leaders—activists who challenged the political sensibilities of the entire community. Given the solidity of the

Nisei political style that had predominated in the post–World War II period and the rigidities of the racial order, Sansei activists participated in a difficult and complex process that was neither culturally or structurally determined. To develop a richer understanding of their changing racial consciousness and political orientation, we will turn to the biographies of two Sansei and see how their lives intersected with the historical and racial dynamics of the times.

Chapter 8

"From Our Own Point of View"

Coming to Terms with the 1960s

THE EMERGENCE OF A NEW POLITICAL ORIENTATION within the Sansei generation was a complex process in which the lives of a number of Sansei resonated with the political ferment and racial destabilization of the 1960s. Of special importance was the emergence of the Asian American movement, because it created a political and cultural space in which Sansei could grapple with their shifting circumstances as they came of age. They rearticulated the meaning of race and ethnicity not only for their generation but for the entire community.[1] These youth developed new political strategies and tactics that offered alternatives to the prevailing political orientation within the Japanese American community.

To develop a fuller understanding of the changing racial consciousness and political style of the Japanese American activists of the late 1960s and 1970s, we will examine the biographies of Fred Ichiyama and Linda Miyano, two Sansei who came of age in that period. Both Ichiyama and Miyano were deeply affected by the forces and conditions impinging on youth during the 1960s, but they got involved in their communities in rather different ways. It is difficult to make the claim that they were "typical" or even "representative." Regional differences certainly set them apart from their southern California counterparts.[2] Still, what happened to them in terms of their consciousness and commitment is revealing, though we cannot overlook the fact that their experience was not widely shared by those members of their generation who were not moved to political action. Thus, in their portraits, we will analyze the impetus for Ichiyama's and Miyano's activism, their changing racial consciousness and social position, and their views about politics and social change.

Coming to Terms with the 1960s

At the time I interviewed Fred Ichiyama, he was a worker for a public utilities corporation in the San Francisco Bay Area. Relative to his education, he was underemployed: he had earned a master's degree in history and had four years of teaching experience at the community college level. Ichiyama considered himself a product of the 1960s. In fact, it was within the racial context of that decade that he got "turned on" to a career in education, a strategy that he used to return to and serve his community. He planned to work with students much like himself—those who found traditional schooling socially alienating and ethnically irrelevant.

During his short teaching career, Ichiyama was also a community activist. Although his political perspective made him a controversial figure, he was committed to the idea of improving the status and welfare of Japanese Americans and other Third World people. His congenial and outgoing personal style enabled him to find acceptance in the community. Unfortunately, Ichiyama's community involvement terminated once he was compelled to change jobs. Full-time teaching positions were difficult to obtain, and he was not content to remain a "part-timer" in a community college system that offered him little security and no future. He settled for unskilled work as a temporary expedient but was determined to find something better.

At that time, Ichiyama was somewhat confused and unsure about the kind of career he should pursue. His initial plan for a career in education had collapsed. He tried several times to get back into the field without success. He became resigned to the fact that teaching was no longer a realistic alternative. He had a sense of guilt about changing his career objectives, because he was no longer able to sustain many of the values that he had developed during the late 1960s and 1970s. Although he was by no means a radical, the notion of participating in efforts to bring about social change had been an important consideration for him. He was more concerned about serving the community than fomenting revolution.

Growing Up in a Suburban Ghetto

Fred Ichiyama was born in a suburb of the San Francisco Bay Area. He grew up in a small Japanese American community located in the "Eastside" of town, a neighborhood that was racially mixed and defined as a "Target Area" by the local Equal Opportunity Commission. In a sense, the Eastside was a ghetto comprised of poor and working-class Asians, blacks, some Chicanos, and a smaller number of working-class whites. *De facto* segregation prevailed in the local school system because housing codes restricted the mobility of Japanese Americans until the late 1950s, a period of economic expansion in light industries in the region.

The major influences in Ichiyama's early life were his parents and community. His Issei father was a gardener and his Nisei mother a domestic worker. The Ichiyamas settled in the Bay Area after returning from camp and worked as domestics. His father then took up gardening, as did many returning internees. He spoke no English and relied on his wife to convey messages to his family, but despite these "communication problems" Fred's parents taught him values that included "neatness, courtesy, and conformity" to the way of life in the Japanese community. Shame was also emphasized. He was constantly reminded, "Don't get into trouble so that everybody in the community will be talking about you." Although Ichiyama complied for the most part with these "commands," he also rebelled against the "regimentation" practiced in his family and community. Ichiyama was influenced by his "peer group," but the mass media and public schooling also had a great impact on him. These conflicting sources of socialization made life perplexing for him. Television, along with magazines and newspapers, introduced Ichiyama to a "lifestyle" with "a white orientation," from "fads to music." The "white influence" really began to dominate during the 1950s after he began attending school. He recalled that from then on "the schools and the teachers" were by far the greatest influence on his thinking. "Individualism" as an approach to life stood out in particular, since the emphasis on personal initiative, self-reliance, personal self-control, and deferred gratification contradicted what he had been taught at home "within the context of the Japanese family and community."

White aesthetics and images of white women as the most desirable female companions also became a key component of that influence. For Ichiyama, "dating white girls" became an important way to achieve assimilationist ideals implicitly transmitted through the mass media and the schools. By establishing relations with whites, in general, he was no longer set apart from other students, so that he no longer felt racially unequal. Yet, there was a paradox. Ichiyama performed poorly in high school, not because he was "stupid," but because he had been "turned off" by a curriculum that lacked ethnic content and relevance—reasons he could not articulate until he began attending college. Extracurricular "social and sports" activities provided a sense of accomplishment and meaning absent from his schooling. Organized athletic leagues operated by the Japanese community provided the stimulation that came from "competing against other people and meeting people from different areas." Besides keeping a working-class kid off the street, sports kept Ichiyama within a community he had begun to reject. Also, because sports were an important source of status and prestige among students, they became a vehicle to meet and date white girls. In the mid-1960s, that was how Ichiyama dealt with race relations.

Realizing Racial Contradictions

After completing high school, Fred Ichiyama attended a local community college because he did not have the grades to gain admission into a four-year university. But he was comfortable with that. One of his big ambitions was to play college baseball. He was a good athlete in high school and he thought he had a chance to "make it" at a small college by taking the junior college route. His dream was short lived when he discovered that the coach built the team around white players. Ichiyama feels he was never given a real tryout.

Although Ichiyama gave up the idea of a possible baseball career, his love of sports made him think about becoming a physical education teacher. If he improved his grades, he believed that he could transfer to a four-year state college and get his teaching credential. Still, he was unsure about his direction; had it not been for the times in which he came of age, he might have dropped out. The Vietnam War had escalated by 1967, and he knew he wanted to retain a 2-S draft status to avoid the military at all cost. He got his deferment and life went on as usual, except that he began to learn that he and his friends could no longer "compete for the white ladies." Interracial dating and relationships became more remote possiblities as he and his female peers began thinking about "marriage and desirable mates." He realized that he did not fall into the "right racial category." In high school, he could "get over" because of his "reputation as an athlete"; but in college he found social relations were clearly "structured" around race. Whites socialized with whites, and it was difficult for Ichiyama to know where he belonged. His explanation for this situation is that he and his friends had been "turned off to Asian sisters" and "highly programmed and influenced by white standards of beauty. Asian women didn't fit into it at the time."

While Ichiyama's social life was in a state of chaos, he began to cultivate an interest in American history through the study of black history and by reading books like *The Autobiography of Malcolm X*. The black experience began to take on a whole new importance for him. When he was growing up, black youths were part of his community. Black families who migrated to the San Francisco Bay Area during World War II to work in war-related industries found housing in neighborhoods vacated by Japanese Americans. During his early youth, his "rapport" with black friends was such that he "did not think about someone being black." Although he was told in subtle ways through his family and community that blacks were "inferior" people, he "resisted these ideas and tried to treat people on an individual basis." "There were dumb white people," too, as far as he was concerned. Ichiyama also understood in retrospect that race relations in his community did not reflect the competition for survival that helped create the racial hostility found in large cities like Oakland or San Francisco. This situation made it easier to make friends with blacks and sensitized him to the fact that blacks were a heterogeneous group. "Black people in the Fillmore and Hunter's Point seemed to be different than blacks in San Jose." Also, there were blacks who were friendly to Japanese Americans. Those who were hostile identified them as exploitative small businessmen similar to Jews in Harlem. Thus, through his study of the black experience, Ichiyama began to form an historical and sociological understanding of the impact of racism on blacks in America. This started him thinking about his own ethnicity and position in society.

Forming an Asian American Consciousness

Fred Ichiyama decided to pursue his incipient interest in American ethnic history at a four-year college. Besides earning good grades as a result of his newfound interest, strong recommendations from his instructors and encouragement from his counselor provided him with the necessary stimulus to apply to a university in Los Angeles, where he was accepted. His first choice, however, was a local state college because it was close to home and friends; the thought of going away to school was intimidating and he questioned his ability to "make it at a university."

The first few months at the university were indeed "terrifying." Lost and disoriented, Fred Ichiyama began to establish a network of friends and developed relationships through courses in which he was enrolled. In contrast to his community college days, Ichiyama started to associate more with Asian Americans and developed a desire "to meet Asian women." He recalled that new friends "turned him on to Asian American Studies," which became a source both for meeting Asian women and learning about his ethnicity. Of particular significance at this point was the study of the internment experience and the underlying racial injustice in American life. This marked the beginning of Ichiyama's ethnic consciousness and political orientation as an Asian American. He also began to develop academic skills—how to write, research, and "to think more critically about racial minorities and the world around us."

His formation of an Asian American consciousness was buttressed both by the unfolding Asian American student movement on campus and in the community, and by his academic study. The organization of Asian student groups, community service agencies, and cultural activities emphasizing the concept of being Asian American seized Fred's attention and motivated him to get involved in the "community." At the same time, he revealed that his study of race relations, labor history, and California history stimulated the evolution of his social consciousness. This was especially true of those courses taught by history professors who introduced him to new ideas about racism and Marxism.

As a result of his contact with the Asian American movement and his course of study, Ichiyama began to connect questions of ethnic identity to problems of racism in American society. Further study of black history

helped build a Third World consciousness that recognized common facets
of racism facing blacks, Chicanos, and Asian Americans. At that historical
juncture, Ichiyama was able to make much more sense of his experience.
He now understood why he had been attracted to white women, why he
had found the community so regimented, and why in the past he had not
fit into any particular social circle. He finally recognized that institutionalized racism had created conditions under which he became detached from
his community and from his ethnic identity.

Finding a Meaningful Line of Work

After completing his B.A. degree in history in 1971, Fred Ichiyama
decided to continue his education in graduate school and to get a master's
degree. "Becoming an instructor in U.S. history" at a community college
seemed to be a meaningful line of work. He reasoned, "I had gone through
those ranks and I knew what students would be like and it would offer me
a greater challenge." He was denied entrance to the university of his first
and only choice. A last-minute decision to apply to a state college proved
useful: he was admitted on a probationary basis.

Nonetheless, Fred Ichiyama felt ambivalent about graduate school
and a professional career. He lacked "self-confidence." He never felt comfortable with many of his Asian American peers who appeared to be more
highly motivated and sure about their career choices. No one in Ichiyama's
family had gone to a four-year college. Without such a precedent, "failure"
was always in the back of his mind. Although he survived the university, he
was surprised that he had gotten as far as he had. Having gone this distance was possibly more significant than setting career goals. His friends
were able to do the same thing easily, but he had a hard time. The fact that
his school friends had come from "middle to upper middle class backgrounds—the sons and daughters of small businessmen . . . lawyers, dentists, and doctors"—might account for their high motivation, according to
Ichiyama. "They had no problems meeting financial problems and making
choices." He recalled, however, that there were Asian American students
like himself, individuals from poorer backgrounds, who were "hungry" to
establish careers for themselves. But these students had not developed the
racial and political consciousness that Ichiyama had. He felt they were simply out for themselves.

The actual process of doing graduate work also made him question
his commitment to teaching. Studying became "a very lonely lifestyle." He
missed learning from fellow students, a facet of his experience within the
student movement that he had found very stimulating and supportive. He
thought his training at the state college was inadequate. Since most of his

classmates worked, the possibilities for "dialogue" with other students were limited. Because interaction was minimal, he felt he was not getting "the whole graduate student trip."

Finding a part-time community college position teaching Ethnic Studies at his alma mater proved to be a temporary solution to his alienation. Teaching gave him the opportunity to improve his ability to articulate his ideas, interact with fellow teachers, and become involved in community activities. At the same time, it gave him valuable experience in moving towards his goal of securing a full-time teaching job. While teaching courses on Asian American history and the Third World experience in America, he realized that he wanted to teach American history from a Third World perspective. This would be his contribution to the conventional history curriculum that, to him, presented a strictly "white perspective."

His attempt to introduce this new perspective to the History Department with the intention of increasing his teaching load to a full-time position met with resistance. He found his colleagues skeptical about his competence in U.S. history as well as the history of Third World minorities. Had he been teaching courses on labor or California history, Ichiyama believed he would have been acceptable to his peers. The best he could do was to get an occasional evening course teaching California history at a nearby college in the same district. Evening courses were less prestigious and paid less than daytime work.

Ichiyama remained committed to the Ethnic Studies program because he believed in the concept and wanted to teach in the program at least half time. But fighting the administration to retain Ethnic Studies became a drain on both his emotions and his time. His community work was also demanding. All these things began to deter him from completing his graduate work. Miserable prospects for finding work in other community college districts because of the constricting economy compounded his problems. A growing emphasis on using part-time teachers to fill positions vacated by retiring full-time instructors, the reduction of salary scales for part-time instructors, and the failure of collective bargaining indicated to Ichiyama that the chances for a full-time job were bleak.

"I Just Completely Started to Lose Touch"

The completion of his master's degree should have inspired Fred Ichiyama to continue with his part-time teaching, but the daily struggles to keep Ethnic Studies alive became too much for him. The concept of developing a Third World Studies program, which he had embraced as an undergraduate student, also started to lose meaning for Ichiyama. It was a good idea "in theory," but in practice it seemed impossible to make it a reality at the community college level. Opposition to Ethnic Studies as a legitimate part of the curriculum was too great; community and student support was too minimal. As a result, Ichiyama experienced a crisis over his future.

Ichiyama became frustrated because "a person with a Master of Arts in History" could not be gainfully employed in a full-time job leading to some kind of career. He realized that he could have become a "migrant teacher," commuting a hundred miles a day to three different schools to make ends meet. But such a compromise was an insult to his dignity. At the same time, former doubts about an academic life took on crisis proportions. The time he spent "indoors teaching and studying" separated him from "the reality outside of the institutions. . . ." "I just started to lose touch," he said. Visual media, newspapers, and magazines became his only channels to the outside world. Teaching "abstract ideas" to students who had more immediate concerns about "finding a job" began to trouble him because he had no answers for them. All he could do was "speculate." Losing touch with the outside world was Ichiyama's way of saying that his current work and lifestyle were becoming a "mental strain." He was tired of being a half-time teacher and tired of "trying to deal with the man."

"Am I Gonna Be a Laborer That Just Works 8 to 5?"

After leaving the community college in 1976, Ichiyama was forced to contemplate his future. He asked himself, "Am I gonna be a laborer that just works 8 to 5?; am I looking for security as far as employment?; am I looking for challenge?; am I looking for money?; am I looking for a career?; what am I looking for?" He had to grapple with these questions. At times, he became depressed because he had not "made it in (his) first career choice." He partly blamed himself, along with "external things such as the job market." Oftentimes he felt that he did not "want to do anything in this society." At other times, he wished he "grew up earlier."

His concern about growing up earlier reflected his disillusionment about the "Movement period" in his life. He had wanted to contribute to the Asian America community, to help build a new society, and to find a meaningful career. Despite his insecurities, he had made a commitment to teaching, but he had been shut out because of a constricting job market. If he had not been involved in the movement, he might have become one of the "hungry ones" who studied business, engineering, or pharmacy, and eventually found a stable career.

Unfortunately, Fred Ichiyama had to settle for less. The labor market was a harsh reality. He had to "clean up his act"—cut his shoulder-length hair, shave his beard, and transform his overall image to one acceptable to the corporate world or to whomever was interviewing him for work. But having a new look was not enough. Ichiyama found himself competing with "many people. . . Many are interviewed and only one is selected."

That experience was "very damaging to the ego." He had to question his "self-worth" all over again. He faced the grim reality of having to "sell" himself to get a job. Given this problem, he was almost relieved that the local telephone company hired him as a "motorized messenger," an unskilled position doing deliveries, but mostly loading and unloading computer tapes that recorded long distance calls. He did this eight hours a day.

Without a doubt, Ichiyama was dissatisfied doing "menial work and collecting a check. . . Hey, what's a couple of hundred or three hundred dollars every two weeks when you're not going nowhere?" Making money to buy a nice house in "the hills" was not Ichiyama's primary motivation. He wanted a career where he could see "personal development," feel "self-satisfaction," and "make decisions." Yet his political consciousness made him question the relevance of joining the "murky waters" of the corporate world. Murky waters for Ichiyama meant the world of business—a world that made him feel "out of place," because Ichiyama had a radical critique of the corporate world. Besides disliking the white middle-class lifestyle associated with business functionaries, he disliked the emphasis of corporate enterprise on competition and production to maintain one's position. In business, "profit is the most important thing," says Ichiyama, and being part of that world would be a problem for him. There was a racial angle, also: in the struggle to produce, he would have to compete with "a white person." Ichiyama felt that whites would have an automatic "edge" for racial reasons. So even if he accepted the need to compete in production, he thought he would be at a disadvantage. He stated, "I haven't found a way to cope with that."

"I Believe Race Is a Factor"

According to Ichiyama, in the corporate world people get sorted out by race in the competition to get ahead and to stay on top. While he hypothesized that this occurs at the management and sales levels, his own experience informed him that this also happened to working class people. Specifically, Ichiyama saw whites advancing faster than people of color. In his judgment, a black worker who put in 18 years of service would receive only the obligatory benefits, whereas a white worker after 9 years on the job could be given a promotion over the black person who possessed the same qualifications and twice the years of experience. It appeared to Ichiyama that people of color must adhere to operational guidelines more closely than whites, and doing so was still no guarantee for advancement. Such observations led him to infer that differential treatment was a reality at his work place.

According to Ichiyama, his employer had an affirmative action program because it had contracts with the government. Given his location, he felt the company disguised differential treatment so that things looked "fine and dandy . . . All the supervisors are white," Ichiyama commented, "and they treat blacks differently than they treat whites." To make it more complicated, supervisors treated Ichiyama differently than they did either blacks or whites. Because he was Asian he occupied a marginal position between blacks and whites. For one thing, he felt that he was expected to do more work than the others:

> It seems like for blacks, they [supervisors] believe that it's good that they show up; and then for whites it's almost a feeling that there's a privilege for them, meaning certain days off, certain times that they don't have to work so hard; little things like that. Treatment by the supervisors towards the employees is an important factor as far as seeing some of the racism.

White and black workers who occupied the same position as Ichiyama could quit work after eight hours and leave whatever work that was not finished, saying "I did the best I could." However, Ichiyama had to develop a different style of handling his job just so that he could keep it. He had to "work harder, with very little complaining" and "take all that shit" given to him "because the supervisors have the arbitrary discretion" to write negative comments in his files. He said, "I have to protect my ass," because "they could get me on the grounds that I don't do my work." He felt that this is less apt to happen to others because his supervisors did not expect the same performance of him.

"I'll Beat the Hell Out of That Ball"

At work, Fred Ichiyama was in a tight spot, and he found it increasingly difficult to cope with his situation. As far as he was concerned, political struggle did not appear to be the way out of this dilemma. Although Ichiyama supported, in theory, the idea of collective organizing to improve the position of nonwhite workers, he believed that it was not realistic at his particular work place. The problem for Ichiyama was that workers seemed divided by race and by their concerns for individual mobility. Whites and blacks were segregated socially, while Ichiyama and a few black friends formed a third group. At lunches, breaks, and informal meetings people socialized with members of their own group. Regardless of race, several workers aspired for management positions, while others had committed themselves to a career with the company. Political organizing would jeopardize their future status. Even if Ichiyama filed a grievance charging his managers with racism, he was not sure that his fellow workers, regardless of their race, would support him. When the "chips are down," he thought that all workers "look out for their own interests."

Moreover, worker interaction was far from congenial according to Ichiyama. Just to maintain some type of "social life" with people on the job, let alone a political one, was problematical. He generally felt "alienated" from his co-workers because he could not engage in some meaningful dialogue with them. Too often conversations became a series of "four letter words [and] complaints." Ichiyama attributes the difficulty of communicating with fellow workers on their terms to his educational training. Known to be a "former teacher," Ichiyama was frequently queried by his co-workers about issues they found puzzling. But in the course of giving explanations, he mentioned that some may have found his vocabulary "pretentious" or may have taken offense at the implicaion that they were stupid if they failed to understand him.

Perhaps Ichiyama was reacting defensively against the fact that he was doing unskilled work despite his level of education. He acknowledged that he was going "downhill as far as (his) achievement orientation" and that he felt trapped between "the economic necessity of having to keep a job and not knowing what to do" to improve his position. This may also explain why he considered himself to be superior to his supervisors and to some workers who had less education than he did but who simply tolerated him.

To rid himself of the frustrations that stemmed from the job, Fred Ichiyama occasionally played racquetball. "I'll beat the hell out of that ball; that's the best therapy there is." This was symptomatic of a retreat into his personal life, particularly during weekends. He was no longer involved in community politics. Keeping his "mental faculties" sharp had become more difficult because the only things he did were "sleep, eat, and work." The main source of weekday entertainment was "the tube." Television, he said, was one of the things that kept him "from going insane."

Community Control and Ethnic Politics

Given his situation, the larger issues of Asian American community, interethnic relations, and social change no longer had the vitality they did when he was teaching. Still, his consciousness about race and political issues seemed to retain a progressive bent. I got the sense from Ichiyama that his disillusionment over his life's circumstances and his desire to improve his economic position helped him crystallize his outlook on the question of social change.

Electoral politics were no longer meaningful to Ichiyama as a means for achieving racial equality. He was no longer a registered Democrat because he did not believe the vote would do very much for common people. The choice of electing a Democrat or a Republican to political office was not really a choice at all. Both parties seemed to represent the same interests and did very little for Asian Americans.

Fred Ichiyama thought that bringing about social change for people of color could best be done through "community control." Although it did mean a certain amount of racial separation and segregation, "community control" appealed to him as a method of gaining political power at the local level. Ichiyama reasoned that "policy decisions, funding" and so forth "center around City Hall." This was one way of saying that Asians and other people of color faced "a Board of Directors" of one form or another if they wished to change the educational or welfare system. Generally, these boards and elected officials do not reflect the needs of oppressed communities. That was why Ichiyama believed that political mobilization at the ethnic community level was an important method to challenge the domination and control of those who had the power to make decisions.

In more practical terms, community control to Fred Ichiyama meant that Japanese Americans needed to mobilize around community issues as well as state and federal issues that affected their interests. "Community" was more than a geographical term. He was talking about a social network based upon ethnic solidarity as a political vehicle to secure some of the resources that tended to be allocated "disproportionately to white society."

The desire for community control and ethnic political mobilization definitely countered assimilation and integration as a race relations ideal. Ichiyama was willing to acknowledge, however, that the choice between community control and integration was rather difficult. He realized that the notion of racial groups integrating at all levels of society mainly "sounds good on paper." But in reality, "there is still segregation," despite programs such as affirmative action. From where he sat, the best method for securing goods and services for Asian Americans in general was to take a community approach, rather than using an individualistic strategy. Someone might be able to "uplift their socioeconomic position" individually, "but it does nothing for everyone else." Individual cases of mobility did no more than become "a display for others to use the same strategy." This approach had been a major tendency among second-generation Japanese Americans, as he observed, but it created problems. For one thing, according to Ichiyama, individual mobility obscured the operation of institutionalized racism for most Japanese Americans. It made them think that they could succeed simply by hard work. Those who sought mobility or experienced some partial mobility were often "put into a little corner in white communities and became alienated from their ethnic community."

Moreover, an individual strategy resulted in Japanese Americans taking a "conservative" political perspective. They tended to "go with the status quo" for safety reasons. With the legacy of the internment experience, most Japanese Americans avoided actions that would bring harm to "them or their children." He thought that concern for security in the future was uppermost in their minds. Ironically, this strategy, according to Ichiyama, often produced negative consequences for their children. Because they remained silent about experiences such as the internment, their children often lost a sense of their family history and ethnic identity.

These were reasons that Ichiyama did not believe Japanese Americans had become a "model minority." He conceded that they were doing well "relative to other racial groups." But, he argued, "they have not been totally accepted by American society." He felt that people who either pushed and/or accepted the success notion had a myopic view. He believed that comparing incomes and educational levels was "an ill-conceived kind of comparison," because "more whites make more money with less education than Japanese Americans do." A more emotional concern for Ichiyama was the reception that Japanese Americans received outside of California— "we all are Chinks" in the eyes of white society. In his view, if social integration were a reality, these subtle forms of racism would not exist and there would not be the need for community control and ethnic politics. In Ichiyama's eyes, there had not been "any great progress as far as making change" for racial groups in America is concerned.

Significance

Fred Ichiyama does not conform neatly to the images of Japanese Americans as an achievement-oriented model minority. He had problems "getting it together" academically before developing some serious interests in teaching history at the community college level. His choice was not determined by traditional culture. On the contrary, Ichiyama's socialization by his family and peer group actually may have made him hesitate about going on to college. Rather, his study of the black experience during the time of the Black Power movement and his subsequent exposure to the Asian American movement were what motivated him to puruse higher education. Through his interaction with the Asian American movement and the university, Ichiyama discovered himself and his community.

A small number of Japanese American activists of Ichiyama's generation have been labeled rebellious, militant, and radical. These images apply to Ichiyama's actions to some extent during the early 1970s. He was politically involved with his community. His teaching in Ethnic Studies emphasized a need for racial equality and community control. But his experience suggested that his racial and political perspectives were quite complicated. He shifted from a preoccupation with sports and the status derived from dating white women to an Asian American identity and a concern for serving the community. He developed strong convictions that Asians are an oppressed group, perhaps not to the same degree as blacks, but victims of racism nonetheless. He thought Asians were neither a model minority nor successful. Community control was his strategy for securing the political power necessary to influence public policy and to achieve racial equality at the local level. This approach would give Asians a voice in local politics, which was monopolized by whites. Ichiyama was not a radical in this respect, that is, he did not call for a restructuring of American institutions; his was a call for institutional access and accountability through ethnic politics. A reflection of the late 1960s, this ideology has remained a central part of his thinking about social change.

Given his model of ethnic community political mobilization, Fred Ichiyama believed that Japanese Americans were too conservative politically, despite their recent visibility in electoral politics. There was a certain irony in his view about the Nisei political style, however, that was related to his changing social position. As a worker for the local telephone company, Ichiyama occupies a precarious position. Perceiving the differential treatment of racial minorities, he felt he had to adopt a "hard work" approach to maintain his job rather than take political action. In fact, he has resorted to an individual strategy of survival used by other Japanese Americans whom he has criticized for their lack of political consciousness and involvement.

In essence, Ichiyama's current situation is very much shaped both by his position at work and by his racial consciousness. He has relinquished many of his political values and community concerns because his work leaves very little time for outside activity. The alienation of his work compels him to seek refuge in his personal life for social support and meaning, rather than engage in collective struggles. Racial separation and tension basically preclude class-based politics for Ichiyama, even though "community control" and "ethnic politics" remain his models for securing social equality and racial justice. As a result, the combination of Ichiyama's racial consciousness and class position as a minority worker prevents him from approaching the question of mobility in collective class terms. He has to resort to an individual strategy of working hard, which can easily shift to a strategy of social mobility through attaining middle-management status. This is the racial and class reality that Japanese Americans confronted several decades ago, when they decided that education, hard work, individual mobility, and conservative political behavior were the most appropriate ways to adjust.

I am not asserting that Fred Ichiyama represents a prototype of all Japanese Americans who were influenced by the 1960s and who later became disillusioned, but his feelings, aspirations, changing radical consciousness, and temporary political involvement are typical of many others of his generational unit. He is unique, however, because he can articulate disappointments, confusion, and more recent changes in his life circumstances that others like him cannot. To say that Ichiyama "sold out" is too simplistic, given the diverse forces operating in his life. He would like to retain the political spirit of the 1960s, but his changing circumstances dictated new priorities. One can sense Ichiyama's feelings of guilt and confusion. He has been left in midstream with many questions unanswered. He now understands institutional racism even better than when he taught about it because he sees it in his daily life. Thus achieving racial equality and social justice are still important goals to him. At this point in his life, he is not sure what to do, given the need to make a living. He is candid about the tensions these contradictions present for him. Hard work was the best strategy available. But he is certainly not among those who could be labeled a model minority, nor would he want to be. Although he is no longer politically involved, he is not ideologically apolitical when it comes to racial issues.

An Asian American Progressive

Linda Miyano, a legal services attorney who specializes in civil rights work, was 29 years old at the time I talked with her. She was single, a dedicated, hard-working person who derived satisfaction from her work. Her father is a second-generation Japanese American from Hawaii; her mother is a war bride from Japan. Although she might be defined as either a Sansei or a Nisei, depending on if one counts her father or her mother, her generational location and experience are more akin to those of Sansei.

The Miyanos moved from Hawaii to the San Francisco Bay Area after the war. They lived in the Japanese community for about 10 years, and then moved to a white middle-class neighborhood. Mr. Miyano held a variety of jobs, mainly white-collar positions requiring business and managerial skills. In this respect, he fitted into the managerial/organizational class that proliferated during the expansion of the postwar political economy. Like other Japanese Americans who benefited from that period of prosperity, the Miyanos experienced some social mobility in the late 1950s. As a result, despite the fact that she attended a Catholic school in Japantown and a Japanese-language school, Miyano never really identified with the Japanese community during her adolescence.

Like many Japanese Americans, Miyano's parents trusted the electoral process and enforcement agencies like the FBI. Mr. Miyano felt leaders like former President Nixon were deserving of respect because of the important decision-making positions they held. Events such as Watergate, however, seemed to have made him much more critical of American politics and perhaps more liberal. Miyano would like to believe that some of the changes in her father's views also stemmed from her own political activism. Recalling her father's interest in her political involvement, she declared,

I knew he was interested because he went to the "Are You Yellow?" symposium at Berkeley. I was real surprised he dragged my mother to that. I didn't put any pressure on him to go, but I made it known that it was happening. He sat through the whole damn thing. He [also] came to the community forums that we had around the [Third World] strike and I'm sure there were times that he wished that I wasn't his daughter but he came.

The Miyanos stressed the importance of a college education for Linda. They did not, however, dictate what she should study or what type of career she should pursue. They were "basically non-directive" and quite supportive of her exploring and finding what was "right" for herself. In this respect, Miyano considered her parents "much more liberal than most other Japanese." Miyano's chances for attending college were quite good, especially after her family moved and she attended a public junior high school comprised of predominantly "upper-middle class Anglos and Jewish Americans." She was a good student and went on to a prestigious public high school that emphasized a college preparatory curriculum. Four years later she attended the local state university because it offered an innovative education in the humanities and social sciences.

Through her schooling and family socialization, Miyano began to develop her racial awareness. As a child she came into contact with blacks who had established their community in the neighborhood that the Japanese American community had occupied before World War II. While growing up, she became quite familiar with her mother's attitudes towards blacks:

> To some extent I was forced to, because my mother would talk, "Oh I don't want you to play with the *kurochan*, or *kuronbo* kids; and I knew that. I knew what those words meant, and what those words mean when you translate them superficially. I don't think they have any particular derogatory meaning, but the negative tone was transmitted.

Also, her interaction with her elementary school peers made her sensitive to her own ethnic background:

> I know when I was a kid, a lot of times I was taunted both by white kids and black kids. Ching, chong Chinaman; that whole business. It tended to happen more often with white kids.

Given these incidents and her mother's admonitions, she began to distinguish among racial groups.

For the most part, however, her awareness of racial differences was still quite undeveloped. She thought that "the world was Japanese and everybody else was non-Japanese." Her political awareness of what it meant to be "black" or what it meant to be "Asian" did not develop until she attended college in the late 1960s.

In the meanwhile, Miyano struggled with the question of personal identity. As a high school student, she adopted an "anti-Asian" perspective because she felt very uncomfortable with Asian "cliques." Becoming part of a clique simply because it was "the social thing to do" made little sense to her. She found it difficult to associate with the Chinese clique, probably due to the fact that there was very little in her past experience that would provide the basis for meaningful ties with other Asians. Since there were very few Japanese American students, that group did not provide a source of association either. For a time she was attracted to the "ruling clique," that group which was "heavily Jewish and upper middle class." They were the "gung-ho, rah-rah" types who ran for and got elected to student body offices. Although she gained acceptance into this clique, Miyano never felt she was completely part of it.

During her junior year, she began to "drift away" from the ruling clique and found that becoming a "loner" was a better way to resolve her problem of where to fit in. At this point, she made some Asian friends, but they, too, were loners who rejected Asian American groupings. During this period of drift, she gravitated towards the "artsy-craftsy types" and politically active students involved in the anti-war movement. At this time, when the United States was escalating the Vietnam War (1966–67), Miyano's political involvement was still minimal. She defined herself much more as a "quasi-hippy" who participated in "Synanon games" and hung around with students who had been defined as the class "weirdos."

Linda Miyano explained her drift towards the artsy-craftsy and political groups in terms of her desire to be "different." This was ironic, because her experience in elementary and junior high school made her feel that "being different was a liability." By the mid-1960s, she wanted to develop an identity as an individual, in spite of her Asian-ness. Thus the desire to be "unique and special" compelled her to associate with "weirdos" who were clearly defined as different, apart from any ethnic identification.

Rise of Racial Consciousness

The resolution of Miyano's identity problem occurred when she developed a racial and political consciousness as a student at a local university. During her freshman year she participated in an experimental program that included 60 students. They were allowed to explore topics and themes of personal interest rather than study the more conventional curriculum. Their loosely structured education included a core curriculum of individualized seminars focusing on a number of themes. Miyano chose the theme of "freedom," a heavy intellectual experience that complemented a growing political awareness emanating from the politicized ambience of the larger campus community and social environment.

In essence, Linda Miyano's politicization was a concentrated process that joined her academic activities with the intense political character of that historical moment. Alternative approaches to education and the formation of community and tutorial programs were some of the politically charged issues stimulating students to become intimately involved in determining the direction of their education. At the same time, the question of Black Studies and the retention of a Chicano professor at her university were "hot" issues that sparked student political activism. Students staged "sit-ins" in response to the Chicano professor's dismissal, to the question of removing ROTC from campus, and to Educational Opportunity Program (EOP) cutbacks. Miyano recalled her participation in the sit-in protesting EOP cutbacks:

> . . . it was the first sit-in I ever participated in. My parents were freaked out. They knew I was at the school and they knew that I was participating in this, and there were people getting busted and stuff, and I guess that was my first heavy political experience.

Miyano's political involvement in Third World student issues with a black student focus, in turn, deeply affected her racial consciousness and made her sensitive to her own ethnicity.

In the summer of 1968, Miyano became involved in the Asian American Political Alliance (AAPA), the first Asian American political organization on her college campus. This organization attracted several Asian American students who were concerned about such issues as the Vietnam War, the question of identity, and the need for a sense of community. The focal point for these interests, however, was the concern for a common racial identity. Students were seeking some agency through which they could express their social and political concerns as "Asian Americans."

The political sophistication among these activists varied, according to Miyano. Some were reading the "Little Red Book" and espoused Maoism. Others advocated Marxism-Leninism. Still others were searching for "community" and "identity." There were also others within the group who were dissatisfied with the orthodox Asian American lifestyle, with its emphasis on material acquisition, status, and mobility. They wanted alternatives.

For Miyano and others who shared her incipient political concerns, a political organization based upon the concept of an Asian American identity—one that united Chinese, Japanese, Koreans, and, later, Filipinos—

offered a vital mechanism for people who were struggling for social change. Though there were some clear differences within this organization, there was a consensus that Asian Americans should become involved collectively in the Asian American movement and develop greater solidarity with other people of color.

In the fall of 1968, Miyano participated in the Third World Liberation Front (TWLF) and the Third World Strike as a member of the Asian American Political Alliance. Among the various demands made by the TWLF was the establishment of a School of Ethnic Studies in which Black, La Raza, Native American, and Asian American Studies would be developed. While the formation of an Ethnic Studies and an Asian American Studies program had not originally been a major focus for Miyano and other AAPA members, she committed herself to the development of Asian American Studies once the TWLF demands became a reality. Those AAPA members who disagreed with the new emphasis on Ethnic Studies pursued "political party" type of work. Others, including Miyano, devoted their political energies to this issue because it offered a forum to continue their community work and to learn about Asian American history from an Asian American perspective. These perspectives reflected the thinking of Third World groups, particularly black activists, at that time. Miyano reflected:

> The whole sense was we need to learn about ourselves from our own point of view, get away from slave history. We took a lot of the rhetoric [of the time], and the themes were sort of almost borrowed from the blacks. It was important to do that. It was important to try to break down the traditional division between college and community, to develop a sense of ourselves. That's one thing that we did real consistently during the strike, to break down that sense [of division]. There were a lot of community people who participated in the strike. By the same token, . . . in our group, AAPA, we made genuine efforts to try to develop more community contacts . . ., and a lot of AAPA people later on did, in fact, go on to become very heavily involved in community organizations.

What appealed to Miyano was the notion of making the college accountable to the concerns of Third World communities and students, which was an important facet of the Ethnic Studies philosophy. Implicit in this philosophy was the idea that the campus could provide important work experience for students—to orient them to the problems and needs of their communities, to train them to return to their communities with skills which would benefit not only their people but also hasten the liberation of all Third World peoples.[3]

Changing Social Position

While the development of her racial consciousness and political style emerged from her generational position and the influence of the social movements of the 1960s, Miyano's entry into the labor market as a professional has also had a profound impact on her political style. In assessing her work and her life, she wondered whether her life was becoming too "compartmentalized" or whether she was simply going through a phase of her life cycle in which her concerns were becoming much "narrower and (more) self-enclosed." Now that she had become part of the work force, she found that the range of choices in her life was "diminishing." In contrast to her college years, her life had become much more routinized. She recalled fondly her student days, not because she was so happy then, but because they were "exciting" and "intense." Also, she had the feeling that "all things are possible, that all options are open to you." Although she thinks that possibility still exists in "an existential sense," it became considerably more difficult to retain that view once she completed school. This is extremely "disconcerting" to her because she feels that "time is running out."

Miyano thought that her emerging perspective stemmed from her abrupt transition from the excitement of the 1960s to the more mundane world of work. As a student, she thought "the revolution was around the corner" and she would "die trying to make the revolution happen." It was extremely difficult to think about being 30 years old. She had a "genuine conviction" that she would be "dead or completely burned out by 30." Now that she was approaching that age (at the time I interviewed her), Miyano thought that she would have to reevaluate her whole life plan, mainly because she had not "thought past 30."

It was not because Miyano lacked vision or foresight that she was facing this dilemma; it had more to do with the priorities she had established during the late 1960s and early 1970s. This was true of the line of work she had chosen:

> I became a legal services lawyer because it was progressive work. [Forget] making money and all that materialistic stuff. Now I'm finding I'm becoming more and more worried about those sorts of things. Other people who were not into social activism, that was never a problem, they had it mapped out. They chose, or they knew that they were going to go in X-line of work and that they were going to make X-amount of money by X-age. They would have a house and they had economic priorities. They were centered around economic progression.

Miyano's game plan was different. She was committed to social change. It had not occurred to her that her game plan did not consider that the "board might be longer or larger." She felt that the plans she had then might seem naive now; but they seemed so real at the time. In one sense, she had a vision of the world and the need to change it that did not include day-to-day realities she would have to face and cope with. Since then she has had to confront those realities and find out what it means to maintain her racial and political orientation in her work and day-to-day life.

Moving Towards a "Progressive" Political Style

When I interviewed her, Miyano's politics were in a state of transition. During the late 1960s and early 1970s she considered herself "a revolutionary," although she was not exactly sure what that meant. Her style of revolutionary activism included participation in protest actions and support for radical groups like the Black Panthers. Marxism-Leninism, however, did not suit her because it implied "a certain amount of doctrinaire inflexibility," but she candidly admitted that she did not think she had a clear understanding of Marxism. She was more comfortable with being "a socialist."

Miyano's style of activism included a rejection of the prevailing political style of Japanese Americans. This rejection was based on the way they had responded to internment. She believed for several years that the Nisei were cowards because "they had not done anything to resist." She could not comprehend how Japanese Americans, after being "kicked down," could then "volunteer to serve in the Army or do anything to help that country that had stripped them of all their civil liberties." Her definition of the Nisei was directly tied to the black liberation movement. "That was the model against which I judged the Nisei." Miyano believed that the Black Power movement had been attractive to her because it was "contemporary and much more." It was a "vital model" compared to the Japanese American tendency to accommodate and to endure (*gaman*). In retrospect, Miyano admitted that she "thought with her heart rather than her head." She saw political issues in their "starkest terms"; everything was "black and white, good and bad." She could not deal with "grays or permutations"; it was simpler to see things "in the most extreme terms." Since then, her view of the Nisei has become much more historical and sociological. Now she understands that their responses to racism were shaped by the prevailing social conditions of the times. She now feels that what was possible for Japanese Americans during the 1960s was very different from what had been possible for the second generation during World War II.

The central feature of Miyano's brand of radicalism was the "Asian American community," but her conception of community was not necessarily *gemeinschaft* in the sense of a highly cohesive and stable rural village.[4] She recognized that the traditional Japanese community had been comprised of institutions such as the Buddhist church. People who were part of this type of community generally attended a language school, belonged to a Japanese Boy or Girl Scout troop, social club, or a church. Those institutions were a central part of the "Japanese American experience." There were other Japanese Americans, however, who were "marginal" to this community either by circumstance or by choice. Because they never had a "community experience," their understanding of it was mostly intellectual.

Now the community had become even more diffuse because of the postwar economic integration that had taken place. Though this bothered Miyano, it did not mean she wanted to recreate the old community. On the contrary, community meant "getting Asians to see beyond difference and to see themselves as Asian American." Hers was now a more inclusive approach to community, one that went beyond Japanese Americans. It derived from her experience and from her political and historical understanding of the common basis of unity among Asian minorities.

In this respect, she felt that the Black Panther Party's theory of fusing Marxism and Third World liberation into a revolutionary nationalism gave her an important handle for developing an Asian American political consciousness. Political mobilization around race-oriented issues within the Japanese American community, for example, could eventually lead to a Third World and then a class perspective on social change.

When the 1960s ended, she no longer defined herself as a revolutionary. To her, revolutionaries built their lives around their political activities. She did not feel that she could structure her life in this way. Consequently, she wondered whether she had become a "liberal," because liberals were not "doctrinaire" and tended to be "pragmatic." Liberalism and pragmatism were both aspects of her political style. But at the same time she had problems with the liberal label because it was ambiguous. Liberals can be so "wishy-washy—not knowing what you want, not really knowing where you're going." And yet, her approach was not ambivalent. Miyano still believes that "a fundamental reordering of our economic system" is necessary before meaningful social change can occur. The issue is the means to be used. She will not work "to promote violent change," even though she suspects "it may take violence to effect the kind of change that would be considered revolutionary, at least within our lifetime."

One way to resolve the tension between her concern for fundamental social change through more practical politics and her rejection of violent revolutionary change is to define herself as a "progressive." This enables her to accept her involvement in ethnic and electoral forms of politics, while retaining the belief that fundamental social change in our economy and institutions is ultimately necessary. Miyano's progressive style seems to entail a two-stage approach to social change. Stage I is the more immediate: it calls for the integration of Asian Americans into all spheres of institutional life. Stage II is much more long range: it suggests that nonviolent structural change can be addressed only after racial integration has been accomplished.

Such an approach probably explains her interest in the politics of the Japanese American community and her participation with a community political organization designed to improve the welfare and status of Japanese Americans in her local community. It also helps us to understand why she supported reform-oriented politicians like Norman Mineta, the first Japanese American Congressman from the U.S. mainland, on the grounds that he had a sense of being "Asian" and was trying "to do good things for Asian Americans," and why she rejected S.I. Hayakawa as a conservative and eccentric person who was insensitive about the Japanese American experience. Hayakawa was originally a Canadian who was never sent to camp, but claims that internment was a blessing in disguise. His views about internment angered Miyano because they ignored the racist roots of internment. If she were a strict cultural nationalist, she could have supported Hayakawa. One might call her a liberal nationalist but this does not take into account her critical posture towards the electoral political process and her belief in the need for long-range structural change.

Her progressive ideological perspective clarifies why she felt that while the election of Mineta and Hayakawa reflected changes in American race relations, they did not mean that Japanese Americans were a "model minority." "Twenty-five years ago," she states, "those same folks could not have been elected, so I think it does reflect a lot more open-mindedness towards Japanese." However, such changes do not mean that Japanese Americans are a success story in American race relations, as many liberal scholars and journalists have suggested. When she was a student, she was aware of the "success theme in the literature." It was a mixed situation that she felt had generated a stereotypic image. She conceded that Japanese Americans had "overcome substantial obstacles and have 'out-whited' the whites in a lot of ways—higher educational level, relative economic affluence." But she knew from her own strategic position and observations that Japanese Americans had "paid" emotionally and "culturally" for what they have managed to achieve. She hypothesized that they must suffer from a higher incidence of stress-related illnesses such as ulcers. Such illnesses, she continued, were probably related to the racism they had endured and their strategies for coping with it. They had paid the price of "community breakdown" and had lost a great deal of respect for their ethnic heritage. In her view, these developments could be attributed to internment and the coerciveness of the integrationist idea that had compelled Japanese Americans "to close the door on their ethnicity."

Thus for Miyano "integration" was not a desirable model of race relations since it denied racial groups the chance to define their own social, cultural, and political priorities. She felt there was a need for ethnic history, cultural expression, and political consciousness. This had become all the more important for Miyano in light of her analysis that Japanese Americans were a "dying community." "Birth rates and immigration rates" were relatively low, while intermarriage rates were increasing. She was not against intermarriage; yet, she felt that in terms of "sheer numbers" and "concentration," the community was growing smaller. "Within the next couple of generations," she commented, "there won't be that many Japanese Americans who have a sense of being Japanese Americans" left.

Still, she believed that the Japanese in America have a heritage worth preserving and she wanted to see it continue. Miyano was "really proud to be Japanese American, not Japanese, but Japanese American," because that experience has been "special and unique." She reasoned that through learning history from a Japanese American perspective, through the development of cultural expressions and political struggles, a sense of community and a special identity could be kept alive.

On the other hand, she did not want to espouse a separatist or cultural nationalist solution either. Miyano thought that it was not desirable for Asians to be "real cliquish." They should be allowed "to function and work well within the mainstream society, but at the same time have a sense of what it means to be Japanese American." She seemed to be suggesting what sociologists call "cultural pluralism"—the option of simultaneously preserving ethnic group integrity with full institutional participation. But she contended that structural change would be necessary in order to achieve this kind of resolution.

Significance

Although Miyano is not a typical Sansei in the conventional sense, her experience informs us about the sociocultural changes impacting on her generational unit. Coming from a family that moved into the ranks of the "middle-class" in the postwar period, Miyano experienced a separation from the Japanese community during her adolescence. Socialized into a white middle-class world through her schooling, she encountered the contradiction of wanting to be "integrated" and finding that she did not fit. For racial and cultural reasons, Miyano attempted to carve out a unique identity by associating with "weirdos" and politically active students. However, this alternative did not seem to assuage her social alienation either.

The actual resolution to her sense of alienation occurred within the context of the social and political upheavals of the 1960s. The emergence of the Black Power movement and the Third World Liberation Front provided an appealing model for developing her own racial and political consciousness. An Asian American identity flowed from this awakening and led to her participation in Asian American Studies as well as student political activities within an emergent Asian American community.

A legal career became an attractive calling during the early 1970s because it offered the manifest opportunity to pursue her political goals of promoting social change and racial equality. It also seems to serve a latent function: Miyano has been able to secure some degree of job stability and satisfaction as a professional, often a key strategy used by Japanese Americans to deal with race relations. Of course, law was Miyano's own choosing, apart from parental pressures; and yet she seemed destined to become a professional, given her experience and family background.

Politics are still important to her and she sustains her commitment to it by practicing civil rights law. She is also involved with community political and professional groups concerned about the status of Japanese and Asian Americans. A one-time radical, her political orientation suggests a "progressive style"—a concern with immediate social changes through established institutions, but informed by an ideology that stresses the need for structural change. Miyano understands that racism is institutional; but she also recognizes that fundamental changes in the labor market, for example, would take time. In the interim, involvement in local politics makes sense to her.

Miyano's political transition, however, may be best understood in terms of her changing social and economic position. Work now occupies a major portion of her time and, in many ways, sets the rhythm of her life. Despite the satisfaction she receives from her job, she does not always control the process of her work. She is accountable to her supervisor and the realities of the cases that she handles. The legal system circumscribes the possibilities for exercising political creativity. Because she wants to balance her life with leisure and personal growth activities, she has only limited time outside of work for political acitivities that she might have considered in the past, for example, mass organizing around race and class issues, a strategy that some of her former contemporaries chose to adopt.

The stress that arises from the convergence of these political, professional, and personal dilemmas often compels politically committed attorneys to seek refuge in their private lives. One might criticize Miyano for pursuing a conventional profession, because the benefits and status she derives from her occupation pushes her towards the rejection of her 1960s ideals. This is a common issue discussed among critical observers of the Asian American movement. The way this issue has been framed, however, grossly simplifies the influence of the times.

While Miyano chose law as a means to serve her community and initiate social change, the *zeitgeist* stimulated her racial and political consciousness. The late 1970s, however, did not provide an ambience of a radical social movement. Because the spirit of the contemporary society had become politically conservative and economically constricted, Miyano had to adjust her political style and redirect her political energies. She reflected the "changes" that many activists had experienced and continued to experience in the wake of the emotionally tense and racially polarized 1960s. Thus she was compelled to grapple with some long-range issues concerning her future security. Hard economic realities had set in, issues that were not salient when she was coming of age. She realizes that she is responsible for herself and that social and financial stability are just as important as political change. By the late 1970s, the time for adhering to the ideals she had acquired as a student, which, though still vital to her, was basically over. Besides her deep concerns for social change, Miyano had to struggle with the politics of work and day-to-day life.

Concluding Remarks

The experiences of Fred Ichiyama and Linda Miyano suggest that, for both of them, the "recovery" of their ethnic identity was critically important. Both are Sansei in terms of their consciousness; but there is some question about whether they are Sansei in terms of birth order. Miyano's mother was an Issei from Japan, while Ichiyama's father, likewise, was an Issei. In this respect, their cases do not simply reflect a Hansenian "third-generation return." This recovery took place within a particular time and geographical context. The portraits of Ichiyama and Miyano indicate that to some extent "replication" took place. Both were influenced by Black Power militance and rhetoric, when they were grappling with their ethnic identity and seeking a more appropriate way to define themselves.

But their political involvement was definitely complex. Like many members of their generation who became activists, Ichiyama and Miyano were not simply moving along an assimilationist trajectory. The process of economic integration and incipient mobility experienced by the second generation, and improved international relations with Japan, did not necessarily mean that all would be well with the third generation. Rather, they experienced the subtle contradictions in terms of racial alienation and socioeconomic uncertainty. Facing such problems as dislocation, rejection, and drift, Ichiyama and Miyano were compelled to find social spaces that were not available in mainstream society, spaces in which they could rearticulate their identities, culture, and politics.

What was unique for people like Ichiyama and Miyano was that they found the model of the "black brother" to be far more vibrant and attractive than the ideal of the "yellow father." This Third World identification was a significant departure from the racial perspective of their parents, particularly Nisei leaders who seemed to have favored white leaders as their role models. The issue of identity was certainly more than a tension between "Americanization" and the concern for their ethnic culture and values. Developing a racial consciousness and embracing their ethnicity were clearly related to the way in which Ichiyama's and Miyano's life course intersected with the racial dynamics of the late 1960s.

Thus Ichiyama's and Miyano's political orientation paralleled those of black and Chicano youth who challenged the integrationist and accommodationist political styles of their community leaders and developed new political approaches to racial change. They viewed assimilation as a coercive process that stripped Japanese Americans of their ethnic heritage. To them, cultural pluralism and racial diversity were more desirable models of race relations because they legitimated the Asian experience in America.

The "community" and higher education also took on new meaning within the changing political orientation of Ichiyama and Miyano. The notion of "community" was not simply a concern for one's ethnic heritage, but also an important focus for political action. Political education and organizing at the community level were important objectives for both Ichiyama and Miyano. Higher education likewise became an arena for racial change rather than simply a vehicle for social mobility. Central to this project was the development of Asian American Studies. This is why Miyano devoted a great deal of her time and energy to such programs. Besides viewing Asian American Studies as an academic program that articulated an "Asian American perspective," she perceived the formation of Ethnic Studies programs, as did Ichiyama, as an important agency for mobilizing students as well as for "community enhancement."[5]

Besides focusing on Asian American issues, Ichiyama and Miyano shared with their racial minority counterparts—blacks, Chicanos, and Native Americans—the vision that Third World groups would eventually come together in one large movement to end the racial stratification in American society. By transcending racial and ethnic boundaries, their perspective contrasted with the more parochial views of their parents' generation. Their militance and radical approach to racial issues clearly contrasted with the views of second-generation individuals like Marshall Endo, and even with activists like Michi Nakada. Although political repression in the 1970s undermined the political movements and the possibilities for implementing such a vision, the events of the 1960s and the "great transformation" generated a new racial context in which Ichiyama and Miyano could develop a very different racial consciousness and political orientation as they came of age.

With their entry into the labor market, however, Ichiyama and Miyano experienced some changes. Whereas their generational location and the times were central to the development of their political orientation, both their work and the changing racial scene made it much more difficult for them to sustain the same level of political activism and commitment to social change. As a professional, Miyano can and does make room in her life for political involvement. Though now more pragmatic in her political orientation, she remains a progressive who maintains a critical consciousness on race issues.

Ichiyama faces a different situation. Being a worker affects what he can do on and off the job. He would like to remain involved in community affairs but his time is limited. Now, such economic realities as limited career opportunities are pivotal for Ichiyama. Though he would like to do more than maintain a livelihood, until he can find a job with career possibilities, it is not clear whether he will be able to resume his activism or community involvement. Still, Ichiyama retains his political consciousness and concerns about racial change, though he expresses them in different ways than before. They play a role in his personal interaction with fellow workers and friends. They also shape the way he now thinks about and relates to the larger society and the world around him.

What emerges from these sociological portraits of Ichiyama and Miyano is a qualitative understanding of the "progressive" Sansei experience. While they are not definitive, they do tell us about the racial and political dynamics operating in the lives of young Japanese Americans in the late 1960s and early 1970s. These portraits also show how they rearticulated their ethnic identity as they came of age, and, in turn, developed a political style oriented towards working for social change in their communities and racial change in the larger society.

Conclusion

FROM THE 1920S TO THE 1970S, JAPANESE AMERICANS HAVE explored and developed ways to make a meaningful place for themselves in American society. Their political styles were neither fixed nor unidimensional. Rather, they represented a rich political diversity that included a range of strategies, perspectives, and orientations that were not always rational or linear in development. At critical historical junctures marked by crisis and change, Japanese Americans actively assessed their economic, political, and racial circumstances, and their political and cultural resources. As individuals and as members of a group, they devised and improvised courses of action that best addressed their concerns or advanced their interests in their struggle for full participation in the larger society.[1] In this respect, their actions were not simply determined by cultural or structural imperatives. Rather, their personal decisions and collective actions were made within specific historical contexts where economic and political forces, as well as cultural and ideological realities, were at play. Thus the outcomes were not always to their choosing or their liking; as historical actors, their efforts to shape their destinies emerged from a complex of generational and racial processes and dynamics that intersected with their lives.

Racial and Generational Change

As our portraits have shown, distinctive generational cohorts of Japanese Americans came of age during periods of major social, cultural, and economic upheavals where shifting concepts of race have been a pivotal part of their experience. It has been within these changing historical contexts that various generations of Japanese Americans developed diverse and sometimes competing political styles where one in particular has come to characterize the predominant orientation for that generation.

Shortly after their entry to American society, various laws and policies, as well as the prevailing racial ideology, served to keep Japanese Americans in a subordinate position and limited the ways in which they pursued the benefits and privileges normally reserved for whites. Land laws, exclusion laws, the denial of citizenship, and occupational segregation were a fundamental part of the racial order preventing the Issei from amassing the "power resources" needed to protect their welfare and improve their social and economic position.[2] Without the vote, numbers, and political contacts, the Issei devised a defensive political style rather than a direct or confrontational one. This often took the form of using the law and the courts, and developing public relations tactics to advance their interests.[3] At the time, a rigid racial structure circumscribed what was possible for people of color and greatly limited their life chances.[4]

While institutional barriers such as the denial of citizenship assumed a formal/legal character for the Issei, the subtle and informal abridgment of their citizenship rights posed a different kind of racial situation for the older Nisei and Kibei who came of age in the 1920s and 1930s. Although citizens by birth, the Nisei and Kibei were still segregated from the social and economic mainstream. Attaining college degrees did not afford them access to "white-collar" work. Aside from having menial jobs, the Nisei were dependent on the Issei economy as their primary source of employment. In response, they struggled to determine how best to promote their interests and gain recognition as American citizens. Their actions, however, were linked to complex dynamics.

The international and domestic crises of the 1930s and the 1940s provided few economic opportunities for Japanese Americans and very little room to affirm their ethnicity. The deterioration of U.S.–Japan relations in the late 1930s and the impending war with Japan revived anti-Japanese sentiment on the Pacific Coast. Nisei leaders like Sakamoto and Akazuki were keenly aware of these international changes as they grappled with such problems as Japan's involvement in Manchuria. Although there were clear political differences between these two men, domestic racial tension that derived, in part, from international conflict placed them in the same racial position: both citizens and aliens of Japanese ancestry were deemed to be undesirable to American society. Within this context, Japanese Americans were compelled to distinguish themselves from Japanese nationals lest they be lumped together as subversive agents of the Japanese government. Any attempt at cultural identification with Japan made their loyalty to America suspect. From the viewpoint of white America, and within the context of the impending war with Japan, any expression of ethnic identity would have made their loyalty even more questionable.

Coupled with the crisis in international relations, the prevailing racial ideology of white America negated the ethnic possibilities open to the Nisei. As our life histories indicated, the views of older Nisei like James Sakamoto resonated with the prevailing ideology and followed the government in this time of crisis. Just as their faith in the American dream, "fair play," and the American way became important ideals undergirding their political outlook, so, too, did the traits embodied in the Protestant Ethic—individualism, self-restraint, progress, hard work, and the accumulation of wealth—impact their consciousness and behavior. By celebrating their American experience, many Nisei, like Mike Masaoka, hoped that the promise of America would be theirs.

Within this racial and political context, Japanese Americans could not publicly affirm their ethnicity or practice ethnic politics. To avoid the charge of ethnic bloc voting, a practice used routinely by European American ethnic groups, the JACL emphasized nonpartisanship in all political matters. In contrast to older Nisei and Kibei political activists like Ruth Kurata and Ken Akazuki, the bulk of the second generation came of age during the wartime crisis and had few opportunities to be exposed to the emerging diversity in political thinking or to participate in the political life of the community. Unlike their white ethnic counterparts, Nisei were not positioned to deal systematically with the oppression that they encountered shortly after the bombing of Pearl Harbor.[5]

In response to Executive Order 9066 and the actual camp experience, the Nisei manifested a variety of political responses. While there were individual instances of protest and legal challenges to the constitutionality of E.O. 9066, the large majority of Japanese Americans practiced some form of "constructive cooperation" or "critical cooperation," strategies that were articulated by the JACL and Nisei progressives, respectively. In the camps, there were instances of mass protest and overt resistance. However, the WRA repressed political protest and rendered it illegitimate by punishing and stigmatizing those who resisted internment. Under such circumstances, the efforts of Japanese Americans to prove to the American public that they were, in fact, loyal American citizens converged with their obedience to the law and ethnic cultural values, and further resulted in the submersion of their ethnic identity.

In the immediate postwar years, the JACL emerged from the wartime crisis as the principal leader of the Japanese American community. For the most part, Nisei progressives and other activists were marginalized and were not a viable political alternative to JACL leaders, like Mike Masaoka, who solidified their position through their legislative efforts and campaign to build the JACL into a national organization. As the only political "game in town," the JACL continued to practice a political style that had been forged during the wartime crisis but continued to reflect the tenor of the times. Their strategy for securing citizenship for the Issei through the passage of the 1952 McCarran-Walter Immigration Act exemplified how their approach dovetailed with a conservative domestic and international racial and political climate.

Concurrently, many of the younger Nisei who came of age during and immediately after World War II varied in political style. As new economic opportunities and political possibilities arose, and racial tensions lessened somewhat for Japanese Americans, the political thinking and perspectives of younger Nisei like Marshall Endo and Michi Nakada revealed changing points of views and orientations. In many ways, both contrasted with their older Nisei leaders and counterparts who came of age in the pre-World War II period. Younger Nisei had access to new forms of economic opportunity in the late 1950s and early 1960s that contrasted with a former reliance on ethnic enterprise. A changing political economy and improving relations between the United States and Japan set a positive stage for domestic race relations; the Korean War precipitated an expansion in the economy that was sustained by the shift to a cybernated "warfare–welfare" economy. Coupled with a repressive Cold War milieu, these political and economic shifts set a context in which Japanese Americans took advantage of new economic opportunities.

Within this changing political economy, the shifting position of Marshall Endo contributed to the development of individual solutions to racial problems. His career transition from professional to petty entrepreneur affirmed the values of individualism, law and order, independence, and the desire for assimilation. Rather than supporting racially based policies, Endo emphasized competence, individual effort, and hard work as the proper approach to race advancement. Yet, such experiences as internment made him sensitive to the problems facing blacks. Also, the persistence of blatant and subtle forms of discrimination made Endo receptive to community involvement and ethnic politics, and kindled a desire to promote racial integration. Caught in this paradoxical situation, he took a "middle of the road" position like many Japanese Americans who adopted a mixed stance towards racial relations in the 1950s.

In contrast, Michi Nakada personified a more liberal style indicative of the progressive orientation exhibited by Nisei and Kibei activists in the late 1930s. While there certainly were ideological variations among these Nisei, Nakada's values and political sensibilities suggest that the younger members of the second generation were neither homogeneous in their political thinking nor uniform in their approach to race issues. She shared with other political activists the fact that she was a minority voice within her community at a time when the political situation did not favor more widespread and collective involvement. It is not surprising, then, that

Nakada and others like her found common political ground with the younger generation of activists.

By adopting a defensive and often conservative style emphasizing the law and the courts, hard work, and a gradualist approach to racial change, the political orientation and practice of Nisei leaders coincided with the Issei in the pre– and post–World War II decade. The Nisei, including the Kibei, also debated differences among themselves as they struggled in various ways to improve their position within a society where white racial privilege predominated. At the same time, the formation of their political styles showed that their choices were not always freely chosen. Within specific historical settings marked by racial and generational changes, activists within each generational group struggled to determine how best to promote their interests and achieve racial equality without reprisal. The possibilities for militancy, protest, and conflict were few. The legal and informal denial of citizenship, the prevailing ideology of white America, and the tenor of international relations set the tone for what was politically possible.

Rearticulation and the Development of New Racial Affinities

As they came of age during the social and cultural turbulence of the 1960s and 1970s, Japanese American youth like Linda Miyano developed a very different political orientation in their respective cultural and organizational spaces. As part of the Asian American movement, Miyano and other activists introduced new perspectives and strategies for dealing with their identity and position in American society, and captured the imagination of others, like Fred Ichiyama, who shared their generational position.[6]

Whether or not they functioned as individuals or members of larger groups and organizations, their efforts challenged the prevailing political wisdom of their parents' generation, especially the Nisei response to the internment experience; and they challenged the authority of American institutions in such arenas as higher education. While not everyone of their generation agreed with or supported their political orientation, these activists, who were largely Sansei, played a major role in shaping the discourse of the entire generation and prompted the larger Japanese American community to reexamine its own political orientation. In fact, various Nisei have acknowledged the important role that Sansei activists have played in voicing racial issues of concern to the community and advocating social change.[7]

Through the development of Asian American studies programs, the formation of alternative community organizations, and the consolidation of Asian American networks, Sansei activists simultaneously rearticulated their individual and group identities to embrace the possibilities represented in the notion of Asian American. Sharing a common generational location with their Chinese, Filipino, and Korean American peers, Sansei activists affirmed their experience to be an integral part of the broader Asian American experience. In this sense, they were not simply a coalition of leaders representing common interest groups, but diverse individuals emerging from common cultural and racial experiences that were crystallized in terms of an Asian American identity.

Thus Japanese American youth from diverse experiences coalesced to forge a new sense of community and cohesion that paralleled and overlapped with the more indigenous communities that were rooted in the pre–World War II era. Also, individuals who were either isolated or alienated from the Japanese American community found these alternatives ways of reconnecting with their ethnicity through the movement to be much more meaningful than having to adhere to norms and practices that previously governed community life. This change posed a marked contrast to the immediate post–World War II years where the racial hostility facing Japanese Americans was still intense, and Nisei and Sansei alike disregarded their ethnicity or handled it privately.[8]

The proliferation of a broader Asian American identity among third-generation Japanese Americans also signaled an important expansion in their racial awareness as they recast their sense of identity and community. Forming a Third World consciousness during the "great transformation" of the 1960s and 1970s, Japanese American youth like Linda Miyano and Fred Ichiyama defined themselves as members of a racially oppressed group. Support for their Third World counterparts and their attraction to the political style and ideas of blacks emphasizing self-determination and community control suggested that a different kind of adjustment was taking place against this historical backdrop marked by "the disorganization of the dominant racial ideology."[9] Although Nisei activists of the pre–World War II period acknowledged the common position between Japanese Americans and "Negroes," and emphasized the need to extend their political understanding of race relations beyond the confines of the Japanese community, they had a limited relationship to black culture and politics.[10] The Nisei generally accepted the prevailing ideology of white America towards blacks and other racial groups, despite their own subordination.[11] During the 1960s, however, Fred Ichiyama and Linda Miyano represented other individuals who became far more empathetic to blacks, Chicanos, and Native Americans in comparison to their parents' generation. Their interest in and ability to relate to black issues through black literature and the Black Power movement were important in the development of their own racial consciousness.

Even prior to the Black Power movement, many Sansei within the Japanese American community identified with "soul" music and used forms of black English to express themselves.[12] In many ways, this form of cultural connectedness prefigured an incipient political awareness and solidarity. The 1960s and 1970s legitimized the alternative of identifying with the black experience as a form of resistance to and protest against "anglo-conformity." The ideological thrust of black politics and celebration of black culture challenged the hegemony of white American culture, and provided an alternative cultural space where Japanese Americans rearticulated their identity and their relations to black Americans and other racial groups. It also became, in part, an impetus for Japanese American youth to develop their own forms of musical and artistic expression.

Generational Convergence

The political and racial transformations of the 1960s simultaneously produced a political space enabling Sansei activists to align themselves with Nisei and Kibei who practiced a progressive political style and espoused similar concerns. The intergenerational linking that resulted from this period of protest and movement for racial equality reconnected Japanese Americans with the struggles and the unresolved debates that occupied Nisei activists, intellectuals, and artists in the 1930s about their position and role in American life. Equally important, second-generation Japanese Americans who did not fit the main currents of the Nisei generation began to express their social and political concerns during this period of racial destabilization and political change. As Nisei and Sansei shared new cultural and political spaces enabling them to discuss and expand upon previous notions of identity, community, and political orientation, they forged a unity that had been previously absent.

The successful campaign to repeal Title II of the 1950 Internal Security Act is one illustration of how politically conscious Nisei who were not a part of the 1960s generation played a mobilizing role within the community.[13] Nisei activists were vitally concerned about the provisions contained in the Act that allowed for the imprisonment of American citizens in concentration camps similar to those built to house Japanese Americans during World War II. Together with Sansei activists, these Nisei sought to educate the Japanese American community about the Act and the need to mobilize in order to rescind it.[14]

Likewise, the campaign to clear Iva Toguri d'Aquino was also a cross-generational effort spearheaded by such Nisei leaders as Dr. Clifford Uyeda and Raymond Okamura and several Sansei.[15] A Nisei stranded in Japan during World War II, Toguri was tried and convicted of treason in 1949 for her wartime role as a broadcaster for Radio Tokyo.[16] Although she was coerced by the Japanese government to broadcast American music to American troops and was one of several English-speaking announcers involved, the U.S. government accused Toguri of being "Tokyo Rose," a name invented by American service men to depict those women who broadcast over Japanese-controlled radio. As a result of her conviction, Toguri automatically lost her American citizenship, and was also fined $10,000 and sentenced to 10 years in prison. After completing roughly 6 years of her prison term, she was released in 1956 and immediately faced deportation by the Immigration Service. With the assistance of her attorney, Wayne Collins, Toguri successfully challenged deportation. After two unproductive attempts to secure a presidential pardon in 1954 and 1968, the incipient movement that arose in 1975 ultimately led to her full and unconditional pardon in 1977.

While a few Japanese Americans were interested in the case, most ignored the Tokyo Rose issue at the outset because it was too close to their wartime experience and much too controversial.[17] Taking refuge in their personal lives after experiencing internment, Japanese Americans did not want to take any risks or "rock the boat" in any way that might jeopardize their interests or status. Even the JACL avoided the issue until the political climate was more permissive. However, after the committee to aid Iva Toguri formed in 1975 and other groups including white veterans backed her cause, many more Japanese Americans extended their support as they sensed a more politically conducive climate.[18] Besides providing the impetus and persevering with the pardon effort, respected Nisei leaders like Uyeda lent credibility to the committee's efforts within and outside the Japanese American community.

The redress and reparations movement also reflected a multigenerational character and a diverse group of leaders who espoused competing views, advocated different strategies, and appealed to varying constituencies.[19] Initially, the Old Guard did not favor seeking redress and reparations, and especially questioned the validity of seeking monetary restitution. In contrast, younger Nisei like Edison Uno, who came of age in the late 1940s and 1950s, assumed an important political role within the Japanese community together with their Sansei counterparts as the redress movement brought generations together both as a political and a cultural project. The common concern to win redress and reparations, despite dividing into at least three distinctive and often competing political trajectories, brought generations and interests together in a loose coalition to advance the movement, and in the process of doing so gave Nisei the opportunity to share their historical memory about the camp experience with the Sansei.

ing different generations together, the redress and repa-
assuaged internal generational splits and gave rise to a
;ive sense of community. The "reassessment of the Nisei
;ers and draft resisters during the wartime period and the
,on given to them by many former hostile Nisei" are per-
of this incipient détente within the community.[20] These
internal political shifts also reflected new internal political alignments and
voices that were largely repressed as a result of the internment experience
itself.

Thus, as the experiences of Japanese Americans between 1920 and
1970 have shown, their efforts to make a place for themselves in American
society have not simply been a linear process in which they move from the
position of racial outsider to mainstream insider, nor do their actions corre-
spond neatly with the view that generational progression necessarily coin-
cides with the process of assimilation. I want to emphasize that their efforts
have been part of a complex process where intragenerational conflict and
intergenerational collaboration have arisen in response to changing historical circumstances.

Emergent and Changing Nature of Japanese American Political Styles

As we move towards the next century, it is interesting to speculate
about the possibilities that the political style of Japanese Americans may
take. Most ethnicity-based studies have approached this issue by posing
such binary alternatives as assimilation or pluralism, although a recent
study suggests that Japanese Americans are moving along the dual trajectories of structural assimilation and ethnic solidarity.[21] It is certainly possible that as individuals and as a group they will approach the larger society
in assimilationist and/or pluralist terms. Yet, the internal political realities
of Japanese American community life have become much more complex.
Sansei activism and the political struggles with which they were involved
during the late 1960s and 1970s were not episodic or incidental, but rather
phenomena that crystallized and gave rise to a new political mosaic within
the Japanese American community. The success of the redress and reparations movement, for example, has certainly generated a sense of political
empowerment as to what a small minority group can achieve during difficult times. Ironically, this success has also created a vacuum in that there is
no longer a central issue to galvanize Japanese Americans as they face the
challenge of regrouping themselves once again on some kind of common
ground.[22] But, it also indicates that Japanese Americans now possess a variety of political and cultural resources that may have a bearing on the kind
of political styles that will emerge. Rather than attempt to forecast what

may transpire, it might be more appropriate to consider what implications a racial-generational perspective has for Japanese Americans as their own position changes and they face the complexities of a changing social and political climate.

In this study, a racial-generational approach revealed the emergent quality of Japanese American political life and ability of Japanese Americans to transform their orientation as new issues arise and historical circumstances change. Indeed, a variety of social indicators suggest that they are in a period of transition and no longer possess the same cultural affinities and economic interests, among others, that had previously helped sustain ethnic community ties. Currently, the "racial residue" that is resurfacing within the context of Asian immigration and the diversification and expansion of new Asian American communities affects all Japanese Americans, despite one's subjective disposition. Coupled with the rise of racial tensions and the movement to reestablish white racial privilege that negatively impacts all racial groups, these developments may again compel Japanese Americans to grapple with the personal significance of their ethnic identity and affiliations, as well as rethink their orientation in the realm of institutional politics.

Thus we cannot assume that the future political style or prospects of Japanese Americans are contingent on the "assimilation" of the fourth generation, *Yonsei,* or the persistence of ethnicity among them. It is very possible in this period of social and political change for a new set of activists and leaders to emerge and new political styles to take shape. Correspondingly, we must keep in mind the political and cultural legacies of the 1970s and 1980s that include the collaborative efforts across generational lines and a heightened consciousness about the racial, class, and gender realities in our society. Both sets of contingencies may come into play as Japanese Americans enter the next century.

The Legacy of the 1970s: Formation of New Spheres of Community and a Cultural Intelligentsia

Unlike the early post–World War II period where there was only one central leadership and organization, today there are many clusters of leaders, community organizations, and a cultural intelligentsia that play a significant role within a community whose spheres of life have become far more intricate and diverse. Alternative community organizations that sprang up in the 1970s and often coexisted with traditional community organizations have now become an established part of the community. Care and nutrition programs for the elderly, legal services, cultural centers, and cultural resources and programs are but a few examples. Also, progressive leaders who emerged from the movement period have taken leadership positions within the larger community and are now active in the political mainstream at the local, regional, and national levels. These newer community institutions and leaders are potential resources for mediating future political action.

The formation of umbrella organizations that have an Asian American and multiracial focus and encompass Japanese American organizations and networks is another important outgrowth of the 1970s. National and local organizations such as the Asian American Education and Legal Defense Fund, Asian Pacific Americans for Higher Education, and the Asian Law Caucus provide new structures for Japanese Americans to interact with other Asian Americans and have become a basis for Asian American political action.[23] This new and broader sphere of community life provides yet another path for Japanese Americans to affirm their ethnic identity and reconnect with their ethnic community.

Besides having new community organizations and leaders that make up new community spheres, Japanese Americans are now part of a cadre of Asian American professionals and intellectuals who inform community politics and impact a range of institutional arenas in which they work. Asian American faculty in Ethnic Studies and the more conventional disciplines have helped to redefine the nature of the broader Asian American experience and the critical issues facing the Japanese American community.[24] Through their teaching, research, and writing, they offer a rich and textured understanding of the Asian and Japanese American experience that was missing for Linda Miyano and Fred Ichiyama when they came of age. As a result, younger generations will have access to a broader knowledge base about themselves and their communities.

On the cultural front, there are artists, musicians, journalists, writers, and media professionals who occupy a new cultural space where issues and perspectives are shared and disseminated to both the community and the larger society.[25] Also, there are other cultural workers who are active in shaping new political alternatives. A number of ethnic-based historical societies, bookstores, professional associations, and community projects have become organizational and institutional sites where Japanese American culture and politics intersect and assume new possibilities.[26] In this sense, there is once again a lively cultural politics going on among Japanese Americans themselves through which they can continue to define themselves and their relations to Asian Americans and other racial groups.

On the electoral political front, it is interesting to note the political transition taking place where former Sansei movement activists are now engaged in the electoral political arena and using their grass roots and community-based organizing skills to promote racial change and social justice. Against a conservative political backdrop and retrenchment on civil rights, old movement activists who were involved in revolutionary party building have now directed their political energies to progressive aspects of electoral politics. Others are involved in community-based organizations and remain active in a wide range of struggles that focus on anti-Asian violence and Japan bashing, media racism, equal employment opportunity, and institutional realms where Japanese Americans continue to seek full and equal participation.[27]

While some have drifted away from the ideological concerns that once informed their political orientation, many others have maintained the political values that they developed then and remain committed to achieving racial equality and social justice for all oppressed groups. What has changed is their economic and social location. As professionals, managers, and technical workers, the time available for political organizing is far more limited that it was two decades ago. Activists of the 1970s generational cohort are older and struggle to balance their political and personal lives. They also confront the dual challenges presented by new arenas in which they work and the task of forging new strategies that address the racial issues and the political conditions of the times. Ironically, these activists may be viewed as reproducing the electoral political tendencies of their Nisei predecessors. What sets them apart, however, is that their progressive perspectives around race, class, and gender continue to guide their work.

At the same time, many Japanese Americans have little or no ties to the networks of professionals, artists, and scholars that formed during the 1960s and 1970s. Rather than engage in these new spheres of community, they favor more privatized lives and diverse social affiliations where ethnicity is also a private matter if it comes into play. Having benefited from social and economic opportunities that arose in the post–World War II period, these mostly younger Japanese Americans have been afforded the position to make such choices, whereas a retreat into private life was not necessarily an option for the older generations of Japanese Americans. This distinctive response to the current period when juxtaposed with the existing array of political styles could make for some interesting community debates around the strategy and direction of Japanese American ethnic politics.

New Generational Realities

Currently, a new generation of Japanese Americans is coming of age that is not just composed of *Yonsei*. While such generational designations as Nisei, Sansei, and Yonsei are still phenomenologically significant within Japanese American culture, one cannot simply assume that the traditional generational designations and their use as analytical categories are still appropriate for this new generational cohort.[28] Now represented in much greater numbers are young second-generation Japanese Americans, *shin Nisei,* whose *shin Issei* parents emigrated to the United States after World War II. Moreover, there is an increasing number of mixed-race and mixed-ethnic youth who are beginning to constitute a critical mass and whose experiences have been quite diverse. These new groupings now make up an increasingly complex and differentiated Japanese American population.

While many of these youth may define themselves as Japanese Americans and share a common generational location with their younger Sansei and Yonsei counterparts, they are linked to the Japanese American community in diverse ways and their experiences and understandings of what it means to be Japanese American seem to vary. Most within this generational cohort have grown up and have attended schools in suburban communities that are primarily white. Fewer seem to be products of "intact" communities whose institutions and practices were grounded in the Issei and Nisei legacy. Except through family ties and networks, ethnicity is not always salient in their early lives. Encounters with racism and an awareness of racial issues is generally limited as well. Several shin Nisei I have interviewed have even intimated how they often rejected their ethnic identity and community ties in their earlier youth in favor of Anglo-conformity.

Among mixed-race Japanese Americans similar issues prevail. Their cultural and racial experiences are certainly not uniform by any means. Some have a solid sense of their ethnic identity and strong ties to ethnic communities, while others do not. Some speak Japanese fluently and have retained their Japanese heritage, while others are far more acculturated and have retained very little of their ethnic values and traditions. Due to critical internal social and racial differences that have shaped their experiences, many have voiced questions about their acceptance in a larger Japanese American community or their ambivalence about belonging. This is understandable given the fact that many members of the older generations seem to retain a very narrow conception of the Japanese American that favors "ethnic purity," and consequently, have had difficulty embracing mixed-race Japanese Americans. Thus, many prefer to carve out their own sense of community among those who share their position and experience.

A pivotal feature for many members of this new generational cohort that may have a bearing on their future ethnic alignments and political style is their student experience. The experiences of Asian American undergraduate students at U.C. Berkeley reveal a set of racial dynamics that seem to be transforming the nature of ethnic affiliations on campus.[29] Moving from high school to the university, their racial and ethnic experiences change somewhat dramatically. Often viewed and characterized in group terms, Asian American students are subject to a racialization process in which other students often define them as a homogeneous bloc and fail to recognize the internal diversity within the Asian American population. They are generally viewed in "model minority" terms and often treated as if they were cut from the same cultural cloth. More disturbing, they report that the racial incivilities and hostilities that Asian Americans experience in the larger society are problems that they encounter at a micro-level on campus.[30]

While experiencing a changing sense of group position vis-à-vis the various ethnic constituencies that make up the campus population, Asian American students undergo an interesting corollary process in which they form ethnic affiliations despite coming from diverse ethnic backgrounds and social experiences. Through a cultural reawakening, prompted partly by racialization, many students have developed an interest in their ethnic roots and its implications for their own ethnic identity. For some, it appears to be merely a stage in their personal and intellectual development where ethnicity will be primarily symbolic.[31] But for others it plays a significant role in shaping their social networks, forming linkages with their community, and thinking about the future. Unlike the 1960s and 1970s where larger social and political movements were a galvanizing force for Asian Americans, current racial conditions on campus seem to lend themselves to the formation of strong ethnic constituencies that serve to crystallize and affirm ethnic ties and cultural values for those whose ethnicity has not been a salient feature of their youth; the legitimacy accorded to ethnic group life also provides a source of support and affiliation for other students who bring with them strong ethnic community attachments.

At first glance, we might expect a different scenario for Japanese American students at U.C. Berkeley. Given their decreasing numbers relative to the overall Asian American undergraduate population, we might have anticipated that there would not be a critical mass to maintain their ethnic cohesiveness. Yet, the students I interviewed have recounted experiences that resonate with their Asian American counterparts. They report that Japanese American students, for the most part, are concerned about the issues of race and ethnicity, especially in connection with the political realities surrounding the relations between the United States and Japan. Besides exploring these issues through relevant academic courses, they join student groups and clubs that provide an ethnic locus for gathering together. The Japanese American student organization on campus gives them an opportunity to interact with other Japanese Americans from diverse generational backgrounds and to explore their ethnic culture. Seemingly, the shin Nisei and Issei, who speak Japanese and have strong ties to Japanese culture, are accorded high cultural status by their more Americanized counterparts. In contrast to the pre–World War II era, this is an interesting cultural reversal considering the fact that Nisei who were Americanized had higher status than their Nisei and Kibei counterparts who exhibited a strong Japanese cultural style and orientation. In some respects, this signals a greater cultural fluidity for these students that is linked to economic globalization and the corresponding transnational realities where knowledge of Japanese adds to one's cultural capital and makes one a more competent world citizen.

Thus many Japanese American youth, within the changing context of higher education, seem to be crystallizing their ethnic identities or negotiating its meaning as they confront the binary options that are often presented to them in the form of "ethnicity" or "mainstream." In such a racialized context, they must determine the nature of their ethnic alignments. At the same time, broadening the span of their ethnic affiliations in new and different ways seems to be a distinct possibility. Through various forms of dialogue and debate about multiculturalism and diversity in higher education, and interethnic contact among Asian American students, they are developing personal and group relations that prefigures a more enduring form of pan-Asian interaction, which, at a political level, is a more complicated issue.[32] From this position, Japanese American youth occupy a positive space to develop a "cultural competency" that will enable them to navigate diverse social, racial, and ethnic situations.[33] Mixed-race and mixed-ethnic Japanese Americans have discussed and organized themselves around such issues. In this sense, ethnic ties can exceed a zero sum situation or extend itself beyond a duality where structural assimilation and ethnicity coexist.[34] Rather, multiethnic and multiracial, mixed-ethnic and mixed-racial possibilities that allow for both the retention and expansion of ethnic specific affiliations may be realities for this new generational cohort.

Regardless of their educational situation, this new generation of Japanese Americans, despite its internal variations, share a common generational location as it comes of age at a time when the racial landscape is changing, the economy is in trouble, and the relations between the United States and Japan have been uncertain at best. In California, the recent passage of Proposition 187 and the movement to dismantle affirmative action have triggered widespread debate within the state and the country around the issue of race. These issues certainly underscore an increasingly conservative racial climate where racial stereotyping, scapegoating, and outright racial violence have increased against a backdrop of anti-Japan bashing that makes many Japanese Americans wary of their current circumstances.[35]

Equally important is the way in which the media have situated Japanese Americans within the context of contemporary race relations. Because the imagery and discourse on race have been cast largely in terms of black and white, Japanese Americans have been rendered "invisible." When Japanese Americans, as part of the larger aggregation of Asian Americans, are given attention, they have been strategically utilized to challenge race-conscious policies and the political efforts of African Americans and others to promote racial change. Their depiction as the "model minority" is an illustration of this situation.

Given the shifting nature of race within this larger context, this younger generational cohort is poised to reassess the political styles of previous generations and, in the process, may develop a new vision and orientation that rearticulates the basis of ethnic affiliation among Japanese Americans and the meaning attached to contemporary Japanese American life itself. From this new generational grouping could also spring new and competing political styles that reshape those established by Sansei leaders who emerged from the 1970s.

Ultimately, Japanese Americans, themselves, must come to terms with their political legacy and the multiple paths before them. Current circumstances, however, make this a formidable challenge. Incipient interracial, gender, and generational differences may further fragment the community, and those who have experienced significant social mobility may retreat further into personal life. The media also continues to represent Japanese Americans in ways that superimpose a definition that is not of their own making. Still, matters of personal and group identity, community, and full citizenship, among others, are not solely contingent upon the external forces that have previously had such major historical impact. Japanese Americans are at a critical juncture where they can make their "political history."[36] The combined features and shared experience of all generations of Japanese Americans can provide a basis for new "racial projects" that are simultaneously ethnic specific, pan-Asian, and multiracial.[37] The possibilities are open as we move towards the twenty-first century.

Notes

Introduction

1. William Petersen, *Japanese Americans: Oppression and Success* (New York: Random House, 1971); Harry H.L. Kitano, *Japanese Americans: Evolution of a Subculture*, 2nd ed. (Englewood Cliffs, NJ: Prentice-Hall, 1976); Gene N. Levine and Darrel Montero, "Socioeconomic Mobility Among Three Generations of Japanese Americans," *The Journal of Social Issues* 1973;20:33–48; Darrel Montero, *Japanese Americans: Changing Patterns of Ethnic Affiliation over Three Generations* (Boulder: Westview Press, 1980).

2. William Petersen, "Success Story: Japanese American Style," *New York Times Magazine*, 9 January 1966.

3. Ibid., and Daniel Okimoto, *An American in Disguise* (New York: Walker, Weatherhill, 1971), 148–149.

4. "Success Story: Outwhiting the Whites," *Newsweek*, 21 June 1971. Also see Ronald O. Haak, "Co-Opting the Oppressors: The Case of the Japanese Americans," *Transaction*, October 1970, 23–31.

5. Nathan Glazer and Daniel P. Moynihan, *Beyond the Melting Pot: The Negroes, Puerto Ricans, Jews, Italians, and Irish of New York City* (Cambridge: M.I.T. Press, 1963); Oscar Handlin, *The Uprooted,* 2nd ed. (Boston: Little, Brown and Co., 1973); Thomas Sowell, *Ethnic America: A History* (New York: Basic Books, 1981). Also see Okimoto, *An American in Disguise*, 173, for a discussion about his socialization as an American.

6. Harry Kitano, "Japanese Americans on the Road to Dissent," in *Seasons of Rebellion*, Joseph Boskin and Robert Rosenstone, eds. (New York: Holt, Rinehart and Winston, 1972) 93–113; Minako K. Maykovich, *Japanese American Identity Dilemma* (Tokyo: Waseda University Press, 1972); Paul Wong, "The Emergence of the Asian-American Movement," *Bridge* 1972;2:33–39; Karen Umemoto, "'On Strike!' San Francisco State College Strike, 1968–1969: The Role of Asian American Students," *Amerasia Journal* 1989;15(1):3–41; Yen Le Espiritu, *Asian American Panethnicity: Bridging Institutions and Identities* (Philadelphia: Temple University Press, 1992); William Wei, *The Asian American Movement* (Philadelphia: Temple University Press, 1993); Amy Uyematsu, "The Emergence of Yellow Power in America," in *Roots: An Asian American Reader,* Amy Tachiki, Eddie Wong, and Franklin Odo, eds. (Los Angeles: UCLA Asian American Studies Center, 1971), 9–13.

7. See Ling-chi Wang, "The ABC's of Asian American Studies," *Asian American Review* 1975;2(1):26–43; and Mike Murase, "Ethnic Studies and Higher Education for Asian Americans," in *Counterpoint: Perspectives on Asian America*, Emma Gee, ed. (Los Angeles: University of California, Asian American Studies Center, 1976), 205–223, for discussions about the early development and role of ethnic studies and Asian American Studies. Also see Sucheng Chan and Ling-chi Wang, "Racism and the Model Minority: Asian-Americans in Higher Education," in *The Racial Crisis in American Higher Education*, Philip G. Altbach and Kofi Lomotey, eds. (Albany: State University of New York Press, 1991), 43–67; and Michael Omi, "It Just Ain't the Sixties No More: The Contemporary Dilemmas of Asian American Studies," in *Reflections on Shattered Windows,* Gary Y. Okihiro et al., eds. (Pullman, WA: Washington State University Press, 1988), 31–36.

8. Umemoto, "On Strike!"; Espiritu, *Asian American Panethnicity*; Wei, *The Asian American Movement*.

9. For a discussion of these facets of the Asian American movement, see Espiritu, *Asian American Panethnicity*; Wei, *The Asian American Movement*; and Glenn Omatsu, "The 'Four Prisons' and the Movements of Liberation: Asian American Activism from the 1960s to the 1990s," in *The State of Asian America: Activism and Resistance in the 1990s,* Karin Aguilar-San Juan, ed. (Boston: South End Press, 1994), 19–69.

10. See Roger Daniels, "The Japanese," in *Ethnic Leadership in America*, John Higham, ed. (Baltimore: Johns Hopkins University Press, 1978), 36–63, regarding the accommodationist nature of Nisei leadership.

11. Raymond E. Wolfinger, Martin Shapiro, and Fred I. Greenstein, eds., *Dynamics of American Politics,* 2nd ed. (Englewood Cliffs, NJ: Prentice-Hall, 1980), 11.

12. Then existent accounts include Alfred H. Song, "Politics and Policies of the Oriental Community," in *California Politics and Policies,* E.P. Dvorin and A.J. Misner, eds. (Reading: Addison Wesly, 1966), 387–411; Kitano, *Japanese Americans;* Gene N. Levine and Colbert Rhodes, *The Japanese American Community: A Three Generation Study* (New York: Praeger, 1981); Vincent N. Parrillo, "Asian Americans in American Politics," in *America's Ethnic Politics,* Joseph S. Roucek and Bernard Eisenbert, eds. (Westport, Conn.: Greenwood Press, 1982), 89–112. Also see Don T. Nakanishi, "Asian American Politics: An Agenda for Research," *Amerasia Journal* 1985–1986;12(2):1–27, for a discussion on the various ways to conceptualize Asian American politics.

13. I need to acknowledge the influence of Herbert Blumer on my thinking and his emphasis on symbolic interaction. See Herbert Blumer, *Symbolic Interactionism, Perspective and Method* (Englewood Cliffs, NJ: Prentice-Hall, 1969); Also see Herbert Blumer and Troy Duster, "Theories of Race and Social Action," in *Sociological Theories: Race and Colonialism* (Paris: UNESCO, 1980). Barbara Ballis Lal was kind enough to share her unpublished paper, "Identity and Social Policy" (1992), on the centrality of Blumer's work for the study of race relations, particularly the importance of "respecting the empirical world" and the point of view of the social actor. I also benefited greatly from Bob Blauner, *Black Lives, White Lives: Three Decades of Race Relations in America* (Berkeley and Los Angeles: University of California Press, 1989); and Frances Fox Piven and Richard A. Cloward, *Poor People's Movement: Why They Succeed, How They Fail* (New York: Vintage, 1979), and their discussion about the influence of structural limitations on collective action.

14. I have benefited from similar approaches that cast Japanese Americans as active participants in the sociohistorical process: Gary Y. Okihiro, *Cane Fires: The Anti-Japanese Movement in Hawaii, 1865–1945* (Philadelphia: Temple University Press, 1991); Evelyn

Nakano Glenn, *Issei, Nisei, War Bride: Three Generations of Japanese American Women in Domestic Service* (Philadelphia: Temple University Press, 1986); and Lane R. Hirabayashi and James A. Hirabayashi, "Ethnic Identity and Social Change: Japanese Americans," San Francisco State University, July, 1984. Also helpful were Eileen H. Tamura, *Americanization, Acculturation, and Ethnic Identity: The Nisei Generation in Hawaii* (Urbana and Chicago: University of Illinois Press, 1994); David Yoo, "'Read All About It': Race, Generation and the Japanese American Ethnic Press, 1925–41," *Amerasia Journal* 1993; 19(1): 69–92; George J. Sánchez, *Becoming Mexican American: Ethnicity, Culture and Identity in Chicano Los Angeles, 1900–1945* (New York: Oxford University Press, 1993).

15. See Yuji Ichioka, Yasuo Sakata, Nobuya Tsuchida, and Eri Yasuhara, eds., *A Buried Past: An Annotated Bibliography of the Japanese American Research Project Collection* (Berkeley and Los Angeles: University of California Press, 1974).

16. Yuji Ichioka, *The Issei: The World of the First Generation Japanese Immigrants, 1885–1924* (New York: Free Press, 1988). Also see John Modell, *The Economics and Politics of Racial Accommodation: The Japanese of Los Angeles, 1900–1942* (Urbana: University of Illinois Press, 1977); Roger Daniels, *Asian America: Chinese and Japanese in the United States since 1850* (Seattle: University of Washington Press, 1988).

17. The term, political history, comes from Robert Blauner, *Racial Oppression in America* (New York: Harper and Row, 1972), 142.

18. Kitano, *Japanese Americans*; Petersen, *Japanese Americans*; Montero, *Japanese Americans*; Levine and Rhodes, *The Japanese American Community*; Ivan H. Light, *Ethnic Enterprise in America: Business and Welfare Among Chinese, Japanese, and Blacks* (Berkeley: University of California Press, 1972).

19. Michael Omi and Howard Winant, *Racial Formation in the United States: From the 1960s to the 1980s* (New York: Routledge & Kegan Paul, 1986).

20. Song, "Politics and Policies of the Oriental Community,"; Parrillo, "Asian Americans in American Politics," Maykovich, *Japanese American Identity Dilemma*; Kitano, "Japanese Americans on the Road to Dissent."

21. Light, *Ethnic Enterprise in America*.

22. Stephen S. Fugita and David J. O'Brien, *Japanese American Ethnicity: The Persistence of Community* (Seattle and London: University of Washington Press, 1991).

23. Edna Bonacich, "A Theory of Middleman Minorities," *American Sociological Review,* 1973;37:546–559; Edna Bonacich and John Modell, *The Economic Basis of Ethnic Solidarity: Small Business in the Japanese American Community* (Berkeley and Los Angeles: University of California Press, 1980). Also see Harry H.L. Kitano, "Japanese Americans: The Development of a Middleman Minority," *Pacific Historical Review* 1974;43(4):500–519. See David J. O'Brien and Stephen S. Fugita, "Middleman Minority Concept: Its Explanatory Value in the Case of the Japanese in California Agriculture," *Pacific Sociological Review* 1982; 25(2):185–204, for an alternative perspective emphasizing the petite-bourgeoisie concept.

24. Bonacich and Modell, *The Economic Basis of Ethnic Solidarity*; Bonacich, "A Theory of Middleman Minorities."

25. Fugita and O'Brien, *Japanese American Ethnicity*, 142, also suggest that in keeping with their petite bourgeois position, Japanese Americans might lean in a more conservative political direction.

26. A critique of ethnicity paradigms have been amply treated elsewhere. See Blauner, *Racial Oppression in America*; and Omi and Winant, *Racial Formation in the United States*.

27. Blauner, *Racial Oppression in America*.

28. For example, Petersen, *Japanese Americans*. For a summary of related studies, see Herbert R. Barringer, Robert W. Gardner, and Michael J. Levin, *Asian and Pacific Islanders in the United States* (New York: Russell Sage Foundation, 1993), 12–13, 164–168.

29. William Caudill, "Japanese American Personality and Acculturation," *Genetic Psychology Monographs* 1952;45:3–102; William Caudill and George DeVos, "Achievement, Culture, and Personality: The Case of the Japanese Americans," *American Anthropologist* 1956;58:1102–1126; Audrey Schwartz, "Traditional Values and Contemporary Achievements of Japanese American Pupils" (Los Angeles: Center for the Study of Evaluation, U.C.L.A. Graduate School of Education, 1970).

30. S. Frank Miyamoto, "An Immigrant Community in America," in *East Across the Pacific: Historical and Sociological Studies of Japanese Immigration and Assimilation*, Hilary Conroy and T. Scott Miyakawa, eds. (Santa Barbara: ABC-Clio Press, 1972), 217–243.

31. Blauner, *Racial Oppression in America*, 10; Omi and Winant, *Racial Formation in the United States*, 14–24. The immigrant model traces the trajectory of social mobility for successive waves of European immigrants who have pulled themselves up from a quagmire of discrimination and have experienced social mobility after undergoing an apprenticeship in the economic and political ways of the city. Such ethnic mobility has shown the uncanny capacity of American society to absorb its immigrants as each group uses its ethnic heritage to its best advantage. The classic case has been New York City where first the Irish, next the Jews, and then the Italians acquired middle-class status by relying on such mechanisms as city politics, ethnic enterprise, and crime. See Glazer and Moynihan, *Beyond the Melting Pot;* Daniel Bell, *The End of Ideology* (New York: Free Press, 1957). Also see Paul Takagi, "The Myth of Assimilation in American Life," *Amerasia Journal* 1973;2:149–158, for a critique of the culture and personality thesis. Omi and Winant, *Racial Formation in the United States*, 21, refer to this situation in terms of the "bootstrap model." The most striking manifestation of this kind of work has appeared in the popular press. In the mid- to late 1960s, scholars and journalists characterized Japanese Americans as a "successful minority" (Petersen, "Success Story," and Haak, "Co-Opting the Oppressors.") This notion of success was a precursor to the model minority theme of the 1970s and 1980s. Keith Osajima, "Asian Americans as the Model Minority: An Analysis of the Popular Press in the 1960s and 1980s," in *Reflections on Shattered Windows: Promises and Prospects for Asian American Studies*, Gary Y. Okihiro et al., eds. (Pullman: Washington State University Press, 1988), 165–174, analyzes the development of the model minority notion.

32. See Blauner, *Racial Oppression in America*, and David Wellman, *Portraits of White Racism*, 2nd ed. (Cambridge: Cambridge University Press, 1993), for a discussion about the rational basis for racism. Omi and Winant, *Racial Formation in the United States*, have provided an excellent critique of theories that conflate race and ethnicity.

33. For a critique of the "model minority" notion, see Bob H. Suzuki, "Education and the Socialization of Asian Americans: A Revisionist Analysis of the 'Model Minority' Thesis," *Amerasia Journal* 1977;4(2):23–51. Also see Daniels, *Asian America*, 317–344; Sucheng Chan and Ling-chi Wang, "Racism and the Model Minority: Asian Americans in Higher Education," in *The Racial Crisis in American Higher Education,* eds. Philip G. Altbach and Kofi Lomotey (Albany: State University of New York Press, 1991): 43–67; Ronald Takaki, *Strangers From a Different Shore: A History of Asian Americans* (Boston: Little, Brown and Co., 1989); and Sucheng Chan, *Asian Americans: An Interpretive History* (Boston: Twayne Publishers, 1991). Don T. Nakanishi and Tina Yamano Nishida, eds., *The Asian American Educa-*

tional Experience: A Source Book for Teachers and Students (New York: Routledge, 1995), 95–164, offers a series of articles that address the model minority issue.

34. Light, *Ethnic Enterprise in America*; Petersen, *Japanese Americans*; Stanford Lyman, "Generation and Character: The Case of the Japanese Americans," in *The Asian in North America*, Stanford M. Lyman, ed. (Santa Barbara: ABC, 1977), 151–176; Montero, *Japanese Americans*; Levine and Rhodes, *The Japanese American Community*.

35. Fugita and O'Brien, *Japanese American Ethnicity*, 141–164. Also see Harry H.L. Kitano, *Generations and Identity: The Japanese Americans* (Needham Heights, MA: Ginn Press, 1993); and Kaoru Oguri Kendis, *A Matter of Comfort: Ethnic Maintenance and Ethnic Style among Third-Generation Japanese Americans* (New York: AMS Press, 1989).

36. Fugita and O'Brien, *Japanese American Ethnicity*, 160–162.

37. Ibid., 162–163.

38. Dorothy Swaine Thomas and Richard S. Nishimoto, *The Spoilage* (Berkeley: University of California Press, 1946); Rosalie H. Wax, *Doing Fieldwork: Warnings and Advice* (Chicago: University of Chicago Press, 1971).

39. Douglas W. Nelson, *Heart Mountain: The History of an American Concentration Camp* (Madison: State Historical Society of Wisconsin, 1976); Daniels, *Asian America*, 257–274; Sue Kunitomi Embrey, Arthur A. Hansen, and Betty Kulberg Mitson, eds., *Manzanar Martyr: An Interview with Harry Y. Ueno* (Fullerton, Calif.: Oral History Program, California State University, 1986); and Richard S. Nishimoto, *Inside An American Concentration Camp: Japanese American Resistance at Poston, Arizona*, Lane Ryo Hirabayashi, ed. (Tucson: University of Arizona Press, 1995).

40. I am indebted to Yuji Ichioka for his insights on this issue.

41. Omi and Winant, *Racial Formation in the United States*, 61.

42. Studying Japanese Americans as part of an interactive process involving major structural changes is similar to Flacks's (1971) theoretical treatment of youth and social change. In fact, Flacks's assumptions about the sources of radicalization among white youth in American society are also important for understanding the politicization of Japanese American youth during the late 1960s. He postulates that key turning points in America's political economy—the passage from competitive capitalism to monopoly capitalism and the creation of massive corporate bureaucracies—created a state of cultural incoherence. The demise of values and meaning that were relevant to entrepreneurial capitalism, the rise of new "yearnings and motives," and the decline of the traditional methods of social control, according to Flacks, were central to this cultural instability which had a radical impact on white middle-class youth. This cultural transformation affected the socialization process within American institutions and established the possibilities within which youth mobilized for change in the 1960s. See Richard Flacks, *Youth and Social Change* (Chicago: Markham, 1971).

43. Antonio Gramsci, *Prison Notebooks* (New York: New World, 1971) points to the strategic role of hegemony achieved by bourgeois culture in winning the loyalty of the citizenry for the purpose of preserving social stability. For an application of the concept of cultural hegemony, see Ronald T. Takaki, *Iron Cages: Race and Culture in Nineteenth-Century America* (New York: Knopf, 1979).

44. Omi and Winant, *Racial Formation in the United States*, 68.

45. Ibid., 93.

46. Ibid., 94.

47. Lyman, "Generation and Character"; Kitano, *Japanese Americans*; Petersen, *Japanese Americans*; Dorothy Swaine Thomas, *The Salvage* (Berkeley and Los Angeles: University of California Press, 1952); Montero, *Japanese Americans*; and Levine and Rhodes, *The Japanese American Community*.

48. Karl Mannheim, "The Problem of Generations," in *Essays on the Sociology of Knowledge*, Paul Kecskemeti, ed. (London: Routledge & Kegan Paul, 1952), 286–312.

49. Ibid., 291.

50. Ibid., 302–312.

51. Richard Sennet and Jonathan Cobb, *The Hidden Injuries of Class* (New York: Random House, 1972); Wellman, *Portraits of White Racism*.

52. C. Wright Mills, *The Sociological Imagination* (New York: Grove Press, 1969), 6.

Chapter 1

1. Roger Daniels, *The Politics of Prejudice: The Anti-Japanese Movement in California and the Struggle for Japanese Exclusion* (Berkeley: University of California Press, 1962), 4–5; Ichioka, *The Issei*, 40. Also see Yamato Ichihashi, *Japanese in the United States* (Stanford: Stanford University Press, 1932), 16–30.

2. Daniels, *The Politics of Prejudice*, 1; Roger Daniels, "Japanese Immigrants on the Western Frontier: The Issei in California, 1890–1940," in *East Across the Pacific: Historial and Sociological Studies of Japanese Immigration and Assimilation*, Hilary Conroy and T. Scott Miyakawa, eds. (Santa Barbara: ABC-Clio Press, 1972), 78. Also see Ichihashi, *Japanese in the United States*, 47–64, and Daniels, *Asian America*, 100–115.

3. Masakazu Iwata, *Planted in Good Soil: The History of the Issei in United States Agriculture*, vol. 1 (New York: Peter Lang Publishing, 1992), 93–94, 97.

4. Ichioka, *The Issei*, 3–4.

5. Yosaburo Yoshida, "Sources and Causes of Japanese Immigration," *The Annals* 1909;34(2):384.

6. Kazuo Ito, *Issei: A History of Japanese Immigrants in North America*, translated by S. Nakamura and Jean S. Gerard (Seattle: Executive Committee for Publication of Issei, 1973), 38; Ichioka, *The Issei*, 7–14.

7. Ichioka, *The Issei*, 42–45.

8. Carey McWilliams, *Factories in the Fields* (1935; reprint, Santa Barbara: Peregrine Publishers, 1971), 60–61; Sucheng Chan, *This Bittersweet Soil: The Chinese in California Agriculture, 1860–1910* (Berkeley and Los Angeles: University of California Press, 1986), 326.

9. Charles A. Beard and Mary K. Beard, *A Basic History of the United States* (Philadelphia: Blakiston, 1944), 300; Chan, *This Bittersweet Soil*, 325; McWilliams, *Factories in the Fields*, 61.

10. Beard and Beard, *A Basic History of the United States*, 296; Chan, *This Bittersweet Soil*, 326.

11. Gerald D. Nash, "Stages in California's Economic Growth, 1879–1970: An Interpretation," *California Historical Quarterly* 1972;51:315–330.

12. Ichihashi, *Japanese in the United States*, 176; McWilliams, *Factories in the Fields*, 106; Iwata, *Planted in Good Soil*, 153–154.

13. Ichihashi, *Japanese in the United States*, 176–177; Iwata, *Planted in Good Soil*, 155–159, 189.

14. Ichihashi, *Japanese in the United States*, 177; Daniels, *Asian America*, 133; Iwata, *Planted in Good Soil*, 155.

15. Ichihashi, *Japanese in the United States*, 137–139, 143–145; Ito, *Issei*, 291–349; Ichioka, *The Issei*, 57–62; Iwata, *Planted in Good Soil*, 119–131. Also see Eliot Grinnel Mears, *Resident Orientals on the American Pacific Coast: Their Legal and Economic Status* (Chicago: University of Chicago Press, 1928), 214–217.

16. Ichihashi, *Japanese in the United States*, 151–155; Ito, *Issei*, 353–365; Ichioka, *The Issei*, 78; Iwata, *Planted in Good Soil*, 111, 131–133.

17. Iwata, *Planted in Good Soil*, 111; Chan, *Asian Americans*, 32–33; Takaki, *Strangers from a Different Shore*, 92–93; and U.S. Immigration Commission, *Reports of the Immigration Commission: Immigrants in Industries*, Pt. 25, "Japanese and Other Immigrant Races in the Pacific Coast and Rocky Mountain States," Vol. 1, "Japanese and East Indians" (Washington: Government Printing Office, 1911), 33.

18. Ichioka, *The Issei*, 72–73.

19. Yuji Ichioka, "A Buried Past: Early Socialists and the Japanese Community," *Amerasia Journal* 1971;1:1–25; Ichioka, *The Issei*, 91–113; McWilliams, *Factories in the Fields*, 104–116.

20. Ichioka, *The Issei*, 113.

21. Ichioka, *The Issei*, 151–152; Daniels, *Asian America*, 133–135; Masakazu Iwata, "The Japanese Immigrants in California Agriculture," *Agricultural History* 1962;36:27.

22. Modell, *The Economics and Politics of Racial Accommodation*, 32.

23. Ibid., 94.

24. Tetsuya Fujimoto, "Social Class and Crime: The Case of the Japanese Americans" (Ph.D. dissertation, University of California, Berkeley, 1975), 142.

25. Iwata, "The Japanese Immigrants in California Agriculture," 29.

26. Robert Higgs, "Landless by Law: Japanese Immigrants in California Agriculture to 1941," *Journal of Economic History* 38(1978):205–225; also see Ichihashi, *Japanese in the United States*, 121.

27. Higgs, "Landless by Law," 210.

28. Ichioka, *The Issei*, 151–153; Iwata, *Planted in Good Soil*, 221–250.

29. Ito, *Issei*, 248, 428, 442, 452, 505; Fujimoto, "Social Class and Crime," 149–150; Leonard Broom and John I. Kitsuse, *The Managed Casualty: The Japanese-American Family in World War II* (Berkeley and Los Angeles: University of California Press, 1956), 10; Mei Nakano, *Japanese American Women: Three Generations, 1890–1990* (Berkeley, Sebastopol: Mina Press Publishing, 1990; San Francisco: National Japanese American Historical Society, 1990), 41; David J. O'Brien and Stephen S. Fugita, *The Japanese American Experience* (Bloomington and Indianapolis: Indiana University Press, 1991), 32–33.

30. Ichioka, *The Issei*, 155.

31. Thomas and Nishimoto, *The Spoilage*, 4; Leonard Broom and Ruth Riemer, *Removal and Return: The Socio-Economic Effects of the War on Japanese Americans* (Berkeley: University of California Press, 1949), 82–83; and Iwata, "Japanese Immigrants in California Agriculture," 32–33.

32. Ichihashi, *Japanese in the United States*, 121; Light, *Ethnic Enterprise in America*, 9–10.

33. Ichihashi, *Japanese in the United States*, 121.

34. Ibid., 129.

35. Ibid., 126.

36. Light, *Ethnic Enterprise in America,* 10.

37. Ichihashi, *Japanese in the United States,* 132.

38. Modell, *The Economics and Politics of Racial Accommodation,* 17–27.

39. Daniels, *The Politics of Prejudice,* 44.

40. Edward K. Strong, Jr., *The Second-Generation Japanese Problem* (Stanford: Stanford University Press, 1924), 89.

41. Thomas, *The Salvage,* 19.

42. Oscar Handlin, *Boston's Immigrants: A Study in Acculturation,* rev. and enl. (New York: Atheneum, 1959), 191–192; Glazer and Moynihan, *Beyond the Melting Pot,* 219–229.

43. See John Higham, *Strangers in the Land: Patterns of American Nativism, 1860–1925* (New York: Atheneum, 1955), for a discussion of the nativist response to immigrants.

44. Ibid., 324.

45. See Will Herberg, *Protestant, Catholic, Jew: An Essay in American Religious Sociology,* rev. ed. (Garden City: Doubleday, 1960).

46. Yuji Ichioka, "The Early Japanese Immigrant Quest for Citizenship: The Background of the 1922 Ozawa Case," *Amerasia Journal* 1977;4:1–22.

47. Handlin, *The Uprooted,* 180–202; John Bodnar, *The Transplanted: A History of Immigrants in Urban America* (Bloomington: Indiana University Press, 1985), 202–204.

48. Edgar Litt, *Ethnic Politics in America* (Glenview, Ill.: Scott, Foresman, 1970), 43–45.

49. Edward T. Kantowicz, "Voting and Parties," in *The Politics of Ethnicity*, Michael Walzer, Edward T. Kantowicz, John Higham, and Mona Harrington, eds. (Cambridge, MA, London: Belknap Press, 1982), 45–46.

50. Lawrence H. Fuchs, "Some Political Aspects of Immigration," in *American Ethnic Politics*, Lawrence H. Fuchs, ed. (New York: Harper, 1968), 15–16; Glazer and Moynihan, *Beyond the Melting Pot,* 209–210. Also see Thomas M. Henderson, "Immigrant Politician: Salvatore Cotillo, Progressive Ethnic," in *Politics and the Immigrants,* George E. Pozzetta, ed. (New York: Garland Publishing, 1991), 127–148.

51. Theodore Saloutos, *The Greeks in the United States* (Cambridge: Harvard University Press, 1964).

52. Ibid., 232–243. Regarding the Americanization movement see Higham *Strangers in the Land*; and Milton M. Gordon, *Assimilation in American Life.*

53. S. Frank Miyamoto, *Social Solidarity Among the Japanese in Seattle* (Seattle: University of Washington Publications in Social Sciences 11, no. 2, 1939), 65, 84–93; Miyamoto, "An Immigrant Community in America," 220.

54. Ichioka, *The Issei,* 146–175.

55. Ibid., 164.

56. Ibid., 173.

57. Ibid., 245–249.

58. Glazer and Moynihan, *Beyond the Melting Pot*; Litt, *Ethnic Politics in America.*

59. Cited in Ichihashi, *Japanese in the United States,* 275.

60. Daniels, *The Politics of Prejudice,* 63; and Ichioka, *The Issei,* 237–248.

61. Ichioka, *The Issei,* 231–232.

62. See Modell, *The Economics and Politics of Racial Accommodation,* 100–106; and Daniels, *Asian America,* 143–147, for a discussion about this issue. Also see Robert M.

Jiobu, "Ethnic Hegemony and the Japanese of California," *American Sociological Review* 1988; 53:353–367.

63. Iwata, "The Japanese Immigrants in California Agriculture," 31–32.

64. Ibid.; Ichihashi, *Japanese in the United States*, 281.

65. Iwata, "The Japanese Immigrants in California Agriculture," 32; Modell, *The Economics and Politics of Racial Accommodation*, 106–107.

66. Ichioka, *The Issei*, 253.

67. Modell, *The Economics and Politics of Racial Accommodation*, 67–93. See Miyamoto, *Social Solidarity Among the Japanese in Seattle*, 70–122, regarding institutional life in Seattle's Japanese community before World War II.

68. Ichioka, *The Issei*, 156–157; Modell, *The Economics and Politics of Racial Accommodation*, 80, 89, 100; Togo Tanaka, "Political Organizations," folder W 1.94, Japanese Evacuation and Resettlement Study, Bancroft Library, University of California, Berkeley (hereafter cited as Japanese Evacuation and Resettlement Study).

69. Modell, *The Economic and Politics of Racial Accommodation*, 80, discusses "the question of defense" in connection with the Central Japanese Association of Southern California. For a fuller treatment of the Japanese Association, see Yuji Ichioka, "Japanese Associations and the Japanese Government: A Special Relationship," *Pacific Historical Review* 1977; 46:409–437; Ichioka, *The Issei*, 156–164. These sources provide the basis for my discussion.

70. Ichioka, *The Issei*, 157.

71. Ichioka, "Japanese Associations and the Japanese Government," 411.

72. Daniels, *Politics of Prejudice*, 21.

73. Michinari Fujita, "The Japanese Association in America," *Sociology and Social Research* 1929;12:211–228; Ichioka, *The Issei*, 186–196; Modell, *The Economics and Politics of Racial Accommodation*, 83–84.

74. Fujita, "The Japanese Association in America." Examples of this kind of literature also include K.K. Kawakami, *The Real Japanese Question* (New York: Mcmillan, 1921); Kiichi Kanzaki, "Is the Japanese Menace in America a Reality?" *Annals of the American Academy of Political and Social Sciences* 1921;93:88–97.

75. Ichioka, *The Issei*, 204.

76. Ichioka, *The Issei*, 206. Also see Ichihasi, *Japanese in the United States*, 323–325.

77. Ichioka, *The Issei*, 200–210. Also see Kawakami, *The Real Japanese Question*, 143–159.

78. Ichioka, *The Issei*, 201.

79. Ibid., 204.

80. Modell, *The Economics and Politics of Racial Accommodation*, 85–87.

81. Sei Fujii, "Letter of Warning from Sei Fujii, Los Angeles," July 1923, Box 6F-7A, folder 307, Survey of Race Relations, Hoover Institution on War, Revolution and Peace, Stanford University (hereafter cited as Survey of Race Relations). Also see Daniels, *Asian America*, 132, regarding the acculturation role of the associations.

82. Ichioka, *The Issei*, 38–39, 86–87, 191–192, 249.

83. Quoted in Robert E. Park, *The Immigrant Press and Its Control* (New York: Harper and Brothers, 1922), 162.

84. Kanzaki, "Is the Japanese Menace in America a Reality?" 94–95.

85. This discussion of Issei's legal efforts draws from Ichioka, "Early Japanese Immigrant Quest for Citizenship"; and Ichioka, *The Issei*, 210–226.

86. Ibid., 11.

87. Ichioka, *The Issei*, 226–243.

88. Ibid., 253.

89. Strong, *The Second-Generation Japanese Problem*, 1–11; Broom and Kitsuse, *The Managed Casualty*, 7; Bill Hosokawa, *Nisei: The Quiet Americans* (New York: Morrow and Co., 1969), 175–176; Modell, *The Economics and Politics of Racial Accommodation*, 128–139; Chan, *Asian Americans*, 113-116; and Takaki, *Strangers from a Different Shore*, 219–220.

90. Dr. Peter S., ca. 1925, Box 6D, folder 246, Survey of Race Relations. At the time Dr. S.'s story was recorded, he had lived in America for 28 years. He had a poor family background, as he described it. Desiring education, he came to America and worked for 15 years as a photographer. He married and had six children. He was a self-educated man in the fields of astronomy, physics, and chemistry and familiar with languages—French, German, English, and Japanese. He studied medicine in America, although his life history did not indicate where or when. Because of his interesting strategy of viewing the situation, I considered it relevant to include this portion of his story. For the most part, his notion of excelling in some special line paralleled many of the ideas advanced by other Issei who were interviewed as part of the Survey of Race Relations. Dr. S's remarks were also quoted in William C. Smith, *The Second Generation Oriental in America* (Honolulu: Institute of Pacific Relations, 1927), 27–28.

91. Colin Greer, *Divided Society* (New York: Basic Books, 1974), argues that the class structure shapes the cultural adaptation of ethnic groups and that the racial structure also shapes the cultural adaptation of racial immigrants.

92. Yamato Ichihashi, n.d., Box 7B, folder 337, Survey of Race Relations.

93. Adjutant M. Kobayashi on the Second Generation, n.d., Box 6D, folder 236, Survey of Race Relations. For a fuller discussion about Kobayashi, see Bryan Masaru Hayashi, "The Japanese 'Invasion' of California: Major Kobayashi and the Japanese Salvation Army, 1919–1926," *Journal of the West* 1984;23(1):73–82.

94. Strong, *The Second-Generation Japanese Problem*, 8–11.

95. Strong, *The Second-Generation Japanese Problem*, 251; Modell, *The Economics and Politics of Racial Accommodation*, 132.

96. Zai-bei Nihonjinkai, *Zai-Bei Nihonjinshi* [The History of the Japanese in America] (San Francisco: Zai-bei Nihonjinkai, 1940), 109–110.

97. Minoru Iino, "My Life History," 12 April 1926, Box 7C, folder 352, Survey of Race Relations.

98. Life of Sakoe Tsuboi, 9 May 1924, Box 5C, folder 58, Survey of Race Relations.

99. Zai-bei Nihonjinkai, *Zai-Bei Nihonjinshi*, 112.

100. Ichihashi, *Japanese in the United States*, 326–328; Strong, *The Second-Generation Japanese Problem*, 168–170.

101. Kitano, *Japanese Americans*, 27; Hosokawa, *Nisei*, 157–158; Tamotsu Shibutani, *The Derelicts of Company K: A Sociological Study of Demoralization* (Berkeley and Los Angeles: University of California Press, 1978), 31.

102. Ito, *Issei*, 592.

103. Interview, Mrs. Nao Tashiro, 28 May 1924, Box 6B, folder 176, Survey of Race Relations.

104. John Modell, "The Japanese American Family: A Perspective for Future Investigation," *Pacific Historical Review* 1968;37:67–81.

105. We should be cautious about characterizing Issei perspectives of success during the early 1900s. Their ideas about *seiko* were solicited in the late 1960s, about 30 years after the Nisei came of age. Also, the long time interval between their entry into America and the actual survey permitted the Issei many years to reflect, to mellow, and to become philosophical about their experiences and their ambitions for the second generation.

106. Modell, *The Economics and Politics of Racial Accommodation*, 13. Also see Ichioka, *The Issei*, 252–254.

Chapter 2

1. Ichioka, *The Issei*, 172. Daniels, *Asian America*, 153, reports that the native-born Japanese population in the U.S. was 29,508 in 1920.

2. Census data reported in Thomas, *The Salvage*, 575–577. A Japanese language source, Zai-bei Nihonjinkai, *Zai-Bei Nihonjinshi* 590, reports fewer Nisei in 1910 (4,413), 1920 (29,508), and 1930 (67,841).

3. In 1910, 1920, and 1930, the Nisei in California constituted 70.5% (3,172), 70.1% (20,814), and 71.7% (48,979) of the total Nisei population in the U.S. (Thomas, *The Salvage*, 577).

4. Thomas, *The Salvage*, 576–577.

5. See Ichihashi, *Japanese in the United States*, 319, for a definition of the second generation which is similar to the one used in this study.

6. See Shibutani, *The Derelicts of Company K*, especially his discussion of pre-World War II Nisei situation in Chapter 2, "The Challenge to Nisei Loyalty," 19–70. Also see Modell, *The Economics and Politics of Racial Accommodation*, 154–172, for a good discussion of the Nisei in Los Angeles.

7. Toshio Mori, interview by author, San Leandro, CA, 16 February 1978. Also see Strong, *The Second-Generation Japanese Problem*, 220; Modell, *The Economics and Politics of Racial Accommodation*, 129.

8. Also see Charles Kikuchi, "Japanese American Youth in San Francisco," folder A1.02, Japanese Evacuation and Resettlement Study.

9. Kikuchi, "Japanese American Youth in San Francisco," 100, stated, "In their democratic education, the Nisei closely ally themselves with American history; similarly, their affinity to Japanese tradition becomes more foreign. George Washington and Abraham Lincoln are much more real to them than Emperor Meiji. Most Nisei can explain the background of the Civil War in the United States fairly well, but very few of those asked could give an account of the Restoration of the Emperor and the subsequent modernization of Japan." Also see Shibutani, *The Derelicts of Company K*, 75.

10. Case History 63, interview by Charles Kikuchi, Case **T, Japanese Evacuation and Resettlement Study. (Case History will hereafter be abbreviated as CH, as in CH-63.) Also, schools were in some ways a safe haven for the Nisei. According to interview with Mrs. K. Iseri and Mrs. Takeyama, 5 January 1925, Box 6D, folder 263, Survey of Race Relations, "The school life of the Japanese children and young people . . . is usually happy. The teachers often seem to take special interest in the children because they are Japanese. It is not in the schools and churches that they encounter prejudice, but outside." Toshio Mori recalled that in the early 1920s Nisei students were on "good behavior" with their teachers and were treated well. He also declared, "I had it very easy because the teacher

trusted me. I had a lot of free time. I finished my assignments early in the term, so I experimented with English and art." In this respect, schooling was a positive experience and it was also an important influence in the lives of the Nisei, especially their teachers. Although their early educational experiences between the sixth and ninth grades were quite encouraging, Nisei like Mori began to raise questions about the relevance of a high school education. The racial climate and prevailing discriminatory barriers meant that these same ambitions and ideals were somehow "impossible goals" to attain in Mori's view. "I felt as if I was studying something in theory which I won't be able to use later." "That's the reason I didn't continue my college education," even though "mother urged me to get at least a college degree."

11. Mori, interview; Joe Oyama, interview by author, Berkeley, CA, 10 July 1978.

12. Many Nisei who went to school to study in the liberal arts field or commerce did not necessarily have a clear sense of their direction. For example, CH-25, interview by Charles Kikuchi, Case **R, Japanese Evacuation and Resettlement Study, stated, "I think they were too immature to really realize what a problem they were up against. They didn't think too much about what they were going to do with their education and when they did talk about it they were most pessimistic." Finances were also a decisive factor. Nisei from families that were better off financially generally had greater opportunities to attend college. Nisei who were less privileged devised a wide variety of strategies such as supporting themselves through school as school boys and school girls, or they pursued vocational training. See Nakano Glenn, Issei, Nisei, Warbride, 124, regarding the experience of Nisei school girls.

13. "A Representative of the Second Generation," 18 April 1924, Box 5B, folder 44, Survey of Race Relations.

14. Interview with Miss Chiyoe Sumi, 21 February 1925, Box 6F-7A, folder 299, Survey of Race Relations.

15. Kazuo Kawai, "Three Roads, and None Easy," Survey, 1 May 1926, 165. See Modell, The Economics and Politics of Racial Accommodation, 164–166, for a discussion about Kawai's views. Also see Strong, The Second-Generation Japanese Problem, 2–7.

16. Shibutani, The Derelicts of Company K, 26.

17. For example, see Interview with Mrs. K. Iseri and Mrs. Takeyama, Survey of Race Relations.

18. Leonard Broom and John I. Kitsuse, The Managed Casualty (Berkeley: University of California Press, 1956), 7; Modell, The Economics and the Politics of Racial Accommodation, 132.

19. See Nakano Glenn, Issei, Nisei, War Bride, for a discussion of Japanese American women in domestic work.

20. Kikuchi, "Japanese American Youth in San Francisco," Japanese Evacuation and Resettlement Study, reported the findings of a 1940 study of the educational and economic status of 133 Nisei in San Francisco: "Of the 80 Nisei employed on full time jobs, 63.8% worked in two broad occupational groups, domestic and personal service workers and sales and clerical work. The salesman group was composed almost wholly of the Nisei youths employed by the small art goods stores in Chinatown." Kikuchi added, "Twenty-nine or 36.3% of the 80 Nisei in full time work were employed by American employers. However, 69% of the twenty-nine workers were engaged in domestic work. Only four . . . Nisei were members of an American labor union."..."Besides domestic work, the Nisei in American companies were engaged as truck driver, dressmaker, seamstress, secretary, typist, stockgirl, blueprint helper, and boxer—one of each."

21. Modell, *The Economics and Politics of Racial Accommodation*, 131–132; Broom and Kitsuse, *The Managed Casualty*, 7–8.

22. Data comes from the U.S. Bureau of the Census, *Sixteenth Census of the United States: 1940, Population, Characteristics of the Nonwhite Population by Race* (Washington, D.C.: Government Printing Office, 1943), 107. Also see Daniels, *Asian America*, 157, for an economic profile of Japanese Americans on the West Coast.

23. Modell, *The Economics and Politics of Racial Accommodation*, 131.

24. Ibid., 132. Also see Louis Adamic, *From Many Lands* (New York: Harper, 1940), 203–234.

25. Modell, *The Economics and Politics of Racial Accommodation*, 132; Strong, *The Second-Generation Japanese Problem*, 241.

26. Thomas, *The Salvage*, 133, and Modell, *The Economics and Politics of Racial Accommodation*, 133.

27. U.S. Bureau of the Census, *Sixteenth Census of the United States: 1940, Population, Characteristics of the Nonwhite Population by Race*, 107.

28. Hosokawa, *Nisei*, 177–178; Strong, *The Second-Generation Problem*, 229–230.

29. Jim Kawamura [pseudonym], interview by author, Berkeley, CA, 18 April 1978.

30. Mori, interview.

31. Thomas, *The Salvage*, 215. This Nisei reported that he was eventually hired by Saburo Kido to work as a reporter on the *New World Sun* newspaper in San Francisco. Also see CH-35, interview by Charles Kikuchi, Case **S, Japanese Evacuation and Resettlement Study.

32. Kawamura, interview. There were, however, a few sectors in the outside economy where Nisei found work. CH-34, interview by Charles Kikuchi, Case **S, Japanese Evacuation and Resettlement Study, stated, "A few of the Nisei were getting into civil service and others were getting into Caucasian businesses, but I would say that the bulk of the Nisei were still frustrated economically as they could not break through the barriers of the Japanese community." Kikuchi, in "Japanese American Youth in San Francisco," also reported that the vast majority of Nisei youth in San Francisco who worked outside the ethnic economy were employed as domestics.

33. CH-34, interview by Charles Kikuchi, Case **S, Japanese Evacuation and Resettlement Study.

34. CH-58, interview by Charles Kikuchi, Case **S, Japanese Evacuation and Resettlement Study.

35. CH-31, interview by Charles Kikuchi, Case **R, Japanese Evacuation and Resettlement Study.

36. U.S. Bureau of the Census, *Sixteenth Census of the United States: 1940, Population, Characteristics of the Nonwhite Population by Race*, 34; U.S. Bureau of the Census, *Sixteenth Census of the United States: 1940 Population, Volume II, Characteristics of the Population, Part I* (Washington, D.C.: Government Printing Office, 1943), 40.

37. Modell, *The Economics and Politics of Racial Accommodation*, 127.

38. CH-59, interview by Charles Kikuchi, Case **S, Japanese Evacuation and Resettlement Study.

39. Ibid. Also, Togo Tanaka, audiotape of lecture, 2 December 1969, Box 398, Japanese American Research Project Collection, University Research Library, University of California, Los Angeles (hereafter materials from this collection will be referred to as Japanese American Research Project). Tanaka discusses his pre-World War II experience and the produce business in Los Angeles.

40. Broom and Kitsuse, *The Managed Casualty*, 7.

41. Interview with G----S----, 19 August 1924, Box 5D, folder 79, Survey of Race Relations.

42. Thomas, *The Salvage*, 389–390.

43. For an interesting personal account of this type of problem, see Thomas, *The Salvage*, 214–215.

44. Saiki Muneno, interview by author, South San Francisco, CA, 16 February 1973.

45. CH-58, interview by Charles Kikuchi, Case **S, Japanese Evacuation and Resettlement Study.

46. Mich Kunitani, interview by author, Berkeley, CA, 28 February 1978.

47. "Life History of—Yamada," n.d., Box 6D, folder 264, Survey of Race Relations.

48. "An American Born Japanese in America," by J. Saito, n.d., Box 6A, folder 107-A, Survey of Race Relations.

49. Michi Nakada [pseudonym], interview by author, 7 March 1978.

50. Carey McWilliams, *Prejudice, Japanese Americans: Symbols of Racial Intolerance* (Boston: Little, Brown and Co., 1944), 97–98; Leonard Broom and John I. Kitsuse, "The Validation of Acculturation: A Condition to Ethnic Assimilation," *American Anthropologist* 57(1955):293–300; Kitano, *Japanese Americans*, 55–68; Shibutani, *The Derelicts of Company K*, 30–31.

51. Interview with Mrs. K. Iseri and Mrs. Takeyama, Survey of Race Relations.

52. Interview with Seichi Nobe, 11 August 1924, Box 5D, folder 78, Survey of Race Relations.

53. Interview with Miss Chiyo Otera, 14 August 1924, Box 5D, folder 80, Survey of Race Relations.

54. Interview with Frank Ishi, 29 December 1923, Box 5D, folder 98-A, Survey of Race Relations.

55. Hosokawa, *Nisei*, 180–181; Shibutani, *The Derelicts of Company K*, 31.

56. Interview with G----S----, Survey of Race Relations. Also see Kitano, *Japanese Americans*, 27; Miyamoto, "An Immigrant Community in America," 229.

57. Interview with Seiichi Nobe, 11 August, 1924, Box 5D, folder 78, Survey of Race Relations.

58. Interview with Frank Ishi, 29 December 1923, Box 5D, folder 98-A, Survey of Race Relations.

59. For example, see CH-32, interview by Charles Kikuchi, Case **R, Japanese Evacuation and Resettlement Study, and CH-48, interview by Charles Kikuchi, Case**S, Japanese Evacuation and Resettlement Study, about the development of "rowdies" in the late 1930s. Also see Isami Arifuku Waugh, "Hidden Crime and Deviance in the Japanese American Community, 1920–1946," (Ph.D. dissertation, University of California, Berkeley, 1978), for a discussion of Nisei gangs.

60. Hosokawa, *Nisei*, 163–166; Kitano, *Japanese Americans*, 50, 60–66. During the formative period of the Japanese American Citizens League, JACL leaders had difficulty developing interest among the Nisei rank and file. According to Bill Hosokawa, *JACL: In Quest of Justice* (New York: Morrow and Co., 1982), 25, "The delegates went away inspired, but once again the inspiration could not be projected to young Nisei who were more preoccupied with baseball and church socials than with their political obligations."

61. Roger Daniels, *Concentration Camps: North America*, rev. ed. (Malabar, Fla: Robert E. Krieger Publishing Co., 1981), 21; Ichioka, *The Issei*, 252–253.

62. *Japanese American Courier*, 13 March 1937.

63. *Japanese American Courier*, 25 March 1939.

64. Thomas, *The Salvage*, 216.

65. Interview with G----S----, Survey of Race Relations.

Chapter 3

1. According to H.H. Gerth and C. Wright Mills, eds. and trans., *From Max Weber: Essays in Sociology* (1946; reprint, New York: Oxford University Press, 1969), 59, "The much discussed 'ideal type,' a key term in [Max] Weber's methodological discussion, refers to the construction of certain elements of reality into a logically precise conception. The term 'ideal' has nothing to do with evaluation of any sort." In this respect, an ideal type is a theoretical construction that approximates historical reality. While it can actually exist in reality, it is generally a heuristic device that helps, according to Weber, "to determine the degree of approximation of the historical phenomenon to the theoretically constructed type." Oftentimes, ideal types can be highly rational constructions that "facilitate the presentation of an . . . immensely multifarious subject matter . . ." (Gerth and Mills, *From Max Weber*, 324). Thus, the most constant and logical features of the subject are identified in order to sort out the various elements of historical reality that are so difficult to capture. Max Weber, *The Protestant Ethic and the Spirit of Capitalism*, trans. Talcott Parsons (New York: Scribner's Sons, 1958), "Bureaucracy," in Gerth and Mills, eds. and trans., *From Max Weber*, 196–244, and "The Social Psychology of the World Religions," in Gerth and Mills, eds. and trans., *From Max Weber*, 267–301, are some examples of his work in which he uses the ideal type method to study such historical phenomena as world religions, capitalism, bureaucracy, and authority.

2. The material used to discuss Kazuo Kawai's life experiences is taken from the following documents: Interview with Kazuo Kawai, 7 August 1924, Box 5D, folder 100, and Life History of Kazuo Kawai, 2 March 1925, Box 6F-7A, folder 296, Survey of Race Relations. Also see Modell, *The Economics and Politics of Racial Accommodation*, 164–166, for a good discussion of Kawai's views.

3. See Higham, *Strangers in the Land*, 234–263, for a discussion about the Americanization movement. Also see Tamura, *Americanization, Acculturation, and Ethnic Identity*, regarding the Americanization movement and the Nisei in Hawaii.

4. The University of California at Los Angeles was previously referred to as the University of California, Southern Branch.

5. Life History of Kazuo Kawai, Survey of Race Relations.

6. Life History of Kazuo Kawai, Survey of Race Relations.

7. *Japanese American Courier*, 1 January 1936. Academic biography listed in Kazuo Kawai, "The Boxer Protocol Negotiations" (Ph.D. diss., Stanford University, 1938), abstract in "Abstracts of Dissertations, Stanford University, 1938–1939," *Stanford University Bulletin*, 1939;14:163–166.

8. *Japanese American Courier*, 21 January 1933. For a fuller discussion of Nitobe's perspective, see Sharlie C. Ushioda, "Man of Two Worlds: An Inquiry into the Value System of Inazo Nitobe (1862–1933)," in *East Across the Pacific*, Hilary Conroy and T. Scott Miyakawa, eds. (Santa Barbara: ABC-Clio Press, 1972), 187–210.

9. *Japanese American Courier*, 17 October 1936.

10. Ichioka, *The Issei*, 252.

11. Saburo Kido, interview, 4 January 1967, Box 381, Japanese American Research Project Collection. Also see Daniels, *Asian America,* 183; Thomas, *The Salvage,* 537. Offering a contrasting view, Hosokawa, *Nisei,* 176, stated, "Since childhood they [Nisei] had been told that they would be a bridge across the Pacific, a link between East and West, the emissaries of understanding between two nations to which they were attached by birth and heritage."

12. Togo Tanaka, "History of the JACL," folder T 6.25, Japanese Evacuation and Resettlement Study; Robert W. O'Brien, "Reaction of the College Nisei to Japan and Japanese Foreign Policy from the Invasion of Manchuria to Pearl Harbor," *Pacific Northwest Quarterly* 1945;36:19–45; Yuji Ichioka, "A Study in Dualism: James Sakamoto and the Japanese American Courier, 1928–1942," *Amerasia Journal* 1986–1987;13(2):49–81; Daniels, *Asian America,* 180–183; and Paul R. Spickard, "The Nisei Assume Power: The Japanese Citizens League, 1941–1942," *Pacific Historical Review* 1983;52(2):147–174.

13. *Japanese American Courier,* 31 August 1929. For a discussion about Sakamoto's background see Ichioka, "A Study in Dualism," 50; Daniels, *Asian America,* 236–237; Hosokawa, *Nisei,* 195–196.

14. Tanaka, "History of the JACL." Also, Saiki Muneno, interview by author, South San Francisco, CA, 16 February 1973.

15. Hosokawa, *Nisei,* 196–197.

16. Tanaka, "History of the JACL."

17. Ibid. Also see Nisei life history in Thomas, *The Salvage,* 547.

18. Tanaka, "History of the JACL"; Yuji Ichioka, lecture Asian American Studies, University of California, Berkeley, 14 March 1973.

19. *Japanese American Courier,* 13 April 1929; Tanaka, "History of the JACL"; Hosokawa, *Nisei.*197.

20. Hosokawa, *Nisei,* 198.

21. *Japanese American Courier,* 6 September 1930.

22. *Pacific Citizen,* September 1940; and Tanaka, "History of the JACL."

23. Miyamoto, "An Immigrant Community in America," 237.

24. *Pacific Citizen,* 1 December 1972.

25. Joe Oyama, interview by author, Berkeley, CA, 10 July 1978; "1936 Revisited," *New World Sun,* 1 January 1937.

26. *Pacific Citizen,* 15 April 1977.

27. *Japanese American Courier,* 31 October 1931.

28. *Japanese American Courier,* 8 June 1929.

29. *Japanese American Courier,* 3 November 1928.

30. *Japanese American Courier,* 29 March 1930.

31. *Japanese American Courier,* 12 July 1941.

32. *Japanese American Courier,* 12 March 1932.

33. Thomas, *The Salvage,* 346.

34. Ibid., 547.

35. Frank F. Chuman, *The Bamboo People: The Law and Japanese-Americans* (Del Mar: Publisher's Inc., 1976), 167.

36. The 1922 Cable Act "provided that any American-born woman who married a person ineligible for citizenship would automatically lose her United States citizenship" (Chuman, *The Bamboo People,* 165). "Oriental veterans of World War I had been denied the privilege of applying for United States citizenship because they were not of the 'white race.' Other aliens were allowed through special legislation passed by Congress to apply for

United States citizenship upon being honorably discharged from military service during World War I" (ibid.).

37. Tanaka, "History of the JACL."

38. Tanaka, "History of the JACL," cites the *Pacific Citizen*, January 1935.

39. *Japanese American Courier*, 18 August 1928; 14 December 1929.

40. *Japanese American Courier*, 26 September 1931.

41. Tanaka, "History of the JACL." For a fuller discussion of Sakamoto's dualism, see Ichioka, "A Study in Dualism."

42. *Japanese American Courier*, 28 August 1937.

43. *Pacific Citizen*, November 1937.

44. Tanaka, "Political Organizations," folder W 1.94, Japanese Evacuation and Resettlement Study.

45. Blauner, *Racial Oppression in America*, 36–44.

46. *Japanese American Courier*, 1 January 1939.

47. *Japanese American Courier*, 2 December 1933.

48. *Japanese American Courier*, 1 January 1934.

49. *Japanese American Courier*, 7 March 1936.

50. *Japanese American Courier*, 23 September 1939.

51. *Japanese American Courier*, 1 January 1939. Sakamoto is referring to the 10-year period between 1929 and 1930.

52. Japanese dignitaries were also featured in the holiday sections but they appeared less frequently in the late 1930s.

53. *Japanese American Courier*, 21 July 1934.

54. *Japanese American Courier*, 16 June 1934.

55. *Japanese American Courier*, 27 August 1938.

56. *Japanese American Courier*, 16 December 1939.

57. *Japanese American Courier*, 22 June 1940.

58. *Japanese American Courier*, 27 January 1940.

59. Daniels, *Concentration Camps,* 50, and Dillon S. Myer, *Uprooted Americans: The Japanese and the War Relocation Authority During World War II* (Tucson: University of Arizona Press, 1971), 18.

60. *Japanese American Courier*, 8 September 1934. Men like Toshio Mori recalled that radicals were severely criticized for their political beliefs and actions (Mori, interview). Joe Oyama pointed out that those who were viewed as "reds" were physically harassed (Oyama, interview).

61. *Japanese American Courier*, 8 September 1934, 10 September 1938.

62. For example, see William Carlson Smith, *Americans in Process: A Study of Our Citizens of Oriental Ancestry* (Ann Arbor, Mich.: Edwards Brothers, 1937), 131–133.

63. *Doho*, 1 February 1940; *Japanese American Courier*, 22 October 1932.

64. *Japanese American Courier*, 9 September 1930.

65. Tanaka, "History of the JACL."

66. Besides being an item of concern for the Pacific Coast, the bloc vote issue and the question of Nisei political allegiance made news in Chicago. On March 2, 1935, an article by Carrol Binder entitled, "Our Japanese Citizens," appeared in the *Chicago Daily News*. Binder argued that Japanese American youth who were coming of age politically did not pose a threat to the government because they would not vote in bloc. Since it was not clear, however, to what degree the Nisei would be influenced by Japan or by Japanese patriotic societies, he asserted that Congress should not yield to Hawaii's demand for statehood,

given the conflict in the Pacific Basin. Though many of the Hawaiian born Japanese were quite "Americanized" in thought and appearance, the fact that there were many Nisei who still pledged their allegiance to Japan presented a definite danger that should not be overlooked from a political standpoint, according to Bender. Japanese Ministry Archives, microfilm reel no. 7, Japanese American Research Project.

67. *Japanese American Courier*, 26 May 1934 and 2 June 1934.

68. *Japanese American Courier*, 21 July 1934.

69. *Japanese American Courier*, 11 August 1934.

70. *Japanese American Courier*, 15 September 1934.

71. *Japanese American Courier*, 12 September 1936.

72. *Japanese American Courier*, 3 April 1937.

73. Literally, Kibei means "returned to America." More specifically, the term Kibei refers to those Nisei who were born in the United States but "educated in whole or in part in Japan" before returning permanently to this country before World War II (Thomas and Nishimoto, *The Spoilage*, 3). Also see Karl Yoneda, *Ganbatte: Sixty-year Struggle of a Kibei Worker* (Los Angeles: Asian American Studies Center, University of California, 1983); William M. Hohri, *Repairing America: An Account of the Movement for Japanese American Redress* (Pullman, Wash.: Washington State University Press, 1988) 175; Ichihashi, *Japanese in the United States,* 319–320; and Broom and Kitsuse, *A Managed Casualty,* 5–6.

74. For a discussion of the Issei Left, see Ichioka, "A Buried Past."

75. *Japanese American Courier*, 24 October 1936; Chris Friday, *Organizing Asian American Labor: The Pacific Coast Canned-Salmon Industry, 1870–1942* (Philadelphia: Temple University Press, 1994), 120–124, 149–171. Also see Yoneda, *Ganbatte,* 85–102.

76. Kenneth Akazuki [pseudonym], interview by author, 10 March 1978.

77. Strong, *The Second-Generation Japanese Problem,* 74–84; Robert A. Wilson and Bill Hosokawa, *East to America: A History of the Japanese in the United States* (New York: Morrow and Co., 1980), 46.

78. Modell, *The Economics and Politics of Racial Accommodation*, 170; *Doho*, 1 November 1938.

79. These figures were quite similar to those reported by two other Nisei progressives whom I interviewed.

80. An interesting exception was the San Francisco Democratic Club, which had been led by professionals and journalists like Tajiri. Dr. Kahn Uyeyama, the first president of the San Francisco Democratic Club, was also a member of the JACL. The difference may be due to the fact that the San Francisco branch was not actually a "Young Democratic" group, but a Democratic club that was "liberal" in perspective as compared to the left orientation of the Y.D.s and thus, compatible with the participation of liberal professionals. Japanese American Young Democrats were probably much more "radical" to the extent that they did have members who were affiliated with the Communist Party. My interviewees indicated that Communist Party members who were active with the Young Democrats did not always disclose their political affiliation. Some progressives were highly critical of this practice and viewed their participation as an attempt to manipulate the Young Democratic Clubs in accordance with the party line.

81. *Doho*, 20 August 1938. The principles of the Democratic Clubs are stated in "An Outline for American Progress," and "Platform, Adopted by the Young Democratic Clubs of California, Inc.," at the convention which met in Hollywood, Calif., 1–3 December 1939.

Also see the Constitution of the Nisei Democratic Club of Oakland. I am grateful to Mich Kunitani for sharing his personal papers regarding the Nisei Democratic Club of Oakland.

82. *Doho*, 20 May 1939; "Publications, press releases, and bulletins," folder T 6.11, Japanese Evacuation and Resettlement Study.

83. *Japanese American Courier*, 11 March 1939; Oyama, interview; and Akazuki, interview.

84. "Staff correspondence," folder T 6.10, Japanese Evacuation and Resettlement Study.

85. *Japanese American Courier*, 11 March 1939.

86. *Doho*, 20 December 1938.

87. Oyama, interview.

88. Oyama, interview. See Modell, *The Economics and Politics of Racial Accommodation*, 141–153, for a good discussion about Nisei labor organizing in Los Angeles; *Doho*, 20 December 1938.

89. *Doho*, 5 December 1938.

90. For Sakamoto's anti-embargo view, see *Japanese American Courier*, 18 March 1939.

91. *Doho*, 1 August 1938.

92. Ibid., 1 January 1939.

93. Tanaka, "Political Organizations." Also see Saburo Kido, interview, Japanese American Research Project, regarding Nisei and Issei relations.

94. Oyama, interview; and Akazuki, interview.

95. *Doho*, 1 February 1940.

96. Sylvia Junko Yanagisako, *Transforming the Past: Tradition and Kinship Among Japanese Americans* (Stanford: Stanford University Press, 1985), 41. Also see Nakano, *Japanese American Women*, 121; Embrey, Hansen, and Mitson, eds., *Manzanar Martyr*, 2–3.

97. Broom and Kitsuse, *The Managed Casualty*, 6; Thomas and Nishimoto, *The Spoilage*, 3; and Shibutani, *The Derelicts of Company K*, 31.

98. Nakano Glenn, *Issei, Nisei, Warbride*, 53; Embrey, Hansen, and Mitson, eds., *Manzanar Martyr*, 10; Thomas, *The Salvage*, 42.

99. CH-13, interview by Charles Kikuchi, Case **R, Japanese Evacuation and Resettlement Study.

100. Embrey, Hansen, and Mitson, eds., *Manzanar Martyr*, 14. Also see Gene Oishi, *In Search of Hiroshi* (Rutland, Vermont and Tokyo: Tuttle, 1988), 15, for a discussion about the problems that his Kibei brother and sister experienced when they returned home from Japan.

101. Nakano, *Japanese American Women*, 122.

102. McWilliams, *Prejudice*, 322.

103. Embrey, Hansen, and Mitson, eds., *Manzanar Martyr*, 16, 22.

104. Hosokawa, *Nisei*, 178.

105. Nakano, *Japanese American Women*, 123.

106. *Doho*, 1 December 1939.

107. See *Doho*, 25 October 1941; 26 December 1941.

108. *Doho*, 1 March 1941.

109. *Doho*, 15 March 1941; 15 May 1941.

110. Thomas and Nishimoto, *The Spoilage*, 53–112.

111. Booker T. Washington, *Up From Slavery: An Autobiography* (Garden City, N.Y.: Doubleday, 1963), 156. Also see Daniels, *Asian America,* 224, regarding the comparison between the accommodationist character of JACL leadership and Booker T. Washington.

112. August Meier, *Negro Thought in America, 1880-1915* (Ann Arbor: University of Michigan Press, 1963), 20–21.

113. Takaki, *Iron Cages.*

114. August Meier and Elliott Rudwick, *From Plantation to Ghetto: An Interpretive History* (New York: Hill and Wang, 1966), 186.

115. Washington, *Up from Slavery*, 51.

116. Meier, *Negro Thought in America*, 110–111.

117. Lewis S. Feuer, *The Conflict of Generations* (New York: Basic Books, 1969); Anthony Esler, ed.; *The Youth Revolution: The Conflict of Generations in Modern History* (Lexington: Heath and Co., 1974); Flacks, *Youth and Social Change*; Todd Gitlin, *The Sixties: Years of Hope, Days of Rage* (New York: Bantam Books, 1987); Carlos Muñoz, Jr., *Youth, Identity, Power: The Chicano Movement* (London, New York: Verso, 1989).

118. A different version of this chapter was previously published as "Japanese American Responses to Race Relations: The Formation of Nisei Perspectives," *Amerasia Journal* 1982:9(1):29–57.

Chapter 4

1. Jacobus ten Broek, Edward N. Barnhart, and Floyd W. Matson, *Prejudice, War, and the Constitution* (Berkeley and Los Angeles: University of California Press, 1954), 124–125.

2. Gordon Hirabayashi (interviews, 29 August 1967 and 5 January, 1970, Box 398, Japanese American Research Project) provides a detailed account of his experience in resisting Executive Order 9066. For a discussion of protests, see Morton Grodzins, *Americans Betrayed: Politics and the Japanese Evacuation* (Chicago: University of Chicago Press, 1949). For a discussion of individuals who resisted E.O. 9066, see Peter Irons, *Justice at War: The Story of the Japanese American Internment Cases* (New York: Oxford University Press, 1983); Daniels, *Asian America,* 220–222.

3. In Gramsci's terms, cultural hegemony refers to "an order in which a certain way of life and thought is dominant, in which one concept of reality is diffused throughout society in all its institutional and private manifestations, informing with its spirit all taste, morality, customs, religious and political principles, and all social relations, particularly in their intellectual and moral connotation." (Gwynn Williams, "The Concept of 'Egemonia' in the Thought of Antonio Gramsci: Some Notes on Interpretation," *Journal of the History of Ideas* 1960;21:587) Of particular importance in this view of culture is the legitimacy of political institutions, which, in times of crisis, are able to command the allegiance of the citizenry. Max Weber referred to this process of achieving domination through consent as "legitimacy." I suggest that the legal-rational form of legitimacy was an important cultural influence in the lives of the Nisei and that the concept of law and obedience to the social order assumed a hegemonic function within American life, particularly during the war.

4. Tanaka, "History of the JACL."

5. Tanaka, ibid., cites the *Pacific Citizen*, September 1940. Also see Mike Masaoka with Bill Hosokawa, *They Call Me Moses: An American Saga* (New York: Morrow and Co., 1987), 48–49.

6. Hosokawa, *JACL*, 106. Tsukamoto also highlighted the grave situation facing the Nisei and urged them to prepare to sacrifice.

7. Tanaka, "History of the JACL."

8. Saburo Kido, interview, 4 January 1967, Box 381, Japanese American Research Project.

9. Hosokawa, *Nisei*, 205. Also see Mike Masaoka, interview, 27 July 1966, Box 390, Japanese American Research Project; Hosokawa, *JACL*, 127; Masaoka, *They Call Me Moses*, 57.

10. Yuji Ichioka, lecture, Asian American Studies, University of California, Berkeley, 12 March 1973. Also see Daniels, *Concentration Camps*, 24–25.

11. Weglyn, *Years of Infamy*, 119; Thomas and Nishimoto, *The Spoilage*, 20–21.

12. The discussion of the JACL response to Executive Order 9066 is based on the Mike Masaoka, "Final Report," 22 April 1944, folder T 6.15, Japanese Evacuation and Resettlement Study; and the Minutes, Special Board Meeting, Japanese American Citizens League, National Headquarters, San Francisco, 8–10 March 1942, reprinted 1971 by the Southern California JACL Office (hereafter this material will be cited as JACL Minutes). Also see Daniels, *Asian America*, 218–224; and Hosokawa, *JACL*, 153–168.

13. JACL Minutes, 10 March 1942; Hosokawa, *JACL*, 158; and Daniels, *Asian America*, 209.

14. Several Nisei observers whom I interviewed referred to such traditional values as *shikataganai* to account for the cooperation of Japanese Americans. Yasuko I. Takezawa, *Breaking the Silence: Redress and Japanese American Ethnicity* (Ithaca: Cornell University Press, 1995), 83, also reports that some of her Nisei interviewees "partially attribute acquiescence" to such traditional values and cultural norms as "perseverance, forbearance, and obedience to authority." Besides identifying such key conditions as political powerlessness and the lack of economic mobility, Kitano, *Generations and Identity*, 62–63, has also emphasized the importance of social-psychological factors to explain the absence of Japanese American resistance. These include the sense of vulnerability linked to the imprisonment of Issei leaders, a range of psychological reasons including "low expectations" for fair treatment and *shikataganai*, and "cultural norms and values emphasizing conformity and nonconflictual behavior."

15. Tanaka, "History of the JACL."

16. Daniels, *Concentration Camps*, 24–25, quotes the creed in its entirety.

17. Masaoka, "Final Report." Also see Daniels, *Asian America*, 221–223, regarding the JACL's efforts to curb resistance to government restrictions.

18. *Japanese American Courier*, 10 April 1942. Also, Daniels, *Concentration Camps*, 80, makes the important point that "for the vast majority of Nisei, at least, loyalty was demonstrated by submissiveness to authority."

19. Gerth and Mills, *From Max Weber*, 78–79.

20. Marshall Endo [pseudonym], interview by author, 31 March, 1978.

21. Selected case studies compiled by Kikuchi are contained in Thomas, *The Salvage*. The entire set of Kikuchi's interviews are part of the Japanese Evacuation and Resettlement Study collection.

22. Thomas, *The Salvage*, 398.

23. Jim Kawamura [pseudonym], interview by author, 18 April 1978.

24. Tamotsu Shibutani and Kian Kwan, *Ethnic Stratification* (New York: Macmillan, 1965), 405–407. In many respects, according to Shibutani and Kwan, this leadership

becomes culturally closer to the dominant class in taste, values, and life style than their own constituency, and in periods of conflict and crisis they tend to side with the leadership of the dominant class. There is an inconsistency within this process of emulation, however. Minority group leaders are generally drawn to values of equality, justice, and freedom professed by the dominant class but find contradictions between these ideals and their social and economic realities. Rather than challenging or confronting the dominant group, petty bourgeois minority leaders prefer a more collaborative strategy in making these values a reality for their communities because such an approach resonates with their own political interests.

25. JACL Minutes, 10 March 1942. The committee was comprised of Dr. T. Yatabe of Fresno; Fred Tayama, small businessman from Los Angeles; Mamaro Wakasugi, small farmer from Portland; Tom Yego, small farmer from Placer; Mas Satow, social worker from Los Angeles; James Sakamoto; and Mike Masaoka. Also see Daniels, *Asian America,* 208–221, regarding the JACL response.

26. Mike Masaoka, interview.

27. Saburo Kido, interview.

28. Modell, *The Economics and Politics of Racial Accommodation,* 122–123; Sánchez, *Becoming Mexican American,* 235–236.

29. CH-31, interview by Charles Kikuchi, Case **R, Japanese Evacuation and Resettlement Study.

30. Karl Yoneda, "A Japanese American Life Struggle," *Daily World,* 16 August 1969.

31. Also see Koji Ariyoshi interview, 24 March 1969, Box 391, Japanese American Research Project. In his interview he stated, "I was opposed to evacuation but since the ILWU, in my opinion, felt that we should go along with the war effort, I concluded that I would evacuate."

32. Karl Yoneda papers, "Racism and Relation to Evacuation," Box 18, folder 2, Japanese American Research Project.

33. *San Francisco Chronicle,* 6 September 1942. See Norman Thomas, *Democracy and Japanese Americans,* The Post War World Council, New York City, 20 July 1942, regarding his views on the internment of Japanese Americans.

34. "Statement of Policy," Nisei Democratic Club, Oakland, CA, 28 February 1942, Mich Kunitani personal papers.

35. Also see *Doho,* 1 June 1940.

36. "Minutes of the Meeting," Sounding Board for the Japanese American Citizens League, Japanese YWCA, San Francisco, CA, 12 March 1942, Mich Kunitani personal papers; *Japanese American Courier,* 13 March 1942.

37. "Minutes of the Meeting," Sounding Board, Kunitani personal papers..

38. *Japanese American Courier,* 3 May 1941.

39. *Japanese American Courier,* 20 March 1942.

40. *Doho,* 13 December 1941.

41. *Nichi Bei Shinbun,* 21 February 1942; and Grodzins, *Americans Betrayed,* 185–187.

42. Cited in Grodzins, *Americans Betrayed,* 196.

43. For a discussion of the loyalty oath issue, see Thomas and Nishimoto, *The Spoilage,* and Grodzins, *Americans Betrayed.*

44. Thomas and Nishimoto, *The Spoilage,* 57; and Morton Grodzins, *The Loyal and the Disloyal: Social Boundaries of Patriotism and Treason* (Chicago: University of Chicago Press, 1956), 110.

45. Thomas and Nishimoto, *The Spoilage*, 62–63.
46. Thomas and Nishimoto, *The Spoilage*, 61, 63.
47. Daniels, *Concentration Camps*, 114.
48. Nelson, *Heart Mountain*, 79.
49. Ibid., 80.
50. For discussions of resistance, see Gary Y. Okihiro, "Japanese Resistance in America's Concentration Camps," *Amerasia Journal* 1973;2:20-34; Arthur A. Hansen and David A. Hacker, "The Manzanar Riot: An Ethnic Perspective," *Amerasia Journal* 1974;2: 112–157; Daniels, *Concentrations Camps U.S.A.*, 122–129; Nelson, *Heart Mountain*, 116–150; Weglyn, *Years of Infamy*; Embrey, Hansen, and Mitson, *Manzanar Martyr*; and Lane Ryo Hirabayashi, *Inside an American Concentration Camp*.
51. Nelson, *Heart Mountain*, 96.
52. Thomas, *The Salvage*, 355. Also see Tetsuden Kashima, "American Mistreatment of Internees During World War II: Enemy Alien Japanese," in *Japanese Americans: From Relocation to Redress*, rev. ed., Roger Daniels, Sandra C. Taylor, and Harry H.L. Kitano, eds. (Seattle: University of Washington Press, 1991), 52–56, regarding mistreatment in the Justice Department detention camps.
53. Thomas and Nishimoto, *The Spoilage*, 65. Also see Richard Drinnon, *Keeper of Concentration Camps: Dillon S. Myer and American Racism* (Berkeley: University of California Press, 1987), for a critical assessment of Myer's role as WRA director.
54. Thomas and Nishimoto, *The Spoilage*, 69. See Weglyn, *Years of Infamy*, 125–126; and Daniels, *Concentration Camps*, 108, regarding the arrest and removal of dissidents from Manzanar. Also see Drinnon, *Keeper of Concentration Camps*, 83–116, regarding the use of isolation centers for "troublemakers."
55. Myer, *Uprooted Americans*, 77; Thomas and Nishimoto, *The Spoilage*, 85. According to Thomas and Nishimoto, the "loyal" were those "who had committed themselves, if citizens, as holding no allegiance to any country other than the United States and willing to serve in its armed forces, or, if aliens, as willing to abide by its laws and to do nothing to hamper its war effort"; the "disloyal" were those "who had either refused to answer the registration questions or had answered them in the negative" (*The Spoilage*, 84).
56. Myer, *Uprooted Americans*, 76.
57. Thomas and Nishimoto, *The Spoilage*, 61.
58. Weglyn, *Years of Infamy*, 167–173, 233–248; Thomas and Nishimoto, *The Spoilage*, 113–146, 184–186, 221–332; Wax, *Doing Field Work*, 118–174; Drinnon, *Keeper of Concentration Camps*, 126–129. For personal accounts and reflections, see John Tateishi, *And Justice For All: An Oral History of the Japanese American Detention Camps* (New York: Random House, 1984); and Sandra C. Taylor, *Jewel of the Desert: Japanese American Internment at Topaz* (Berkeley and Los Angeles: University of California Press, 1993), 151.
59. Thomas and Nishimoto, *The Spoilage*, 361.
60. Weglyn, *Years of Infamy*, 249–265.
61. George Kagiwada, "Thoughts on the Political-Economic Context of Japanese America," University of California at Davis, September 1976. Kagiwada has argued that deportation eliminated many advocates of resistance to the domination of Anglo-American culture. While his interpretation of the actual role of these "disloyals" may be debated, he does inform us about the consequences of resistance in a time of national crisis.

62. Thomas, *The Salvage*, 108; Myer, *Uprooted Americans*, 127–143; Drinnon, *Keeper of Concentration Camps*, 50–61. Also see Taylor, *Jewel of the Desert*, 177–178, 185–189 regarding the apprehensions and reluctance of internees to resettle.

63. Thomas, *The Salvage*, 105–128.

64. Robert W. O'Brien, *The College Nisei* (Palo Alto: Pacific Books, 1949), 55–59.

65. Bradford Smith, *Americans from Japan* (Philadelphia: Lippincott, 1948), 369.

66. Monica Sone, *Nisei Daughter* (Boston: Little, Brown and Co., 1953), 219, 236.

67. Carey McWilliams, *Prejudice: Japanese Americans: Symbol of Racial Intolerance* (Boston: Little, Brown and Co., 1944), 225.

68. Ibid., 224.

69. Ibid., 223.

70. Chizu Iiyama, interview by author, El Cerrito, CA, 10 March 1978. Also see Thomas James, *Exile Within: The Schooling of Japanese Americans, 1942-1945* (Cambridge and London: Harvard University Press, 1987), 120–125.

71. Alexander Leighton, *The Governing of Men* (Princeton: Princeton University Press, 1945), 46. Also see Taylor, *Jewel of the Desert*, 165–200, regarding such issues as dissension and demoralization.

72. *Tanforan Totalizer*, 15 May 1942.

73. Ibid., 30 May 1942.

74. Mary Oyama, "This Isn't Japan," *Common Ground* 1942;3:34.

75. *Heart Mountain Sentinel*, 7 February 1943, 6 March 1943.

76. Ibid., 17 July 1943.

77. Monika Kehoe, "Education for Resettlement," *Common Ground* 4 (Spring, 1944): 101. Also see James, *Exile Within*, 71, 87–89, 134–137; and Daniels, *Asian America*, 232.

78. *Topaz Times*, 25 November 1942.

79. *Tanforan Totalizer*, 11 July 1942. Approximately 360 Issei and Kibei were reported as having participated in these classes.

80. James, *Exile Within*, 37–39. See Taylor, *Jewel of the Desert*, 81–83, 119–133, regarding schooling and adult education in Topaz. Also see Lane Ryo Hirabayashi, "The Impact of Incarceration on the Education of Nisei Schoolchildren," in Daniels, Taylor, and Kitano, eds., *Japanese Americans*, 44–51, regarding racism and the impact of camp education on the Nisei.

81. James, *Exile Within*, 40.

82. Taylor, *Jewel of the Desert*, 121; *Trek*, December 1942, 9.

83. Cited in John Modell, ed., *The Kikuchi Diary: Chronicle from an American Concentration Camp, The Tanforan Journal of Charles Kikuchi* (Urbana: University of Illinois Press, 1973), 106.

84. *Topaz Times*, 24 November 1942.

85. Edward H. Spicer, Asael T. Hansen, Katherine Luomala, and Marvin K. Opler, *Impounded People: Japanese-Americans in the Relocation Center* (Tucson: University of Arizona Press, 1969), 227; Kitano, *Japanese Americans*, 75–77. Also see Kitano, *Generations and Identity*, 42–52, for the author's personal account of camp life.

86. Ibid., 228.

87. Audrie Girdner and Anne Loftis, *The Great Betrayal: The Evacuation of the Japanese-Americans During World War II* (London: Macmillan Co., 1969), 307–310; Spicer, et al., *Impounded People*, 216–229.

88. Leighton, *The Governing of Men*, 20.

89. Spicer, et al., *Impounded People*, 209–215; Thomas and Nishimoto, *The Spoilage*, 29. Built to house 250 internees, each block contained 14 barracks.

90. Michio Kunitani, "Tanforan Politics," folder B 8.29, Japanese Evacuation and Resettlement Study.

91. *Tanforan Totalizer*, 13 June 1942.

92. Ibid., 6 June 1942.

93. Ibid., 25 July 1942.

94. Ibid., 1 August 1942.

95. Leighton, *The Governing of Men*, 110–111.

96. Daisuke Kitagawa, *Issei and Nisei: The Internment Years* (New York: The Seabury Press, 1967), 86.

97. Modell, *Kikuchi Diary*, 157–158.

98. Leighton, *The Governing of Men*, 129. Also see Taylor, *Jewel of the Desert*, 133–136, 184.

99. Leighton, *The Governing of Men*, 12.

100. Ibid., 120.

101. Girdner and Loftis, *The Great Betrayal*, 292.

102. "The Case for the Nisei," "Publications, press releases, bulletins," folder T 6.11, Japanese Evacuation and Resettlement Study.

103. Mike M. Masaoka letter to Milton S. Eisenhower, 6 April 1942, folder T 6.10, Japanese Evacuation and Resettlement Study. Also see Drinnon, *Keeper of Concentration Camps*, 67. See Spickard, "The Nisei Assume Power," 165, regarding Eisenhower's views about Masaoka.

104. See Daniels, *Concentration Camps*, 104–129, and Daniels, *Asian America*, 240–241, 258–282, regarding the role of the JACL.

105. E. Franklin Frazier, *Black Bourgeoisie: The Rise of the New Middle Class* (New York: Free Press, 1957); Charles Flint Kellog, *NAACP, Vol. I, 1909-1920* (Baltimore: John Hopkins Press, 1967).

106. Ralph Guzman, "The Function of Anglo-American Racism in the Political Development of Chicanos," *California Historical Quarterly* 1971;50(3):321–337.

Chapter 5

1. Daniels (*Asian America*, 288) reported that "more than two-thirds of Japanese Americans did return to the Pacific Region" after the war ended. The return was a slow process that Girdner and Loftis (*The Great Betrayal*, 424) described as follows: "In the spring of 1945, only 1,500 or so evacuees had ventured to return to the Coast out of 55,000 cleared for return; 40,000 were residing in other states. By August 5,000 were reestablished on the Coast, representing 5 per cent of the American Japanese population. By January, 1946, 50 per cent were back, and another 25 per cent were expected to come gradually from the Midwest and the East." As a result of their wartime experience, Japanese Americans were no longer as concentrated along the Pacific Coast as they were prior to their evacuation. In 1950, 69.3 percent (98,310) of the Japanese American population resided in the Pacific region, a drop from the 88.5 percent (112,353) living there in 1940 (Daniels, *Asian America*, 289).

2. Paul Takagi, interview by author, Berkeley, CA, 22 February 1978. Also see Tetsuden Kashima, "Japanese American Internees Return—1945–1955: Readjustment and

Social Amnesia," *Phylon* 1980;41(2):107–115, regarding the "crisis of readjustment" for Japanese Americans during the postwar decade.

3. Daniels, *Concentration Camps*, 159–161.

4. Ibid., 159.

5. Ibid., 169; Chuman, *Bamboo People*, 201. Hosokawa and Wilson (*East To America*, 257) estimated that approximately 200 escheat cases were filed during this period. Key cases were *Oyama v. State of California* (1948) and *Fujii v. State of California* (1952).

6. Broom and Riemer, *Removal and Return*, 198–204. Also see Girdner and Loftis, *The Great Betrayal*, 433–438; and Daniels, *Asian America*, 296–298 regarding the claims issue.

7. Report of the Commission on Wartime Relocation and Internment of Civilians, *Personal Justice Denied* (Washington, D.C.: Government Printing Office, 1982), 241–242.

8. Florence Hongo, interview by author, San Mateo, Calif., 23 February 1978; and *Starting Over: Japanese Americans After the War*, produced and directed by Dianne Fukami, 60 min., Bridge Media, Inc., 1996, videocassette.

9. Broom and Riemer, *Removal and Return*, 64.

10. U.S. Bureau of the Census, *Sixteenth Census of the United States: 1940, Population, Characteristics of the Nonwhite Population by Race* (Washington, D.C.: Government Printing Office, 1943), 107; U.S. Bureau of the Census Reports, *U.S. Census of Population: 1950, Vol. IV, Special Reports, Part 3, Chapter B, Nonwhite Population by Race* (Washington, D.C.: Government Printing Office, 1953), 78.

11. Broom and Riemer, *Removal and Return*, 66–67; Bonacich and Modell, *The Economic Basis of Ethnic Solidarity*, 108–109, 134–141.

12. Broom and Riemer, *Removal and Return*, 64, 110.

13. Data from U.S. Bureau of the Census, *Sixteenth Census of the United States: 1940, Population, Characteristics of the Nonwhite Population by Race*, 107; U.S. Bureau of the Census Reports, *U.S. Census of Population: 1950, IV, Special Reports, 3-B, Nonwhite Populations by Race*, 78. Also see Bonacich and Modell, *The Economic Basis of Ethnic Solidarity*, regarding the changing economic position of Japanese Americans after World War II.

14. See Nakano Glenn, *Issei, Nisei, War Bride*, 83, 128–131. Data for women domestic workers from U.S. Bureau of the Census, *Sixteenth Census of the United States: 1940, Population, Characteristics of the Nonwhite Population by Race*, 107; U.S. Bureau of the Census Reports, *U.S. Census of Population: 1950, IV, Special Reports, 3-B, Nonwhite Population by Race*, 78.

15. Broom and Riemer, *Removal and Return*, 94.

16. Ibid., 113.

17. Ibid., 64.

18. Ibid., 123.

19. Data from U.S. Bureau of the Census Reports, *U.S. Census of Population: 1950, IV, Special Reports, 3-B, Nonwhite Population by Race*, 78; U.S. Bureau of the Census, *U.S. Census of Population: 1960, Subject Reports, Nonwhite Population by Race, Final Report PC(2)-1C* (Washington, D.C.: Government Printing Office, 1963), 244. See Nakano Glenn, *Issei, Nisei, Warbride*, 79–96, for a discussion of the occupational changes of Japanese American women during the post-World War II period.

20. Barbara F. Varon, "The Japanese Americans: Comparative Occupational Status, 1960 and 1950," *Demography* 1967;4:811.

21. Ibid., 813. Data for this discussion is from Varon, "The Japanese Americans."

22. For an example of this perspective, see Petersen, "Success Story: Japanese American Style," For a summary of related studies that address such issues as success and achievement, see Herbert R. Barringer, Robert W. Gardner, and Michael J. Levin, *Asian and Pacific Islanders in the United States* (New York: Russell Sage Foundation, 1993), 12–13, 164–168.

23. For example, see Amado Y. Cabezas and Harold T. Yee, *Discriminatory Employment of Asian Americans: Private Industry in San Francisco-Oakland SMSA* (San Francisco: Asian Inc., 1977); Governor's Asian American Advisory Council, *Report to the Governor on Discrimination Against Asians* (Seattle, State of Washington, 1973); United States Commission on Civil Rights, *Social Indicators of Equality for Minorities and Women* (Washington, D.C.: Government Printing Office, 1978). For a summary of the criticism directed at the model minority thesis, see Chan, *Asian Americans,* 168–171.

24. Gabriel Kolko, *Main Currents in Modern American History* (New York: Harper and Row, 1976); and Douglas F. Dowd, *The Twisted Dream: Capitalist Development in the United States Since 1776* (Cambridge: Winthrop, 1974).

25. Richard J. Barnet, *The Economy of Death* (New York: Atheneum, 1969); Charles Nathanson, "The Militarization of the American Economy," in *Corporations and the Cold War*, D. Horowitz, ed. (New York: Monthly Review Press, 1969); James L. Clayton, "Defense Spending: Key to California's Growth," *Western Political Quarterly* June 1962;15:280–293; Gerald D. Nash, "Stages in California's Economic Growth, 1879–1970: An Interpretation," *California Historical Quarterly* 1972;51:315–330. Franz Schurmann, "System, Contradictions, and Revolution in America," in *The New American Revolution*, Roderick Aya and Norman Miller, eds. (New York: The Free Press, 1971), 34, discusses the importance of war and technology for economic growth and stability.

26. David Horowitz, ed., *Corporations and the Cold War* (New York: Monthly Review Press, 1969); Richard Edwards et al., *The Capitalist System* (Englewood Cliffs, NJ: Prentice Hall, 1972); Dowd, *The Twisted Dream*; Schurmann, "System, Contradictions, and Revolution," 38.

27. Nathanson, "The Militarization of the American Economy," 210.

28. Schurmann, "System, Contradictions, and Revolution in America," 22. Also see Franz Schurmann, *The Logic of World Power* (New York: Pantheon Books, 1975), for a historical discussion of these developments.

29. Schurmann, "System, Contradictions, and Revolution in America," 27, cites the *Handbook of Labor Statistics*, 1968, 67.

30. Caudill, "Japanese American Personality and Acculturation"; Caudill and DeVos, "Achievement, Culture, and Personality."

31. See Isao Horinouchi, *Educational Values and Preadaptation in the Acculturation of Japanese Americans* (Sacramento: The Sacramento Anthropological Society, Sacramento State College, 1967), for a study of the importance of education among Japanese Americans.

32. This formulation stems from Greer, *Divided Society*.

33. For a case study of this problem, see Cheryl Cole, *A History of the Japanese Community in Sacramento, 1883-1972* (San Francisco: R and E Associates, 1974).

34. Mori, interview; Oyama, interview; and Kawamura, interview. Also see Fisk University, Social Science Institute, *Orientals and Their Cultural Adjustment: Interviews, Life Histories and Social Adjustment Experiences of Chinese and Japanese of Varying Backgrounds and Length of Residence in the United States* (Nashville: Social Science Institute, Fisk University, 1946), for case histories of Nisei who discuss their employment options.

35. Ichihashi, *Japanese in the United States*, 351–352. My interview with Toshio Mori, 16 February 1978, revealed Nisei experiences with segregation in primary school. Also see Charles Wollenberg, *All Deliberate Speed: Segregation and Exclusion in California Schools* (Berkeley and Los Angeles: University of California Press, 1976).

36. Ichihashi, ibid., 336–340; Strong, *The Second-Generation Japanese Problem*, 184, 187–207. Strong's study suggested that the Nisei had better quantitative and technical capabilities as compared to white students, who were supposed to have superior conceptual and theoretical skills.

37. Strong, *The Second-Generation Japanese Problem*, 220; Modell, *The Economics and Politics of Racial Accommodation*, 129. Also see Broom and Riemer, *Removal and Return*, 43, regarding the occupational aspirations of the Nisei in the postwar period.

38. Saloutos, *The Greeks in the United States*; and Christie W. Kiefer, *Changing Culture, Changing Lives: An Ethnographic Study of Three Generations of Japanese Americans* (San Francisco: Jossey Bass, 1974).

39. Strong, *The Second-Generation Japanese Problem*; 219; L.G. Portenier, "Abilities and Interests of Japanese-American High School Seniors," *Journal of Social Psychology* 1947;25:53–61.

40. Strong (*The Second-Generation Japanese Problem*, 232–233) suggested that the Nisei would be much better off pursuing occupations practiced by the Issei. In his view, "agriculture offers the greatest opportunity for employment, the establishment of homes, and the chance to prosper. Here the Japanese are wanted, for they are among the best workers and come into the least competition with the Occidental elements of the population. The second generation can lease and buy land and thus establish permanent homes and prosper according to their industry."

41. For a discussion of occupational changes see Broom and Riemer, *Removal and Return*, 32–68; Bonacich and Modell, *The Economic Basis of Ethnic Solidarity*, 93–102. Also see Kitano, *Japanese Americans*, 98–99, for a good discussion about the "occupational strategy" of Japanese Americans.

42. Henry M. Takahashi, interview, 14 September 1967, Box 389, Japanese American Research Project.

43. Paul Takagi, interview by author, Berkeley, CA, 22 February 1978.

44. Henry Wakayama [pseudonym], interview by author, 10 March 1978.

45. Data for discussion for U.S. Bureau of the Census, *Census of the Population: 1970, Subject Reports, Final Report PC(2)-1G, Japanese, Chinese, and Filipinos in the United States* (Washington, D.C.: Government Printing Office, 1973), 17, 31.

46. Colin Watanabe, "Culture and Communication: Self Expression and the Asian American Experience," *Asian American Review* 1972; Spring: 1–2. Also, Martin Trow, "Education and Survey Research," in Charles Y. Glock, ed., *Survey Research in the Social Sciences* (New York: Russell Sage, 1967), 363, stated, "We may note further that where Orientals comprise a sizeable proportion of the student body, as they do at the University of California at Berkeley, Oriental boys are disproportionately enrolled in the engineering courses."

47. Derald W. Sue and Austin C. Frank, "A Typological Approach to the Psychological Study of Chinese and Japanese American College Males," *Journal of Social Issues* 1973;29(2):136. Also see D.W. Sue and B.A. Kirk, "Differential Characteristics of Japanese and Chinese American College Students," *Journal of Counseling Psychology* 1973; 20:142–148.

48. Bob H. Suzuki, "Education and the Socialization of Asian Americans: A Revisionist Analysis of the 'Model Minority' Thesis," *Amerasia Journal* 1977;4:23–51. Also see Chancellor's Advisory Committee on Asian American Affairs, *Asian Americans at Berkeley*, University of California, Berkeley, May 1989, for recent patterns.

49. Daniels, *Asian America*, 295.

50. Miyamoto, "An Immigrant Community in America," 240.

51. Broom and Riemer, *Removal and Return*, 52.

52. Wilson and Hosokawa, *East to America*, 245.

53. *JACL Press Release*, 9 September 1944, folder T 6.11, Japanese Evacuation and Resettlement Study; Hosokawa, *JACL*, 282; Masaoka, *They Call Me Moses*, 191.

54. Hosokawa, *JACL*, 276, 283–293; *Pacific Citizen*, 25 December 1969. For a discussion of the politics surrounding the Japanese American Evacuation Claims Act of 1948, see Daniels, *Asian America*, 296–299.

55. *Pacific Citizen*, 25 December 1969; Hosokawa, *Nisei*, 435–455.

56. *JACL Reporter*, January 1949.

57. *JACL Reporter*, October 1950.

58. *JACL Reporter*, January 1949; *Pacific Citizen*, 13 December 1947; Hosokawa, *Nisei*, 450–451; Hosokawa, *JACL*, 294.

59. Daniels, *Asian America*, 296. Also see Chuman, *Bamboo People*, 309.

60. Statement of Mike Masaoka, Joint Hearings before the Subcommittees of the Committees on the Judiciary, 82nd Cong., 1st sess., on S. 716, H.R. 2379, and H.R. 2816, Revision of Immigration, Naturalization, and Nationality Laws 6–9, 12–16, 20–21 March, 9 April, 1951, 69.

61. Ibid., 69.

62. Ibid., 74.

63. Ibid., 49.

64. Mas Tamura [pseudonym], interview by author, Berkeley, CA, 30 March 1978.

65. Togo Tanaka, "How to Survive Racism in America's Free Society," in *Voices Long Silent: An Oral Inquiry into the Japanese American Evacuation*, Arthur A. Hansen and Betty E. Mitson, eds. (Fullerton: California State University, 1974).

66. *JACL Reporter*, June 1952.

67. Kunitani, interview.

68. *JACL Reporter*, June 1952. Also see Masaoka, *They Call Me Moses*, 217–238.

69. See Daniels, *Asian America*, 305–306, regarding the Cold War and the passage of the McCarran-Walter Immigration Act of 1952.

70. Eric F. Goldman, *The Crucial Decade—and After: America, 1945–1960* (New York: Vintage, 1960); Dowd, *The Twisted Dream;* Horowitz, ed., *Corporations and the Cold War;* William Appleman Williams, *The Contours of American History* (1961, reprint, New York: Franklin Watts, 1973).

71. American Council of Race Relations, *Report,* August 1950.

72. Ibid., January 1949.

73. Arthur M. Ross, "The Negro in the American Economy," in *Employment, Race, and Poverty,* Arthur M. Ross and Herbert Hill, eds. (New York: Harcourt, Brace and World, 1967), 5–6, 17; Herbert Hill, "The Racial Practices of Organized Labor—the Age of Gompers and After," in *Employment, Race, and Poverty,* Arthur M. Ross and Herbert Hill, eds. (New York: Harcourt, Brace and World, 1967), 396; August Meier and Elliot Rudwick,

From Plantation to Ghetto, rev. ed. (New York: Hill and Wang, 1970), 256; William J. Wilson, *Power, Racism, and Privilege* (New York: The Free Press, 1973), 127–128.

74. Wilson, *Power, Racism, and Privilege*, 129–130; Meier and Elliot, *From Plantation to Ghetto*, 254.

75. American Council of Race Relations, *Report*, October 1949. Also see Donald R. McCoy and Richard T. Ruetten, *Quest and Response: Minority Rights and the Truman Administration* (Lawrence: The University Press of Kansas, 1973), 45–46, 65, 93, regarding activities of ACRR.

76. American Council of Race Relations, *Report*, August 1950.

Chapter 6

1. For example, Thomas, *The Salvage*; Petersen, *Japanese Americans*; Montero, *Japanese Americans*; Hosokawa, *Nisei*; Hosokawa and Wilson, *East to America*; Sowell, *Ethnic America*; and Parillo, "Asian Americans in American Politics."

2. *Hakujin* is the Japanese term for white people.

3. *Buddhahead* is a Nisei slang expression for a person of Japanese ancestry.

4. At the time of my interview, the Bakke case, *Regents of the University of California v. Bakke*, 438 U.S. 265 (1978), was big news and generated a lot of discussion about affirmative action. According to William T. Trent ["Student Affirmative Action in Higher Education: Addressing Underrepresentation," in *The Racial Crisis in American Higher Education*, Philip G. Altbach and Kofi Lomotey, eds. (Albany: State University of New York Press, 1991), 126], "Allan Bakke, a white male, brought suit seeking relief under the equal protection clause of Title VI of the Civil Rights Act of 1964. He contended that the UC Medical School at Davis, having voluntarily established admissions procedures setting aside sixteen places for underrepresented minorities, having employed lower standards for admission to those places and having restricted white access to those places, had denied him access solely on the basis of race. A badly divided Supreme Court, in deciding in Bakke's favor, rendered a narrow ruling based on the reasoning supplied by Justice Powell. The ruling in the case decided three issues: (1) in the absence of a finding of specific discrimination traceable to a particular institution, race could not be used as a criterion for remedial benefits; (2) a person's race or ethnic background could not be used as a sole criterion for admissions decisions; and (3) race or national origin, along with other criteria, could be a factor in admissions where those criteria are intended to meet certain institutional needs or priorities."

5. Suzuki, "Education and the Socialization of Asian Americans," 44–45. Also see Magali Sarfatti Larson, *The Rise of Professionalism: A Sociological Analysis* (Berkeley and Los Angeles: University of California Press, 1977), 232–233, regarding the growth of professionals employed by private employers and the government in the immediate post–World War II period.

6. Samuel Bowles and Herbert Gintis, *Schooling in Capitalist America: Educational Reform and the Contradictions of Economic Life* (New York: Basic Books, 1976), 202.

7. See Nathan Glazer, *Affirmative Discrimination: Ethnic Inequality and Public Policy* (New York: Basic Books, 1975), for an early critique of affirmative action as a social policy. See Troy Duster, "The Structure of Privilege and Its Universe of Discourse," *The American Sociologist* II 1974:73–78, for a critique of Glazer. Since I first wrote this chapter, the debates on affirmative action have intensified and expanded. *The Diversity Report*, Institute for the Study of Social Change, University of California, Berkeley, 1991, provides a useful summary

of the issues. Also see Dana Y. Takagi, *The Retreat From Race: Asian-American Admissions and Racial Politics* (New Brunswick: Rutgers University Press, 1992).

8. Wellman, *Portraits of White Racism*, 141.

9. Wellman, *Portraits of White Racism*, 221.

10. Stokely Carmichael and Charles V. Hamilton, *Black Power: The Politics of Liberation in America* (New York: Random House, 1967).

11. *Shikataganai*, a Japanese term meaning "it can't be helped," refers to a sense that a situation is beyond one's control.

Chapter 7

1. Kitano, *Japanese Americans*, 196–197; Petersen, *Japanese Americans*, 115–116; Gene N. Levine and Darrel M. Montero, "Socioeconomic Mobility among Three Generations of Japanese Americans," *Journal of Social Issues* 1973;29(2):45.

2. Wong, "The Emergence of the Asian-American Movement"; Umemoto, "'On Strike!' San Francisco State College Strike, 1968–1969"; Wei, *The Asian American Movement*, 19; Omatsu, "The 'Four Prisons' and the Movements of Liberation," 24–26.

3. Kitano, "Japanese Americans on the Road to Dissent," provides a useful discussion of the resurgence of ethnic identity and the appearance of political dissent among third-generation Japanese Americans. He proposes that this changing pattern might be best understood in terms of an interactive model emphasizing generation and acculturation, and hypothesizes that "the most active dissenters are those whose parents (the Nisei) were the most assimilationist in their orientation" (p. 113).

4. Maykovich, *Japanese American Identity Dilemma*.

5. Marcus L. Hansen, "The Third Generation in America," *Commentary* 1952;14: 492–500; Stanford Lyman, *The Asian in the West* (Reno: Desert Research Institute, University of Nevada, 1970). Stanford Lyman noted that the "mild anxiety" felt by Sansei over the loss of their cultural heritage had induced a "Hansen effect—a desire to recover selected and specific elements of old Japan." Lyman went on to say, however, that because of their Americanization, Sansei had been ineffective in their recovery. George Kagiwada, "The Third Generation Hypothesis: Structural Assimilation Among Japanese Americans" (Paper presented at the Pacific Sociological Association meeting, San Francisco, CA, March 1968), also applied the Hansen hypothesis in an attempt to understand why Sansei detoured from an assimilationist path in a quest for their ethnic roots. Although Lyman and Kagiwada did not refer specifically to the behavior of political activists, their observations offer grounds for hypothesizing that militant Sansei were motivated by their concern for recovery.

6. George Kagiwada ["Assimilation of Nisei in Los Angeles," in *East Across the Pacific: Historical and Sociological Studies of Japanese Immigration and Assimilation*, Hilary Conroy and T. Scott Miyakawa, eds. (Santa Barbara: ABC-Clio Press, 1972), 268–278] makes an important point in this regard. He argued that the Hansen hypothesis is subject to question because it applied only to "a small segment of the total generation." He suggested, as an alternative, that Mannheim's concept of a generational unit could prove to be more useful, because it points to the possibility of diverse and competing generational patterns that stem from changing social and cultural dynamics in a specific historical period.

7. Maykovich, *Japanese American Identity Dilemma*, 67–74; Takezawa, *Breaking the Silence*, 127–153. Regarding the impact of the camp experience on the Sansei, see Donna Nagata, *Legacy of Injustice: Exploring the Cross-Generational Impact of the Japanese American*

Internment (New York and London: Plenum Press, 1993); and Nobu Miyoshi, "Identity Crisis of the Sansei and the American Concentration Camp," *Pacific Citizen,* 19–26 December 1980.

8. Omi and Winant, *Racial Formation in the United States,* 86.

9. U.S. Bureau of the Census, *Census of Population: 1970, Subject Reports, Final Report PC(2)-1B, Negro Population* (Washington, D.C.: Government Printing Office, 1973), 1; U.S. Bureau of the Census, *Census of Population: 1970, Subject Reports, Final Report PC(2)-1C, Persons of Spanish Origin* (Washington, D.C.: Government Printing Office, 1973), 1; U.S. Bureau of the Census, *Census of Population: 1970, Subject Reports, Final Report PC(2)-1F, American Indians* (Washington, D.C.: Government Printing Office, 1973), 1; U.S. Bureau of the Census, *Census of Population: 1970, Subject Reports, Final Report PC(2)-1G, Japanese, Chinese, and Filipinos in the United States* (Washington, D.C.: Government Printing Office, 1973), 1, 60, 199; U.S. Bureau of the Census, *Historical Statistics of the United States: Colonial Times to 1970, Bicentennial Edition, Part I* (Washington, D.C.: Government Printing Office, 1975), 14.

10. Robert W. Gardner, Bryant Robey, and Peter C. Smith, "Asian Americans: Growth, Change, and Diversity," *Population Bulletin* 1985;40(4):8 (Washington, D.C.: Population Reference Bureau, Inc.).

11. U.S. Department of Health, Education, and Welfare, *A Study of Selected Socio-Economic Characteristics of Ethnic Minorities Based on the 1970 Census, Volume II: Asian Americans* (Washington, D.C.: Government Printing Office, 1974), ii.

12. Barringer, Gardner, and Levin, *Asians and Pacific Islanders in the United States,* 25, 31.

13. U.S. Bureau of the Census, *Census of Population: 1970, Subject Reports, Final Report PC(2)-1G, Japanese, Chinese, and Filipinos in the United States,* 2; Gardner, Robey, and Smith, *Asian Americans,* 16.

14. Department of Health, Education, and Welfare, *Asian Americans,* 16–17. Although Hawaii had the largest Japanese American population (217,175) according to the 1970 Census, California had the largest mainland Japanese American population (213,277), followed by Washington (20,188), New York (19,794), and Illinois (17,645). Japanese Americans were still an urban population clustered in three major Standard Metropolitan Statistical Areas (SMSA): Honolulu (169,025), Los Angeles-Long Beach (104,994), and San Francisco-Oakland (33,587). (U.S. Bureau of the Census, *Census of Population: 1970, Subject Reports, Final Report PC(2)-1G, Japanese, Chinese, and Filipinos in the United States,* 1, 50).

15. Department of Health, Education, and Welfare, *Asian Americans,* 88. Statistics apply to U.S.-born Japanese American men.

16. Department of Health, Education, and Welfare, *Asian Americans,* 88. Statistics apply to U.S.-born Japanese American women.

17. Department of Health, Education, and Welfare, *Asian Americans,* 84.

18. Department of Health, Education, and Welfare, *Asian Americans,* 17; O'Brien and Fugita, *The Japanese American Experience,* 95.

19. Bonacich and Modell, *The Economic Basis of Ethnic Solidarity,* 122–123.

20. O'Brien and Fugita, *The Japanese American Experience,* 95–96; Kitano, *Japanese Americans,* 104. Also see Bonacich and Modell, *The Economic Basis of Ethnic Solidarity,* 108–127.

21. U.S. Bureau of the Census, *Census of Population: 1970, Subject Reports, Final Report PC(2)-1G, Japanese, Chinese, and Filipinos in the United States,* 17. The median figure is for Japanese Americans, 16 years and over. For Japanese Americans, 25 years old and over, the median years of school completed is 12.5 (Ibid., 9).

22. Ibid., 9; O'Brien and Fugita, *The Japanese American Experience*, 94, 144.

23. U.S. Bureau of the Census, *We the Asian Americans* (Washington, D.C.: Government Printing Office, 1973), 9. Barringer, Gardner, and Levin, *Asians and Pacific Islanders in the United States*, 238–239, reported that in 1969, the median person incomes (adjusted to 1980 dollars) for Japanese American men and women, 15 years and over, were $14,998 and $6,408, respectively; for white men and women, the figures were $12,579 and $4,609, respectively.

24. See, for example, Petersen, *Japanese Americans*; Haak, "Co-Opting the Oppressors." See Nakanishi and Nishida, eds., *The Asian American Educational Experience*: 95–164, regarding the model minority debate.

25. United States Commission on Civil Rights, *Social Indicators of Equality for Minorities and Women* (Washington, D.C.: Government Printing Office, 1978).

26. Ibid., iii.

27. Ibid., iii. For each of these social indicators, the Commission found that "women and minority men have a long to go to reach equality with majority men, and, in many instances, are relatively further from equality in 1976 than they were in 1960."

28. Ibid., 24. Statistics reported were for 1975.

29. Ibid., 27.

30. Ibid., 54.

31. Ibid., 44.

32. Ibid., 42.

33. Espiritu, *Asian American Panethnicity*, 20–25. Wong, "The Emergence of the Asian-American Movement," 34, also suggested that the ethnocentrism practiced by such ethnic groups as the Japanese and Chinese, national political differences, and communal separation were deterrents that kept a movement from developing any sooner.

34. Wong, "The Emergence of the Asian American Movement," 34.

35. Evelyn Yoshimura, "How I Became an Activist and What It All Means to Me," *Amerasia Journal* 1989;15:106–109.

36. Espiritu, *Asian American Panethnicity*, 27–29.

37. Ibid., 25.

38. Wong, "The Emergence of the Asian American Movement," 33–39; Glen Omatsu, "The 'Four Prisons' and the Movements of Liberation"; Espiritu, *Asian American Panethnicity*, 42–49; Wei, *The Asian American Movement*, 37–43. Also see Omi and Winant, *Racial Formation in the United States*, 1, 2, 108.

39. Group interview by author, Berkeley, CA, 19 March 1978.

40. Wong, "The Emergence of the Asian American Movement," 39; Omatsu, "The 'Four Prisons' and the Movements for Liberation," 20–21; Wei, *The Asian American Movement*, 41–42.

41. Omi and Winant, *Racial Formation in the United States*, 98–99. For a discussion of Black Power, see Stokely Carmichael and Charles V. Hamilton, *Black Power: The Politics of Liberation in America* (New York: Vintage Books, 1967); Robert Allen, *Black Awakening in Capitalist America: An Analytic History* (Garden City, New York: Doubleday, 1969); Blauner, *Racial Oppression in America*.

42. Omatsu, "The 'Four Prisons' and the Movements of Liberation," 21–28; Takezawa, *Breaking the Silence*, 147–148.

43. Philip Vera Cruz, Lillian Nakano, Happy Lim, Lori Leong, May Chen, Alan Nishio and Wes Senzaki, "Personal Reflections on the Asian National Movements," *East Wind*, Spring/Summer 1982, 37.

44. Omi and Winant, *Racial Formation in the United States*, 103.

45. Ibid., 104–105.

46. Wong, "The Emergence of the Asian American Movement," 35–36; Chan, *Asian Americans*, 174; Wei, *The Asian American Movement*, 41.

47. Yuji Ichioka, telephone conversation with author, 6 January 1994. Also see Espiritu, *Asian American Panethnicity*, 34–35.

48. Omi and Winant, *Racial Formation in the United States*, 105.

49. Wong, "The Emergence of the Asian American Movement," 36; Wei, *The Asian American Movement*, 39–40; Weglyn, *Years of Infamy*, 279.

50. Mike Murase, "Toward Barefoot Journalism," in *Counterpoint: Perspectives on Asian America*, Emma Gee, ed. (Los Angeles: Asian American Studies Center, University of California, Los Angeles, 1976), 312.

51. "Students Organize for Asian Unity," *The Daily Californian*, 26 May 1970.

52. "'Rap Session' on Cambodia Issue Set for Nihonmachi," *Hokubei Mainichi*, 9 May 1970.

53. "30 Individuals, 10 Groups Back SF Rap Session," *Hokubei Mainichi*, 13 May 1970; "500 Young Audience Packs Buddhist Church Hall," *Hokubei Mainichi*, 20 May, 1970.

54. Espiritu, *Asian American Panethnicity*, 35–38; Wei, *The Asian American Movement*, 132–161; Omatsu, "The 'Four Prisons' and the Movements of Liberation," 25.

55. Espiritu, *Asian American Panethnicity*, 35–36.

56. Chan and Wang, "Racism and the Model Minority," 46; Lane Ryo Hirabayashi and Marilyn C. Alquizola, "Asian American Studies: Reevaluating for the 1990s," in *The State of Asian America: Activism and Resistance in the 1990s,* Karen Aquilar-San Juan, ed. (Boston: South End Press, 1994), 354-357; Michael Omi, "It Just Ain't the Sixties No More," 32. Also, Omatsu, "The 'Four Prisons' and the Movements of Liberation," 27, emphasized the activists efforts to build organizations designed to "serve the people" and the "*mass* character of community struggles."

57. Espiritu, *Asian American Panethnicity*, 47; Wei, *The Asian American Movement*, 72; Esther Ngan-Ling Chow, "The Feminist Movement: Where Are All the Asian American Women?" in *Making Waves: An Anthology of Writings by and about Asian American Women*, Asian Women United of California (Boston: Beacon Press, 1989), 362–377.

58. Susie Ling, "The Mountain Movers: Asian American Women's Movement in Los Angeles," *Amerasia Journal* 1989;15(1):53.

59. Wei, *The Asian American Movement*, 77–78.

60. Espiritu, *Asian American Panethnicity*, 49.

61. Espiritu, *Asian American Panethnicity*, 48–49.

62. Espiritu, *Asian American Panethnicity*, 48; Wei, *The Asian American Movement*, 73–74; Ling, "The Mountain Movers," 63.

63. Espiritu, *Asian American Panethnicity*, 49; Wei, *The Asian American Movement*, 81–90; Chow, "The Feminist Movement," 364–365.

64. "Students Organize for Asian Unity," *The Daily Californian*, 26 May 1970.

65. Yoshimura, "How I Became an Activist and What It All Means to Me," 108.

66. Vera Cruz et al., "Personal Reflections on the Asian National Movements," 37.

67. Omatsu, "The 'Four Prisons' and the Movements of Liberation," 21.

68. Yoshimura, "How I Became an Activist and What It All Means to Me," 109.

Chapter 8

1. Wong, "The Emergence of the Asian American Movement," 33; Espiritu, *Asian American Panethnicity*, 31–33; Omatsu, "The 'Four Prisons' and the Movements of Liberation," 20.

2. Within the context of the Asian American movement, activists in the Japanese American community acknowledged differences in the political orientation between Bay Area and Northern California activists, on one hand, and Los Angeles and Southern California activists, on the other. Historical and cultural developments, as well as differential developments within the larger political economy, have something to do with these differences. As Lane Hirabayashi has pointed out, future research needs to address these internal regional differences.

3. Omi, "It Just Ain't the Sixties No More," 32; Umemoto, "'On Strike!' San Francisco State College Strike, 1968–69," 4; and Omatsu, "The 'Four Prisons' and the Movements of Liberation," 24–28. Also see K. Hekymara, "The Third World Movement and Its History in the San Francisco State College Strike of 1968–1969" (Ph.D. diss., University of California at Berkeley, 1972).

4. T.B. Bottommore, *Sociology: A Guide to Problems and Literature* (London: George Allen & Unwin, 1962; New York: Random House, Vintage Books, 1972), 100; Robert A. Nisbet, *The Social Bond: An Introduction to the Study of Society* (New York: Alfred A. Knopf, 1970), 105–106.

5. George Woo, "Service and Action," in *Tool of Control? Tool of Change?: Proceedings of National Asian American Studies Conference II*, 6–8 July 1973, 29.

Conclusion

1. The notion of improvisation as defined by Pierre Bourdieu (*In Other Words: Essays Towards a Reflexive Sociology*, Stanford: Stanford University Press, 1990, 61) has positive implications that I have not been able to develop in this study.

2. Wilson, *Power, Racism, and Privilege*, 16.

3. James Coleman ["Conflicting Theories of Social Change," *American Behavioral Scientist* 1971;1(2):633–650] examines the use of legal strategies in social structures where a fixed hierarchy prevails.

4. Tomás Almaguer (*Racial Fault Lines: The Historical Origins of White Supremacy in California*, Berkeley and Los Angeles: University of California Press, 1994) provides an insightful analysis of the racialization process in California and the differential subordination of Mexicans, Native Americans, and Asian immigrants.

5. See Irons, *Justice at War*, regarding the failure of the legal system to uphold the civil rights of Japanese Americans during the wartime crisis.

6. Interviewees mentioned that many Sansei during this period made pilgrimages to Japan in search of their ethnic roots. The times also allowed Sansei to celebrate their culture, invoke community, and affirm ethnic values and ties to one's community. Although he is writing in a different historical context, David Mura (*Turning Japanese: Memoirs of a Sansei*, New York: Atlantic Monthly Press, 1991) offers insight into this process of redefining one's ethnic identity.

7. For example, Yoshiko Uchida, *Desert Exile: The Uprooting of a Japanese American Family* (Seattle and London: University of Washington Press, 1982), 147; and Weglyn, *Years of Infamy*, 278–281. Also see Wilson and Hosokawa, *East to America*, 296–298.

8. See Espiritu, *Asian American Panethnicity*, 25–31, regarding the common experience among Chinese, Filipino, and Korean American peers that led to increased interaction during the rise of the Asian American movement.

9. Omi and Winant, *Racial Formation in the United States*, 86.

10. McWilliams, *Prejudice*, 284–285.

11. Ibid., 286.

12. Warren Lee (*A Dream for South Central: The Autobiography of an Afro-Americanized Korean Christian Minister*, 1993), provides an insightful account of this kind of experience for a Korean American that easily applies to the experience of many Japanese Americans who grew up in communities that were adjacent to black communities.

13. Raymond Okamura, "Background and History of the Repeal Campaign," *Amerasia Journal* 1972;2:73–94. Also see Masaoka, *They Call Me Moses*, 303–311; and Hosokawa, *JACL*, 323–324.

14. "Youth Rededicate Manzanar Camp Cemetery," *Pacific Citizen*, 2–9 January 1970.

15. I owe a debt of thanks to Isami Arifuki and Clifford Uyeda for discussing and sharing their insights on this issue with me.

16. This summary of the Tokyo Rose case is based upon the following sources: David A. Ward, "The Unending War of Iva Ikuko Toguri D'Aquino: The Trial and Conviction of 'Tokyo Rose,'" *Amerasia Journal* 1971;1(2):26–35; Isami Arifuku Waugh, "The Trial of Tokyo Rose," *Bridge* 1974;3(1):5–12, 40–46; The National Committee for Iva Toguri, *Iva Toguri (d'Aquino): Victim Of A Legend*, San Francisco, Japanese American Citizens League, 2nd ed., May 1976; Clifford I. Uyeda, "The Pardoning of 'Tokyo Rose': A Report on the Restoration of American Citizenship to Iva Ikuko Toguri," *Amerasia Journal* 1978; 5(2): 69–93; Masayo Duus, trans. Peter Duus, *Tokyo Rose: Orphan of the Pacific* (Tokyo: Kodansha International, 1979); Russell Warren Howe, *The Hunt for "Tokyo Rose"* (Lanham, New York, and London: Madison Books, 1990).

17. Waugh, "The Trial of Tokyo Rose," 45; Duus, *Tokyo Rose*, 227; Uyeda, "The Pardoning of 'Tokyo Rose,'" 70–71.

18. Uyeda, "The Pardoning of 'Tokyo Rose,'" 82–85, discusses the political mobilization for Iva Toguri's case.

19. Daniels, *Asian America*, 330–341; Takezawa, *Breaking the Silence*, 28–59. Also see Hohri, *Repairing America*; John Tateishi, "The Japanese American Citizens League and the Struggle for Redress," 191–195, in *Japanese Americans*, Daniels, Taylor, and Kitano, eds.; Dale Minami, "Coram Nobis and Redress," 200–202, in *Japanese Americans*; and Leslie T. Hatamiya, *Righting a Wrong: Japanese Americans and the Passage of the Civil Liberties Act of 1988* (Stanford: Stanford University Press, 1993).

20. I am indebted to Yuji Ichioka for raising this point (letter to author, 1 November 1989).

21. Fugita and O'Brien, *Japanese American Ethnicity*.

22. I am indebted to Michael Omi for his insights on this particular point.

23. Yuri Kochiyama, "A Quick Reflection," *Amerasia Journal*, 15:1 (1989):101; Espiritu, *Asian American Panethnicity*, 65–69, 82–111; Wei, *The Asian American Movement*, 169–202; Nakanishi, "Asian American Politics," 20.

24. Chan, *Asian Americans*, 181; Sucheng Chan, "On the Ethnic Studies Requirement," *Amerasia Journal*, 1989;15(1):267–280; Espiritu, *Asian American Panethnicity*, 35–38; Takaki, *Strangers from a Different Shore*, 486; Wei, *The Asian American Movement*, 132–161.

25. Kochiyama, "A Quick Reflection," 101; Chan, *Asian Americans*, 181–185; Takaki, *Strangers from a Different Shore*, 486; Omatsu, "The 'Four Prisons' and the Movements of Liberation," 28–30.

26. O'Brien and Fugita, *The Japanese American Experience*, 122.

27. Chan, *Asian Americans*, 177–179; Espiritu, *Asian American Panethnicity*, 134–160; Takaki, *Strangers from a Different Shore*, 482–484; Wei, *The Asian American Movement*, 241–270.

28. I am indebted to Lane Hirabayashi for his insights on this issue. Also see Kitano, *Generations and Identity*, 202–203.

29. At the University of California, Berkeley, Japanese Americans were estimated to be the largest Asian Pacific American undergraduate student group in the early 1970s. By 1980, they were the fourth largest Asian Pacific group. In 1995, they were the sixth largest.

30. Chancellor's Committee on Asian American Affairs, *Asian Americans at Berkeley*, Yuan T. Lee and Janice Koyama, co-chairs, University of California, Berkeley, 1989; Institute for the Study of Social Change, *The Diversity Project: Final Report*, University of California, Berkeley, 1991, 21–27.

31. O'Brien and Fugita (*The Japanese American Experience*, 120–124) discuss the applicability of symbolic ethnicity to Japanese Americans; Mary C. Waters (*Ethnic Options: Choosing Identities in America*, Berkeley and Los Angeles: University of California Press, 1990) examines symbolic ethnicity in relation to European American ethnic groups.

32. Espiritu, *Asian American Panethnicity*, 161–176.

33. The notion of cultural competency comes from Institute for the Study of Social Change, *The Diversity Project*, 53–57.

34. Michael Omi ("Out of the Melting Pot and into the Fire: Race Relations Policy," LEAP Asian Pacific American Public Policy Institute and UCLA Asian American Studies Center, *The State of Asian Pacific America: Policy Issues to the Year 2020*, 1993, 201) assesses the zero-sum nature of assimilation theory.

35. U.S. Commission on Civil Rights, *Civil Rights Issues Facing Asian Americans in the 1990s* (Washington, D.C., February 1992), 22–48.

36. This expression comes from Blauner, *Racial Oppression in America*, 142.

37. Michael Omi and Howard Winant, *Racial Formation in the United States: From the 1960s to the 1990s*, 2d ed. (New York: Routledge, 1994), 56–61.

Index

Also in the *Asian American History and Culture* series: